COFFEE CULTURE NEW ORLEANS

SOFAB SERIES ON THE CULTURE OF FOOD AND DRINK

The SoFAB Series on the Culture of Food and Drink explores the techniques, traditions, and histories of southern food, along with the people who create and perpetuate them. Grounded in robust research and accessible to a wide audience, these books celebrate the diverse and ever-changing food stories that have shaped not only the South, but also the entire nation and beyond.

COFFEE CULTURE NEW ORLEANS

MARIELLE SONGY

LOUISIANA STATE UNIVERSITY PRESS | BATON ROUGE

Published with the assistance of The Noland Fund

Published by Louisiana State University Press
lsupress.org

Manufactured in the United States of America
First printing

Designer: Michelle A. Neustrom
Typefaces: Calluna, text; Le Havre Layers, display
Printer and binder: Sheridan Books, Inc.

Cover images (coffee beans, cup, banana leaves): Adobe Stock

The manufacturer's authorized representative in the EU for product safety is Mare Nostrum Group B.V., Doelen 72, 4831 GR Breda, The Netherlands. Email: gpsr@mare-nostrum.co.uk.

Cataloging-in-Publication Data are available from the Library of Congress.

ISBN 978-0-8071-8621-3 (cloth: alk. paper) — ISBN 978-0-8071-8722-7 (pdf) —
ISBN 978-0-8071-8721-0 (epub)

To the coffee growers, brokers, importers, roasters, baristas, and enjoyers who are a part of New Orleans coffee history

and

In memory of my father, whose endless support made this work possible

CONTENTS

LIST OF ILLUSTRATIONS
· ix ·

INTRODUCTION
A City Built on Coffee
· 1 ·

1. A MAGICAL FRUIT
The Origins of Coffee
· 5 ·

2. COFFEE IN THE CRESCENT CITY
Importation and the Port That Shaped New Orleans
· 27 ·

3. A MODERN EXCHANGE
The Role of Coffee in New Orleans Social Life
· 53 ·

4. HEADING TO MARKET
Coffee Business and Customs of Early New Orleans
· 69 ·

5. ROAST OF THE TOWN
Specialty Coffee and Roasters in Modern-Day New Orleans
· 94 ·

6. VIETNAM TO VERSAILLES

Vietnamese Coffee and Culture in New Orleans

• 149 •

7. BEYOND THE BIG EASY

New Orleans Coffee Makes a National Name for Itself

• 160 •

8. BREW IT YOURSELF

Grinding and Brewing Coffee at Home

• 181 •

CONCLUSION

Still Brewing After All These Years

• 195 •

ACKNOWLEDGMENTS

• 197 •

SOURCES

• 203 •

INDEX

• 215 •

Illustrations

Coffee at Cherry Coffee
· XII ·

Coffee cherries on a tree
· 6 ·

Green coffee beans
· 9 ·

Roasted coffee beans in the cooling bin,
Congregation Coffee
· 11 ·

Roasted coffee beans
· 13 ·

Newspaper display at NOLA Coffee Festival 2023
· 38 ·

Café du Monde, French Market
· 79 ·

Morning Call Coffee Stand postcard,
French Market
· 83 ·

Coffee at French Truck Coffee
· 97 ·

Coffee assortment at Cherry Coffee
· 105 ·

Seventy-five-pound San Franciscan Coffee Roaster, Orleans Coffee

· 113 ·

Bellwether Coffee Roaster, Coffee Science

· 116 ·

Loring Coffee Roaster, French Truck Coffee

· 123 ·

Coffee at CR Coffee Shop

· 128 ·

Bagged coffee beans, French Truck Coffee

· 145 ·

Café du Monde Coffee and CDM Coffee

· 156 ·

Vietnamese coffee preparation with a phin filter

· 158 ·

Oji Tower producing cold brew coffee, French Truck Coffee

· 165 ·

Bagged Community Coffee

· 173 ·

Moka pot

· 190 ·

COFFEE CULTURE NEW ORLEANS

Coffee at Cherry Coffee.
Photo by David Rodrigue.

INTRODUCTION

A City Built on Coffee

> I think coffee is one of the best things about being alive.
>
> —COMEDIAN STEVEN WRIGHT,
>
> *The Late Show with Stephen Colbert,* January 18, 2024

What is your coffee order? In New Orleans, the answer can tell you as much about a person as another popular question, "Where did you go to high school?" Whether your answer is "black," "café au lait," or "a café latte made with beans from a small farm in Guatemala," the type of day we have is often determined by that first cup of coffee. In New Orleans, coffee is a way of life, and many New Orleanians will tell you that their day (or favorite dessert) isn't complete without a cup of coffee.

If you're an avid coffee drinker, you likely started drinking coffee when you were young. Maybe your father snuck some to you when your mother wasn't looking. Maybe your grandmother mixed it into a cup of milk to make you feel grown-up. If you're of a certain age, you probably enjoyed your first "fancy" coffee drink at Starbucks. No matter how you discovered your love of coffee, that warm, roasty brew became a part of your routine—and I'm so glad because it's a part of mine, too.

I became a regular coffee drinker in 2005 after Hurricane Katrina. I had dabbled in coffee before, often enjoying sugary drinks closer to milkshakes than actual coffee, but after Katrina my coffee addiction flourished. My family and I had evacuated to a hotel in Birmingham, Alabama, and, of course, I was glued to the news, clinging to every morsel of information about what was happening back home. A little coffee maker in the hotel's lobby made cheap, no-frills coffee in about three minutes. I drank coffee from tiny Styrofoam cups and watched the news. I drank coffee and searched for updates about home on the hotel's computer. I drank more coffee. When I returned home to New Orleans, my new coffee habit stuck with me. I bought a small, cheap drip machine and started brewing it myself. To this day, I brew my coffee at home, but I truly enjoy dipping into coffee shops and trying different types of coffee from places like Brazil, Ethiopia, Guatemala, and Peru. These countries, so far away, tell their story through coffee.

I always knew New Orleans was significant in the world's coffee story. It wasn't until I started researching this book, though, that I realized what an integral part the city and, more specifically, the Port of New Orleans played in the coffee industry developing into what it is today. From the eighteenth century to now, New Orleans, its people, and the companies that operate here have profoundly impacted the coffee industry in the United States and the coffee trade as we know it.

In the early nineteenth century, as New Orleans's love affair with coffee flourished, coffee exchanges and coffeehouses became social hubs where important decisions were made over coffee. Over time, coffee drinking became even more of a social affair when it was served at home during events and at the markets where people did their weekly shopping. No day of shopping was complete without stopping at a coffee stand, such as those in the French Market. Here, the enslaved took the opportunity to sell coffee to save money to purchase their freedom. Pioneers like Rose Nicaud paved the way for the coffee stands we are familiar with today, such as Café du Monde and Morning Call.

The coffee most closely associated with New Orleans is coffee with chicory, in which roasted chicory is added to coffee grounds. Although many believe that this practice began in New Orleans during the Civil War, it can be traced back to the Prussian Empire in the eighteenth century. The French later adopted the custom during Napoleon's Continental System, which placed an embargo on multiple imports, including coffee. Because New Orleanians held an allegiance to France, it made sense that citizens would begin integrating chicory into their own coffee.

The different waves of coffee changed the New Orleans coffee scene throughout the twentieth century. Coffee lovers who were no longer satisfied with just grabbing a cup of black coffee at a diner frequented second-wave coffee shops such as True Brew Coffee House, which offered espresso and cappuccino in a social, cozy atmosphere. While many of these coffeehouses leaned more on the casual vibe of their shops than on their coffee to draw customers, they paved the way for the third wave of coffee, which focuses more on specialty coffee and sustainability.

These days, coffee drinkers in New Orleans and beyond are branching out from their traditional "store-bought" coffee and embracing specialty coffee. Modern coffee drinkers are thoughtful about where their coffee comes from, who grows it, and the different flavor notes that vary by a coffee's region of origin. Coffee is so much more than what you find at the grocery store; it's become an industry as multifaceted as wine, and no matter your taste, you are bound to find a coffee that speaks to your soul.

Even beyond New Orleans, finding coffee connected to the city is relatively easy. Folgers, the best-selling brand of store-bound ground coffee in the United States, roasts its coffee in New Orleans. PJ's Coffee, a local coffee brand founded by Phyllis Jordan, has expanded outside Louisiana and boasts nearly two hundred locations nationwide! Community Coffee, a Baton Rouge coffee brand with connections to New Orleans, is the largest family-owned coffee company in the United States and is enjoyed in multiple states outside of Louisiana. Café du Monde coffee, served at the famous coffee stand, is the essential ingredient in Vietnamese coffee throughout the United States. When Vietnamese refugees emigrated to the United States for new opportunities, the richness of Café du Monde coffee reminded them of their coffee from back home.

Since the beginning, New Orleanians have embraced coffee and woven it into their story; coffee is a part of the fabric that makes the city unique. Some of the most intriguing people are "coffee people," and the best ideas have been exchanged over a cup of coffee. Even if you aren't a New Orleanian, there's a good chance that the coffee you enjoy has a connection to New Orleans.

1

A Magical Fruit

The Origins of Coffee

For many, coffee is more than just a start to the day; it's a ritual. Whether you're a one-cup person or drink it all day, when you enjoy coffee in New Orleans, you connect with a piece of the city's history. It's hard to believe that the simple coffee bean has had such significant impact on the growth of New Orleans's industry. While New Orleans was responsible for importing many products in the eighteenth and nineteenth centuries, coffee made New Orleans a major player in trade at this time. Before diving into the ins and outs of New Orleans's coffee history, the industry, and its incredible impact on the city's commerce, it's important to become familiar with some basic coffee information.

The Beginning of a Coffee Bean

The "beans" we use to make our daily coffee begin as fruit seeds inside coffee cherries. Coffee trees average about thirty feet in height and are covered in waxy leaves that grow in pairs. Before a tree can produce the fruit needed for coffee beans, it must reach maturity, which takes about four years. The skin of a coffee cherry is called the exocarp and ripens from green to a bright color like yellow, orange, or red, and the shape is reminiscent of a cranberry. The pulp,

Coffee cherries on a tree.
Wikimedia Commons.

or mesocarp, is just beneath the cherry's skin, as are the mucilage and pectin. These layers contain sugars that aid in the fruit's fermentation process. Finally, the seeds or beans are the innermost part of the coffee cherry.

When coffee is harvested, coffee beans go through a purification process called dry milling during which they are first sorted according to size. Impurities are removed from the beans through a cleaning technique: Fibers and dirt are vacuumed off the beans during the precleaning process, a magnet removes any metallic fragments from the beans, and a vibrating belt shakes the beans to ensure that they are separated from any stones that might have been in the batch. Beans are hulled, and the parchment surrounding the bean is removed to reveal the green coffee bean so familiar to coffee lovers. The beans then pass through a polisher to remove any other impurities that may have slipped past the other processes, and finally, they are sorted and graded by size, weight, and color. For specialty coffee, an added step includes hand sorting, in which trained coffee bean sorters pick out any beans that aren't the same size as the rest. When that process is complete, the coffee beans are loaded into bags, which are sewn, weighed, and shipped to their next destination.

TYPES OF COFFEE BEANS

Two types of beans are typically used for coffee—arabica and robusta. Arabica is the most popular type of coffee and is made from the beans of the *Coffea arabica* plant. Arabica, also known as Arabic coffee, originated in the southwestern highlands of Ethiopia. It is grown in dozens of countries in the Bean Belt between the Tropic of Capricorn and the Tropic of Cancer and accounts for 60 percent of the world's coffee. While the United States is not typically known for its coffee production, an arabica coffee tree was introduced to Hawaii in 1813. Of course, this was well before Hawaii was a part of the United States. By 1850, coffee was being widely grown in Hawaii, especially in Kailua-Kona, a town on the west coast of the Big Island. Kona coffee is rare, highly sought after, and has a chocolate-like flavor profile. Today, Kona coffee is so highly regarded that laws state that any coffee sold as Kona coffee must be no less than 100 percent Kona coffee grown in Kona.

Robusta is made from the beans of the *Coffea canephora* plant and originated in central and western sub-Saharan Africa in places like Liberia and Tanzania. It is also found in Brazil, India, Indonesia, and Vietnam, where French colonists introduced it in the nineteenth century. Once introduced, coffee became the preferred drink in Vietnam, unlike in other Asian nations, where tea is the drink of choice. Robusta coffee makes up about 45 percent of global coffee production. Arabica coffee tends to have a sweeter taste, whereas robusta has a more earthy, bitter taste.

Two other types of coffee beans used less often than arabica and robusta are liberica and excelsa. Native to central and western Africa, especially Angola, Liberia, and Uganda, liberica, or *Coffea liberica,* tends to be inconsistent in flavor but usually has a floral aroma and a bold, smoky taste. Because it's rare, making up just 2 percent of the world's coffee supply, it costs more than arabica or robusta coffee beans. Liberica was unheard of in the Western world until the late 1800s and is scarce in North American and European markets. Today, it is grown in Indonesia, Malaysia, and the Philippines.

Excelsa coffee, or *Coffea dewevrei,* was discovered in Africa in 1903 as a tree-like plant rather than a shrub that requires vertical space to grow. According to *Perfect Daily Grind,* excelsa is frequently cultivated in Southeast Asia, including India, the Philippines, and Vietnam. It wasn't until 2006 that British botanist Dr. Aaron P. Davis discovered that *Coffea dewevrei* was not its own coffee plant genus but a variety of *Coffea liberica.* As a result, quality-control measures for excelsa coffee are lax, and it isn't easy to find official statistics on how much of coffee produced is excelsa, as it's been grouped into the liberica category. However, other researchers argue that excelsa should be recognized as its own species due to its complex growth patterns and unique bean variety. Excelsa coffee beans are lower in caffeine than arabica and robusta, and the plant tends to be heartier than its counterparts. When the beans are roasted light to medium, excelsa tastes tart and fruity; when the beans are roasted dark, flavors of chocolate and cream can be detected.

THE COFFEE-ROASTING PROCESS

Until I began my research for this book, I had no idea about the personal touch that goes into roasting coffee. I thought it was as simple as loading green coffee beans into a big roaster, pressing a button, and letting the machine do all the work. I was wrong—coffee roasting is an intricate and skilled process that is learned and perfected over time. Each roaster's style is personal, and roasters have their own techniques for roasting coffee to their liking.

Green coffee beans.
Photo by the author.

Before coffee can be consumed, green coffee beans must be roasted. Like everything in coffee making, roasting has evolved from basic to more advanced. While there is a science to obtaining the perfect roast, anyone can roast coffee beans in a cast-iron skillet or wok. Small air roasters are available online for home roasting, and some even roast their coffee in a popcorn popper. As William Ukers explains in *All About Coffee,* the first cylindrical coffee roaster was developed in 1650 in Cairo, Egypt. It consisted of a tinned copper or cast-iron cylinder, a lid, and a long handle used to roast coffee beans over an open fire. The idea was improved in 1660, when Elford's white iron roaster equipped with a sliding door was invented in England. The sliding door allowed the beans to be contained while the apparatus rotated for an even roast. Between 1700 and 1800, coffee roasting leaped forward with the invention of an iron roasting stove that roasted coffee in a handled cylindrical rotating drum over burning charcoal. Today's sizeable commercial-grade coffee roasters are advanced variations of this same concept.

Modern coffee roasting is a very specific technique, and roasting style can vary depending on who is doing the roasting. Greg Rodrigue of HEY Coffee Co. in New Orleans walked me through how he roasts his company's coffee on a twelve-kilogram Diedrich Coffee Roaster. At the top of the roaster is a hopper and a large drum that contains a ceramic heating element heated by a flame and propane. After the drum is preheated to 415°F, green coffee beans go from the hopper into the drum for the drying stage, the first four to eight minutes of roasting. During the process, gas pressure and temperature are monitored. Rodrigue explains that he starts roasting with a lot of heat and gradually reduces the heat as the roasting continues. Because the coffee beans start at room temperature, the drum's temperature will drop significantly when the beans are added. After about five minutes of roasting, the beans are at about 275°F. From there, heat is reduced, and 50 percent airflow control is imparted. Rodrigue says that the coffee beans begin to change color at this point. This stage, called the browning stage, starts the Maillard reaction, which brings out the sweetness of the sugars within the coffee bean. The goal is to bring out the best flavors of the coffee without burning it. During the roasting process, key points happen that the roaster is trained to recognize, such as color changes in the beans and scents that come from the roasted beans.

Roasted coffee beans in the cooling bin, Congregation Coffee.
Photo by the author.

One of the roles of the roaster is to control the rate of rise, which is how many degrees the coffee increases every thirty seconds.

First crack—when most of the moisture in the coffee beans evaporates, causing the bean to crack, thus signaling the beginning of the light roast or roasting stage—happens after about ten minutes of roasting, when the beans reach 385°F. When that happens, heat is reduced, and airflow is increased. This process prolongs the first-crack stage and adds to the coffee's sweetness. Rodrigue ends the roasting process for HEY's coffee at around eleven or twelve minutes but explains that the roasting time can depend on the coffee's country of origin or what type of roast level the roaster prefers. After the roasting process is complete, the beans drop into the cooling bin, which, with the help of a rotating agitator that spreads the beans, quickly cools the coffee with airflow in five or six minutes. To get the most flavor out of your coffee, experts recommend that you grind and brew roasted coffee beans within a week or two of their roast date. Many recommend storing roasted coffee beans in the freezer to prolong their freshness.

COFFEE ROASTS

There are four coffee roast types, each with a different aroma, appearance, and flavor.

- Light coffee roasts are roasted for the least amount of time to an internal temperature of 356°F to 401°F or right after the bean cracks. Light roasts are high in caffeine and acidity, and origin flavors of the coffee are more detectable because an extended roasting process hasn't compromised its flavor.
- Medium coffee roasts reach internal temperatures of 410°F to 428°F and have more body and less acidity than a light roast. This tends to be the preferred roast of most casual coffee drinkers.
- Medium-Dark coffee roasts reach an internal temperature of 437°F to 446°F. Due to the high internal temperature, this roast brings the beans' oils to the surface. This roast has a rich, full flavor, more body, and less acidity.
- Dark coffee roasts reach an internal temperature of between 464°F and 482°F. The roasting process itself produces the essential flavors you taste in a dark roast because the origin flavors have been compromised during roasting. Due to the caramelization of the sugars in the coffee beans, dark coffee roasts tend to be sweeter, with a richer flavor and fuller body. This roast produces the least acidic coffee, has a smoky flavor, and contains the least caffeine because it is lost during the roasting.

COFFEE CUPPING

The professional practice of observing brewed coffee's fragrance, aroma, and flavor is coffee cupping or coffee tasting. Anyone can in-

Roasted coffee beans.
Photo by the author.

formally perform the practice, but it is mainly done by professional coffee graders known as "Q Graders" and other coffee professionals such as producers, importers, exporters, brokers, roasters, and baristas. Coffee cupping is a meticulous ritual, an excellent way to build your coffee palate, and a method to learn what makes a specific coffee taste a certain way and what goes into a good cup of coffee.

During a coffee cupping, evaluators assess the coffee's aroma when brewed, acidity, body, flavor, fragrance when dry, and sweetness. Results are scored on a coffee-cupping form or recorded in a coffee journal. Evaluators often compare coffee aroma and flavors to foods to adequately explain the flavors they pick up from the coffee cupping. A coffee flavor wheel, which was developed by the Specialty Coffee Association in 1995 and contains a variety of descriptive flavors and tastes, is also used to convey what flavors the coffee taster is getting from the coffee.

When conducting a coffee cupping, you will need at least two different coffees, bowls, a grinder, a scale, a timer, cups, hot water, and cupping spoons. "Coffee Cupping: A Step-by-Step Guide," on the *Methodical* blog, explains the process of conducting a coffee cupping:

- Place the bag of coffee you'll be cupping in front of your bowls. Fill one bowl with hot water to rinse your spoon between tastings.

- Weigh out 10 grams of coffee to be brewed in 180 milliliters of water in each bowl at a ratio of 1:18.

- Grind enough coffee to fill two bowls.

- Once the coffee is ground, smell the grounds and observe the fragrance. Shake the bowl to agitate the aroma of the grounds.

- Brew your coffee by pouring hot water on the grounds in each bowl. Brew for four minutes.

- After the coffee is brewed, break the crust on top and release the coffee's aroma. As you break the crust, bring your nose close to the bowl to observe the aroma, noting your observations.

- Breaking the crust releases foam, which should be discarded. At this point, the crust is gone, and grounds have settled to the bottom of the bowl. The bowl should look like a regular cup of coffee.

- Taste the coffee by slurping and spreading the coffee over your palate, making a note of your observations.

- Taste the coffee again as it cools, ensuring it passes over your taste buds. Make a note of any differences in your previous tasting.

The Three Waves of Coffee

In modern coffee culture, professionals refer to three waves when describing the evolution of the coffee business and coffee consumption. The first, second, and third waves are definitive moments in the industry that trace how far the coffee industry has come and where it's going. The difference in these waves is based on how coffee is prepared and sourced, its quality, and how it is consumed.

The first wave of coffee was commodity coffee. This is mass-produced coffee, sometimes considered low-quality, that comes from a factory. First-wave coffee was a means to an end; people wanted to consume coffee quickly and easily, so they bought whatever was available at the grocery store. The coffee came preground, was often dark and bitter, and sometimes flavored. Consumers didn't know exactly where their coffee came from and didn't care; they were just happy to get the caffeine that coffee provided. This wave also marks the beginning of instant coffee, which is prepared by adding boiling water to freeze-dried coffee. Many coffee professionals consider the first wave of coffee to have begun in the late 1800s and lasted until the early 1960s.

In the second wave of coffee, beginning in the 1960s and lasting into the 1990s, consumers started caring more about where their coffee came from, but they were more interested in fancy coffee drinks than quality coffee. This was when specialty coffee began to take shape. A good example of second-wave coffee is Starbucks, which marketed gourmet coffee drinks to young people starting in the early 1990s. There was *some* focus on good-quality coffee, but that came with brands focusing more on the café atmosphere than serving the best coffee available. Some good things that came with the second wave were coffee companies selling individual brands and baristas trained to make more intricate coffee drinks than typical black coffee. The introduction of cappuccino and espresso to a larger market is widely associated with the second wave.

The third wave of coffee began in the late 1990s and early 2000s and is marked by a community of passionate roasters and coffee professionals dedicated to buying and selling the highest-quality coffee beans and focusing on specific flavor notes. Coffee enthusiasts are now more interested in single-origin coffee, knowing exactly where their coffee comes from, manual brewing methods, and sustainable farming practices. Those in the coffee industry hold trade shows and competitions to meet, hone their skills, and trade inside information on coffee farming, hold coffee cuppings, exchange roasting tips, and support co-ops and women-owned farms. Getting your hands on a good cup of quality coffee has never been easier, thanks to people who have dedicated their lives to improving the world's coffee and sharing the bounty of small farms with their customers.

What lies ahead in the fourth wave of coffee has yet to be seen. Some coffee professionals think we are entering the fourth wave of coffee due to the new generation's interest in coffee preparation and their focus on roasting and brewing methods. Some coffee makers are already beginning to change their roasting practices to be more environmentally friendly and produce coffee more sustainably. Some in the industry believe that science will take a front seat in the next wave as coffee enthusiasts study the chemistry behind coffee. Furthermore, people will take their home coffee brewing more seriously, focusing on specialty equipment and high-quality beans.

Decaffeinated Coffee

Most coffee contains caffeine, a stimulant, which is why people drink it to start their day. Caffeine has a lot of perks, no pun intended—it can keep you focused and wake you up, but it can also lead to nervousness and insomnia. If you're sensitive to caffeine but enjoy coffee, it would make sense that you'd want to reach for the decaf, especially if you're an afternoon coffee drinker. It should be noted that decaffeinated coffee isn't 100 percent caffeine-free and can contain small traces of caffeine. How is coffee decaffeinated, anyway?

There are different ways to get the caffeine out of coffee, but here are the basics. The direct-solvent method was developed by a German merchant named Ludwig Roselius in 1903. In this process, coffee beans are steamed with acids and bases and then rinsed with benzene or other solvents to extract the caffeine from the coffee. This process is repeated multiple times until 97 percent of the caffeine is removed from the coffee beans. According to "Understanding the Weird History of Decaffeinated Coffee and How It's Made," on the *Compass Coffee* blog, Roselius marketed his decaffeinated coffee in Europe as Kaffee HAG. This method is still used to decaffeinate coffee; however, ethyl acetate or methylene chloride is now used instead of benzene.

In the indirect-solvent method, coffee beans are soaked in hot water for hours. The water in which the beans were soaked is treated with methylene chloride or ethyl acetate to extract the caffeine through hydrogen bonds. The same water is used to soak more batches of coffee beans until equilibrium is reached and the caffeine is removed from the beans. *Compass Coffee* likens this process to washing rice; essentially, coffee beans are soaked in the water solution until they are decaffeinated.

The Swiss Water Process was developed in Switzerland in 1933. Green coffee beans are soaked in hot water, producing a green coffee extract, which is filtered through activated charcoal to remove the caffeine molecules. Freshly steamed beans are added to the filtered green coffee extract and, like the indirect-solvent method in which batches of coffee beans seek equilibrium, caffeine molecules migrate from the coffee beans to the green coffee extract solution. Because the water is oversaturated with coffee compounds, the flavor components of the coffee beans remain in the beans while caffeine is released into the water. Once again, the solution is passed through activated charcoal filters and is repeated until the coffee beans are decaffeinated.

One of the more modern methods of extracting caffeine from coffee is the supercritical carbon dioxide extraction method developed by Kurt Zosel in 1967. Green coffee beans are soaked in water and added to a high-pressure vessel where water and carbon dioxide are circulated at 300 atm and 149°F. Caffeine dissolves in the carbon dioxide, producing a supercritical fluid, while other flavors and compounds remain in the coffee bean. The carbon dioxide and coffee are moved to another chamber, the pressure is lowered, and the supercritical carbon dioxide turns gaseous and evaporates. The remaining caffeine is removed from the carbon dioxide with water.

WHERE DID COFFEE ORIGINATE?

I first heard the story about the origins of coffee and the Ethiopian legend credited for the discovery from Prince Lobo, the co-owner of Addis NOLA, an Ethiopian restaurant in New Orleans. The story of how coffee became the staple of our mornings (and after-mornings) begins in Abyssinia, which is modern-day Ethiopia, where lived a goat herder named Kaldi (or Khalid) in AD 700. Kaldi was known to be a dreamer; he worked as a goat herder, but his passions were poetry and music. At the end of a long workday, he would play his pipe and summon his goats back home.

One day Kaldi played his pipe as usual, but the goats didn't come. Concerned, he searched and found them down a trail. The goats were playing and frolicking; they seemed to have more energy than they typically had at this time of day. Kaldi grew especially concerned when he noticed that one of the goats had chewed the green leaves and red berries from an unknown bush. He was convinced that his goats had been poisoned and would surely die.

Hours later, Kaldi was able to wrangle the goats back home. Not only did they live, but the goats ran back to the bushes the next day to, once again, munch on these mysterious cherries. Curious, Kaldi decided to try this plant for himself. First, he chewed on some leaves and then the berries. While the leaves were bitter, the berries were sweet, and Kaldi was filled with inspiration he had never felt before. He felt happy and full of life and was creatively inspired to write poetry and music in a way he never had. When Kaldi told his father about the trees he had discovered, the secret was soon revealed, and the coffee produced by these magical cherries became an integral part of Ethiopian life.

Whether that story is true or not is up for debate, but what is a fact is that coffee was first cultivated in Ethiopia and, later, Yemen and the Levant. In the sixteenth century, coffee reached Italy through commercial Mediterranean trade routes, and it had reached India by the mid-seventeenth century. By the late seventeenth century, coffeehouses were popping up in western Europe, and coffee spread quickly to the Caribbean and Mexico.

According to *Uncommon Grounds: The History of Coffee and How It Transformed Our World* by Mark Pendergrast, the word "coffee" comes from *qahwa* (or *kahwa*), the Arab word for wine. He also notes that some believe that "coffee" could be a derivative of the Kaffa region of Ethiopia, *quwwa*—the Arab word for power, or a tea-like drink made from the khat plant called *kafta.* In Turkey the drink is called *kahveh;* in the Netherlands it is known as *koffie.*

Upon discovering coffee, the Ethiopians began trading it with Arabs through the Red Sea. Pendergrast speculates that when the Ethiopians invaded and ruled Yemen in the sixth century, they set up coffee plantations. The Arabs embraced coffee and considered it a medicinal and religious aid. Due to its stimulating properties, coffee was a part of their daily routine, allowing them to stay awake for midnight prayers. The wealthier members of society had rooms in their homes dedicated to coffee consumption, while others enjoyed coffee in coffeehouses called *kaveh kanes.* By the end of the fifteenth century, coffee had become profitable in trade, spreading throughout the Islamic world to Egypt, North Africa, Persia, and Turkey.

TURKISH COFFEE

It's believed that Turkish coffee was brought to the Ottoman Empire in 1540, when the Ottoman governor of Yemen, Ozdemir Pasha, introduced it to Sultan Suleiman the Magnificent. The sultan made the hot beverage a part of his daily routine, and it was brewed for him by coffee makers called Kahveci Usta. The Kahveci Usta, usually high-ranking citizens trusted to brew the coffee correctly, prepared the sultan's coffee by grinding coffee beans to a fine powder in a mortar and brewing it in a pot called an ibrik. As the sultan enjoyed the coffee, the elites followed suit, and Turkish coffee became a popular delicacy. However, in the mid-seventeenth century, Murad IV, the sultan of the Ottoman Empire from 1623 to 1640, closed coffeehouses, believing they were gathering places for dissenters. The punishment for drinking coffee in a gathering was severe beatings and even death. The sultan's coffeehouse ban lasted into the eighteenth century.

Today, Turkish coffee is an integral part of Turkish marriage customs. The bride-to-be prepares coffee during the meeting of her parents and the bridegroom's parents. After enjoying a cup of Turkish coffee, some even tell fortunes with the leftover grounds. In a practice known as tasseography, the coffee grounds are turned over onto a saucer and interpreted.

Turkish coffee is prepared with cold water, finely ground coffee, and a copper wide-bottomed pot, or cezve. It is served in two-ounce Turkish coffee cups, or finjans, with sugar if preferred. Turkish coffee is not filtered; the superfine grounds settle to the bottom of the finjan after it is served.

Here are the steps in preparing Turkish coffee:

- Use the coffee cup in which you will be serving the coffee to measure 1.5 cups of water.
- Measure a heaping tablespoon of coffee into the water-filled cezve. If you're preparing the coffee with sugar, mix the sugar into the grounds before brewing. If some guests prefer their coffee with sugar and others without, prepare it separately. Sometimes cardamom or cinnamon is also added to the mixture.
- Heat the cezve on a burner and allow the coffee to brew for

three to four minutes until dark foam forms on top of the mixture.

- Before the mixture boils, scoop some of its foam into each finjan.
- Return the cezve to the burner and boil the remaining coffee for ten to fifteen seconds.
- Pour the coffee over the foam in the cups to the cup's rim. Wait about five minutes before drinking so the coffee can cool, and the grounds can settle.

Turkish coffee is traditionally served with water to allow the person consuming it to clean their palate before taking the first sip. The eldest in the group is served first, and because the coffee is strong, only one cup is usually enjoyed. Turkish coffee is frequently served with something sweet like candy or Turkish delight.

COFFEE IN EUROPE

Arabia is the mother of the modern version of roasted coffee. According to Tori Avey in her essay "The Caffeinated History of Coffee," not a single coffee plant existed outside of Arabia or Africa until the 1600s, when an Indian pilgrim named Baba Budan left Mecca with fertile coffee beans that would eventually lead to the European coffee trade. After successfully transporting a coffee tree from Aden to Holland in 1616, the Dutch became responsible for the first European-owned coffee estate in Sri Lanka after an offspring of that tree was transported to Ceylon in 1658. By 1699, more trees were planted in Bali, Celebes, Sumatra, Timor, and the East Indies. Pendergrast notes that coffee production in the Dutch East Indies set the price in the world's coffee market.

When coffee made its way to Europe in the seventeenth century, it was considered an exotic beverage. However, by midcentury, it was being sold on the street alongside lemonade, chocolate, and liquor. Venice opened its first coffeehouse in 1683, and the "caffé," as it was called, became a social destination where people could enjoy coffee, conversation, and food. The people of France were more resistant to coffee than other European countries; doctors questioned the medicinal properties others claimed, and winemakers feared that this new drink would draw people's attention away from wine consumption.

As Julia Landweber writes in "Domesticating the 'Queen of Beans': How Old Regime France Learned to Love Coffee," the French people's attitude toward coffee began to soften when Louis XIV discovered that he could use the coffee trade to pay for the Nine Years' War. In 1692, he passed an edict to control the import and distribution of coffee into the country and listed an official price on whole and ground beans. France was a player in the international coffee trade by the eighteenth century. In the early 1700s, Jean de la Roque led two expeditions into the Red Sea to better establish a coffee trade relationship there. Landweber explains that in 1713, the Royal Botanical Garden in Paris received a gift from the Botanical Garden of Amsterdam in the form of a coffee bush; from the plant's cuttings, the first French coffee plantations were established in 1715 in Saint-Domingue. Coffee production soon exploded in French-owned Saint-Domingue, with seventy-seven million pounds of coffee beans exported annually, accounting for 60 percent of the world's coffee consumption.

In 1689, Francois Procope, an Italian immigrant, opened Café du Procope, Paris's first coffeehouse. Located across the street from Comédie-Française, a theater founded in 1680, the coffeehouse began catering to actors, authors, and musicians, who would gather to enjoy coffee and conversation. From there, coffee spread to Vienna, with coffeehouses popping up in the late seventeenth century. Like their French predecessors, the Viennese gathered in coffeehouses to talk, write, and read the newspaper. Around the same time, coffee and coffeehouses were taking hold in Germany, and Pendergrast writes that by 1721, most major German cities had a coffeehouse. He explains that, like the winemakers in France, German beer brewers were wary of coffee, concerned that it would cut into the public's beer consumption. By 1781, Frederick the Great had forbidden coffee roasting outside government establishments, forcing people experiencing poverty to substitute their coffee with chicory root, dried fig, barley, wheat, or corn.

England opened its first coffeehouse in 1650, and the phenomenon exploded there, with eighty-two coffeehouses opening in central London by 1663. The British immediately took to coffee and the coffeehouse culture, and by 1700, London boasted more than two thousand coffeehouses. Known as "penny universities" due to the price of a cup of coffee, the coffeehouses became social hubs where one could consult a physician, have religious discussions, meet for business, trade goods, or chat with strangers. Upon the advent of coffee, alcohol consumption in England decreased, and coffeehouses became lively spots where people preferred to start their day. Instead of having ale or wine first thing in the morning, businessmen chose to consume coffee and found their day to be better for it.

Not everyone in England, however, was a fan of coffeehouses. "The Women's Petition Against Coffee" complained that men-only coffeehouses and the coffee therein were crippling society. The petition argued that when men weren't in taverns getting drunk, they were in coffeehouses trying to sober up. They would then find their way back to the tavern, and the cycle continued. The petition also suggested that coffeehouses would lead to the downfall of the cohesive family. It is widely believed that this was a satirical piece likely not written by women at all but rather by members of society who opposed such establishments. Its goal was to reduce the popularity of coffeehouses, which were seen as places where politicos gathered to fan the fires of unrest with the public. In 1676, King Charles II attempted to ban coffeehouses in "A Proclamation for the Suppression of Coffee Houses," claiming that they led to an idle public and merchants neglecting their affairs. However, due to public outcry, the king backed down on this proclamation two days before it was scheduled to take effect.

Coffee's Introduction into the United States

Across the pond, interest in coffee was gaining momentum in the American colonies. According to Pendergrast, the first American coffeehouse opened in Boston in 1689. Unlike their British counterparts, coffeehouses in the American colonies not only served coffee but ale, beer, and tea as well. The American love of coffee was solidified in the late eighteenth century when King George attempted to enact the Stamp Act of 1765, a tax paid for British military troops stationed in the American colonies after the French and Indian War. The act imposed a tax on the British colonies in America, requiring materials such as legal documents and magazines to be printed on embossed stamped paper. It was required that the tax be paid in British currency and not colonial paper money. In 1767, the Townshend Acts took it a step further and imposed taxes on glass, lead, paint, paper, and tea.

Eventually, the Stamp Act of 1765 and the Townshend Acts were lifted, but the tax on 1.2 million pounds of tea that colonists consumed yearly remained. More specifically, the Tea Act of 1773 reduced the amount of tea held by the British East India Company and helped the company make ends meet. Colonists opposed the act, and tea that arrived in New York and Philadelphia was returned to Britain. Rather than pay a tax to the Crown, the colonists smuggled tea from Holland. In Charleston, British tea sat untouched on docks, and things reached a head in December 1773, when Boston colonists raided tea-filled ships and tossed 342 chests of the stuff into Boston Harbor during what is now known as the Boston Tea Party. Not only did this act lead to the American Revolution, but it solidified coffee as the drink of choice for the colonies. Colonists began enjoying coffee regularly before the Boston Tea Party as a protest against the Tea Act of 1773. By the time the tea hit the harbor, drinking coffee was seen as an American thing to do, and no one benefited more than the coffeehouses.

During the Industrial Revolution of the eighteenth and nineteenth centuries in both Europe and North America, coffee was a sustaining force. Workers migrated to cities to work in deplorable conditions in textile factories and iron mills. Before this time, most people had worked at home or in craft workshops. An organized workforce meant no longer being your own boss, working at your own leisure, and enjoying meals in a smoothly run household complete with home-cooked meals. Those who chose to continue working at home were making less money. Pendergrast explains that lacemakers survived on bread and coffee in the nineteenth century, which gave an illusion of nutrition due to its warmth. Coffee, an appetite suppressant, also did an excellent job of keeping hunger at bay.

Today, over 2.25 billion cups of coffee are consumed daily worldwide. It is the one of the most traded commodities in the world, with 9.9 million tonnes of coffee beans produced annually. Brazil was responsible for the most coffee production in 2021, producing 3 million tonnes. According to Airi Ryu's graphic in *Visual Capitalist,* the world's number-one importer of coffee is the United States, which imported 1.47 million tonnes of it in 2019. Germany is the top importer in Europe, importing 1.08 million tonnes in 2019; many of the top importing companies reexport coffee under private brands.

In the United States, coffee and soft drinks are neck and neck for the second-most-consumed beverage after water, with Americans enjoying 400 million cups of coffee a day, or 146 billion cups a year. That averages out to about three cups of coffee a day. Furthermore, the National Coffee Association reports that the economic impact of the United States coffee industry was $343.2 billion in 2022, and the industry generates more than $100 billion in wages annually in 2.2 million of the country's jobs, including importing, roasting, maintenance, transport, and general coffee-related food service.

On September 29, 2005, the National Coffee Association honored coffee's popularity in the United States by declaring the first National Coffee Day. The National Coffee Association notes that the day was declared to "promote coffee consumption and raise awareness about the economic, social, and environmental issues faced by coffee farmers and workers worldwide." This day is not to be confused with International Coffee Day, which was declared by the International Coffee Organization (ICO) on October 1, 2015, as a worldwide celebration allowing coffee lovers and professionals to share their love of coffee and support coffee farmers who make their living growing the world's coffee.

2

COFFEE IN THE CRESCENT CITY

Importation and the Port That Shaped New Orleans

In the eighteenth century, trade was quickly becoming New Orleans's lifeblood, and coffee would play an essential role in the city's position on the national and international stage. As the United States headed into the nineteenth century, those who were thinking of coffee were thinking of New Orleans. The city was the place to come to make money in an industry that was taking the country by storm. Throughout the nineteenth and early twentieth centuries, the New Orleans coffee industry would survive hardships such as importation and trade restrictions imposed during the Civil War and World War I. In 1925, a coffee dock fire caused millions of dollars in damage. However, the New Orleans coffee industry would bounce back by introducing a new coffee shed and new trade opportunities. All of these events would usher in the new era of New Orleans coffee, with companies new and old ensuring the city remains a viable part of the national coffee industry.

LIFE IN NEW ORLEANS IN THE NINETEENTH CENTURY

New Orleans, or La Nouvelle Orléans, was founded in 1718 by the French under the guidance of Louisiana Governor Jean-Baptiste Le

Moyne, Sieur de Bienville. The city was named in honor of Philip II, Duke of Orléans, who served as Louis XV's regent from 1715 to 1723. New Orleans's location appealed to Bienville due to high ground at the mouth of the Mississippi River, a natural levee in the river's bend, and the city's ideal position as a trading post. New Orleans's position between the Mississippi River and Lake Pontchartrain made it easy to access the Gulf of Mexico without interference from colonial English and Spanish settlements. By 1722, New Orleans was named the capital of French Louisiana, relieving Biloxi of the title, and was already experiencing hardship in the form of a hurricane that destroyed most of the city's structures and the port's ships. The French ruled the Louisiana territory from 1682 to 1762 before it was relinquished to Spain from 1763 and 1803 as a condition of the Treaty of Fontainebleau.

Coffee was first introduced to New Orleans in the eighteenth century. The city received its supply from Cuba and Caribbean Islands such as Saint-Domingue, a colony that, like Louisiana, was under French rule. In post–Revolutionary War New Orleans, the city and its trade and travel position had much potential. New Orleans was a city where people wanted to do business, and agricultural products such as corn, potatoes, wheat, flour, and whiskey, and livestock such as chicken, pigs, and cows were first shipped into the port via flatboats, a one-way, downstream vessel with a rectangular, flat bottom and square ends.

Flatboats were impractical in the long term. The boats were typically around twenty feet wide so that they could easily weave their way along the river and twenty to one hundred feet long. The boats were somewhat awkward and designed to move only downriver quickly and were often salvaged for lumber once they reached New Orleans. Making matters more treacherous, farmers who accompanied their goods to New Orleans were forced to return to their original starting point on a keelboat, a type of man-powered riverboat that was difficult to maneuver against the river's powerful current.

Keelboats were around eighty feet by fifteen feet, with a long, narrow shape, and propelled by setting poles pushing against the riverbed. The locomotion of a keelboat depends on the water's current, and, as a result, keelboat trips were expensive and could take up to three months. Because of the limitations of flatboats and keelboats, New Orleans was only involved in domestic trade into the early nineteenth century. Something had to be done to make the process easier for all involved and expand New Orleans's trade options.

STEAMBOATS BRING NEW POSSIBILITIES

The use of the steamboat brought New Orleans into modern times in the trade world. As the name suggests, steamboats are powered by steam and driven by propellers or paddlewheels. Although other vessels had dabbled with the idea of using steam to move from one place to another quickly, an American named Robert Fulton revolutionized the steamboat, which would change New Orleans trade forever. Inspired by the *Charlotte Dundas,* a boat that contained a horizontal steam engine directly linked to a crank, an invention patented by William Symington, Fulton enlisted the help of Scottish engineer Henry Bell to design his own steamboat.

Michael Gershon reports, in "Steamboats: The Engine That Drove Economic Development in New Orleans," that the first record of a steamboat being employed was in 1811, when Nicholas Roosevelt, the great-granduncle of President Theodore Roosevelt, piloted the aptly named *New Orleans* along the Mississippi River from Pittsburgh, Pennsylvania, to New Orleans. The introduction of steamboats was a revolution, and the *New Orleans*'s trip sparked excitement for the future of travel and trade.

The Port of New Orleans and steamboats stimulated New Orleans's growth as a trade city, with more than four hundred steamboats eventually working the Mississippi River, easily importing and exporting products. Investments were made in the production of steamboats, and their construction kicked into high gear, with

$5.6 million spent on it between 1817 and 1829. By 1835, New Orleans had reached $54 million in commerce. Much of that money was from cotton, the South's most profitable commodity, and by the 1840s, the Port of New Orleans was the second-largest port in the country and the fourth-largest in the world.

New Orleans exported cotton to Britain and France in exchange for salt and other manufactured items, according to Thomas E. Redard in "The Port of New Orleans: An Economic History, 1821–1860." While cotton was the leading export to foreign ports, coffee was the leading import into the United States. After introducing steamboats to trade, New Orleans went from importing 1,438 bags of coffee in 1802 to over 500,000 bags from Cuba and other Caribbean islands by 1840. This number increased to 531,236 bags by 1857. With that, New Orleans became the second-largest importer of coffee into the United States, after New York. Thanks to its proximity to the Caribbean, Cuba, and Central and South America, New Orleans earned the nickname "the logical port," receiving shipments of green coffee from suppliers who were happy to establish a business relationship with the city.

In 1840, the population of New Orleans was around 100,000, and it was the third-most-populous city in the United States. By 1860, the population had grown to over 168,000. The citizenry comprised immigrants and their descendants from all over the world, including France, Italy, Spain, Ireland, Africa, Germany, and Haiti. New Orleans was a bustling city that was the center of trade and immigration in the United States, and it wasn't just immigration that New Orleans played an essential role in—with one of the busiest ports in the world, all roads into business seemed to lead to and from the Crescent City.

COFFEE AND THE NEW ORLEANS BOOM

As Suzanne Stone and David Feldman report in *New Orleans Coffee: A Rich History,* coffee importation into New Orleans had grown to over 531,000 bags annually by 1857. At that time, coffee was being exported from New Orleans to the rest of the United States, increasing coffee consumption per capita from three pounds annually in 1830 to eight pounds by 1859.

One of those responsible for the success of coffee in New Orleans and the rest of the United States was importer Henry T. Lonsdale. Lonsdale, a first-generation American born to British parents in Brooklyn, got a job working on the docks in New Orleans as a teenager. He first found success making burlap packaging from jute fiber after his parents had sent him some of it during one of their trips to India. The burlap business was good for Lonsdale and solidified his name in the import circles, and his burlap sacks were responsible for the successful shipping of two million sacks of shelled corn into the city.

However, when the Panic of 1837, a financial crisis that lasted until the mid-1840s, hit, Lonsdale lost his burlap fortune. With youth and time on his side and seeing the money to be made in the coffee trade, Lonsdale quickly pivoted from the burlap business into importing, making deals throughout the South and West. Lonsdale excelled at his new venture, producing weekly and annual reports of the city's coffee trade, including imports, exports, and the amount of coffee stored. According to Stone, the reports show that coffee importing and exporting grew exponentially when Lonsdale took over; imports from 1852 to 1853 increased by 20 percent from more than two years prior. In that same period, one-third of the country's coffee stock of 230,000 bags was in New Orleans.

Westfeldt Brothers, Inc., and J. Aron and Company

In 1851, Gustavus Adolphus George Westfeldt moved from Sweden to the United States to act as a Swedish ambassador. He formed a freight forwarding company in Mobile, Alabama, which became one of the nation's first green, or unroasted, coffee importers. In

1853, Westfeldt moved the company to New Orleans to profit from the city's coffee trade, occupying the warehouse and offices of a bankrupt debtor. His brothers joined the company after moving from Sweden to New Orleans, and Westfeldt Brothers, Inc., was officially formed.

The Westfeldts found success by selling coffee to towns established along the Mississippi River and peddling their coffee to local grocers. The brothers also had a diplomatic relationship with Brazilian importers and their home country of Sweden, which helped them build their business; today, Westfeldt Brothers, Inc., still operates in New Orleans in a building on Gravier Street. The company continues to hold a position as one of New Orleans's largest coffee importers and is still family-owned, with Thomas Westfeldt acting as the company's CEO and his daughter, Shelby Westfeldt Mills, a sixth-generation Westfeldt, holding the position of company president. Westfeldt Brothers, Inc., is a major player in coffee importation in modern-day New Orleans, buying green coffee mainly from Central and South America and selling it to roasters. While some of Westfeldt's customers are on the international market, the primary buyers they handle are in the United States.

Another importer that influenced New Orleans's renewed trade success was J. Aron and Company. Founder Jacob Aron learned the commodities trade from his uncle, a meatpacking agent in Chicago. According to the Louisiana State Museum online exhibit *Coffee Trade and Port of New Orleans,* in 1898, he partnered with his brother-in-law, Leon Israel, to import coffee into New Orleans. Although his partnership with Israel was short-lived, Aron found success in 1905, when a yellow fever epidemic made it difficult for ships to land their commodities. This wasn't the first time this has happened; quarantine for the disease had previously affected business and trade in 1853. Aron turned the shortage of coffee into profits for his company as coffee prices increased. Later that year, Aron hired William B. Burkenroad as his business partner. Aron then relocated to New York to be closer to the New York exchanges, leaving Burkenroad in charge of the company. Burkenroad's son took over J. Aron and Company in the 1930s and ran it until the company left the coffee business in 1978. Today, J. Aron and Company is located in New York and serves as the commodities arm of Goldman Sachs, which trades in precious and base metals, crude oil, natural gas, agriculture, and other goods.

Along with importers like Westfeldt Brothers, Inc., and J. Aron and Company, the early New Orleans coffee trade boasted a selection of coffee roasters and brokers. William Ukers enumerates the roasters in *All About Coffee* as Shaw's Louisiana Coffee and Spice Mills, Ruliff, Clark and Company, R. Poursini and Company, and Smith and McKenna. He says that New Orleans Coffee Company, Southern Coffee Polishing Mills, and Cage and Drew were added to the roasting scene between 1876 and 1900. In 1865, Daniel H. Hoffman began working for the only coffee broker in New Orleans, E. P. Cottraux. By 1894, he had opened the Southern Coffee Polishing Mills, which later became the Southern Coffee Mills, Incorporated. Furthermore, W. T. Jones, a coffee broker from Iowa, founded the New Orleans Coffee Company in 1890. By 1900, New Orleans employed twelve green coffee importing and roasting firms, and by 1920, this number had increased to fifteen.

THE CIVIL WAR

Due to rationing, coffee consumption in the United States decreased from 1861 to 1865 during the Civil War. Furthermore, the Union imposed a four-cent tax on imported coffee beans and blockaded southern ports. According to the World Port Source website, the Confederacy left the Port of New Orleans vulnerable at the start of the war, and by 1862, a Union fleet led by Admiral David Farragut had placed the port under military command. Mark Pendergrast explains that coffee producers began to increase their prices because of the conflict. For example, throughout the war, Brazil gradually increased its coffee prices from fourteen cents a pound to forty-two cents a pound, eventually reducing prices to eighteen cents a pound when the war ended.

As the war raged on, Union soldiers enjoyed coffee in their rations, with each soldier given one-tenth of a pound of green coffee beans daily. Coffee was serious business in the Union camps; it was equally divided, and beans were ground as needed to ensure freshness. Each company was fitted with its own coffee grinder, and soldiers took the stuff black with hardtack, a biscuit made with flour, water, and salt. Meanwhile, the Confederates were less fortunate when it came to coffee, or rather, coffee substitutes. Real coffee was scarce and cost as much as five dollars a pound in Richmond, Virginia. Instead, soldiers were forced to drink concoctions made from peanuts, wheat, dandelion roots, beans, corn, or chicory.

After the war ended, the South's coffee economy was slow to recover, as a Union naval blockade cut off the port, decreasing trade. In 1866, only 55,000 bags of coffee came into the Port, while coffee importation into New York and Baltimore thrived. While Caribbean blockade-runners could sneak in items such as rifles, medicine, and brandy to other Southern ports, the New Orleans port was almost entirely cut off. For years, no coffee was moving through the New Orleans port, causing financial distress to those who had made money in the coffee trade. However, by the end of 1865, New Orleans had seemingly bounced back and was trading coffee again, thanks to tenacious importer Henry T. Lonsdale, who wouldn't let a small thing like losing a war cut into his profits.

After the coffee trade took a hit due to the Civil War, importers had yellow fever to contend with. Before the war, in 1853, yellow fever claimed 7,849 New Orleans residents due in part to the fact that the public was only alerted of the outbreak after more than one thousand people had already died. Businesses feared that a quarantine would put a dent in local trade and stopped short of calling yellow fever what it was—an epidemic. When the city was forced to quarantine, ports were shut down for months at a time. The combination of war woes and yellow fever restrictions meant that the New Orleans coffee trade numbers did not surpass New York's numbers for decades.

A Brief Background on the New York Coffee Exchange

The New York Coffee Exchange was the first coffee exchange to be organized in the United States. Founded on March 7, 1882, it became one of the world's most important exchanges for trading in coffee and, later, sugar. In "The New York Coffee and Sugar Exchange," E. M. Brunn notes that the reasons for the creation of the Exchange date back to the Civil War. Between 1861 and 1865, coffee prices significantly increased except for a short time in 1862. This price increase naturally led to a rise in profits in the years before the end of the war. After the Civil War, coffee prices decreased steadily until 1870, when short crops caused prices to increase again. The crop shortage continued until 1875, and immediate price increases indicated that the market was being manipulated.

Meanwhile, in Brazil and South America, coffee planting increased due to the stateside coffee shortage, and by 1878, coffee that had been planted in 1870 was ready to be harvested. That year, Brazil exported 206,329 tons of coffee, setting a record at the time. Brazilian coffee became a commodity while the prices of Java coffee declined. The various unregulated firms dealing in coffee noted that coffee prices seemed to fluctuate with little explanation. Coffee traders created a board to ensure fairness in the purchase, sale, handling, and distribution of coffee. The board also established a well-organized market with a regulated procedure.

Trading of coffee contracts initially took place in coffeehouses until it was decided that a more centralized site should be used as the demand for coffee grew. Brunn explains that "through the establishment of a well-organized market with regulations for a uniform procedure, a group of the most prominent men in the coffee trade formulated plans for the organization of an exchange in the City of New York." When the New York Coffee Exchange opened at 135 Pearl Street, it was under the guidance of Exchange President Benjamin G. Arnold. There were 112 members of the Exchange, with the first hundred seats sold for $250 each and the second hundred seats sold at $1,000 each. With two calls daily—one at 11:00 a.m. and another at 1:00 p.m.—arrangements were made to receive daily telegrams from Rio de Janeiro, Santos, London, Havre, Antwerp, Amsterdam, and Hamburg regarding the conditions of trade there.

The Exchange concentrated on the coffee trade in New York, the leading coffee port during the Civil War, with the institution creating fixed standards for coffee grades. Pendergrast explains that in the Exchange, a buyer would sign a contract with a seller and agree to purchase a predetermined number of bags of coffee sometime in the future. Over time, the value of the contract changes, depending on the market. The Exchange would protect the coffee trade from abuse, set standards for coffee quality, settle disputes, offer prices for coffee contracts based on coffee quality, origin, and future delivery dates, and arrange for large roasting plants to buy futures and protect legitimate profits through hedging. It also provided a regulated marketplace in which prices were determined through the interaction of supply and demand. Over time, the Exchange helped set global coffee prices and served as a benchmark for coffee contracts.

In 1914, sugar contracts were added to the market, and in 1916, the New York Coffee Exchange became the New York Coffee and Sugar Exchange. In 1979, the New York Coffee and Sugar Exchange merged with the New York Cocoa Exchange to form the Coffee, Sugar, and Cocoa Exchange, Inc., which became one of the largest trade markets in the world. In 1998, the Coffee, Sugar, and Cocoa Exchange and the New York Cotton Exchange were acquired to form the New York Board of Trade. Today, the organization trades cocoa, coffee, cotton, frozen orange juice concentrate, sugar, and wood pulp.

RAILROADS PROVIDE NEW OPTIONS

William Ukers writes that by the mid-1800s, the Erie Canal, which connected Albany to Buffalo, was posing a threat to New Orleans coffee importation. In addition, railroads were expanding east and west, creating easy access to the Baltimore, Boston, New York, and Philadelphia ports. While these railways produced shipping booms for these cities, the construction of rails in the North and South was all but forgotten. If railroads created more accessible access to ports in other cities, then New Orleans trade would undoubtedly take a hit. In response, the Louisiana legislature authorized the Pontchartrain Railroad Company to build a four-and-a-half-mile railroad from New Orleans to Lake Pontchartrain. The Pontchartrain Railroad ran to the lakefront town of Milneburg from 1831 to 1930, connecting the port to the rest of the city. Milneburg was located at the end of what is now Elysian Fields Avenue, and ships came into Lake Pontchartrain and docked at the Milneburg pier. From there, goods were loaded onto the Pontchartrain Railroad and transported into the city.

Rail expansion continued; in 1835, the New Orleans and Carrollton Railroad was built, connecting New Orleans to the Carrollton neighborhood via four and a half miles of track. In "St. Charles Avenue Streetcar Line, 1836," the American Society of Mechanical Engineers Regional Transit Authority notes that today, this is the St. Charles Avenue Streetcar Line, the world's oldest continuously operating streetcar line. By 1860, the city had 143 miles of railroad, and by 1880, New Orleans boasted four railroad lines. When the Illinois Central connected to New Orleans, imports and exports by train expanded, and by 1890, five times more freight was being carried by railroad rather than by water. In 1881, the Southern Pacific rail system expanded to include New Orleans, connecting the city to El Paso across New Mexico and through Tucson to Los Angeles, San Francisco, and Sacramento.

By the early 1870s, New Orleans coffee importation was again

THIRD PART

The Daily Picayune.

THIRD PART

VOL. LXXIV.

NEW ORLEANS, LA., SUNDAY, JUNE 26, 1910.

NO. 153

COFFEE

From: "Coal" to "Brick Dust"

New Orleans Pushing New York for First Place as Port of Entry for the Enticing Bean

UNBAGGING A CARGO OF COFFEE AT THE JULIA ST LANDING NEW ORLEANS

SORTING COFFEE BEANS, GUATEMALA

THE DRYING PATIOS AT STA. EMILIA GUATEMALA

INTERIOR OF THE JULIA ST. SHED WHICH HAS A CAPACITY OF [illegible] BAGS OF COFFEE AND IS SERVED BY THE PUBLIC BELT RAILROAD

A COFFEE-CART TRAIN IN GUATEMALA

"LA CHINA" THE MODEL COFFEE FINCA OF GENERAL REGALDO EX-PRESIDENT OF EL SALVADOR

MULES LADEN WITH COFFEE GUATEMALA

Newspaper display at NOLA Coffee Festival 2023.
Photo by the author.

on the upswing. Ukers writes that New Orleans coffee numbers had reached 250,000 bags by 1871 and rapidly increased from there. From 1893 to 1894, coffee imports reached a total of 337,000 bags; in 1900, that number had increased to 514,000 bags, and by 1903, one million bags, one-quarter of the country's coffee, were being imported into New Orleans. This uptick in success was thanks, in part, to New York coffee dealers Anson Wales Hard and George C. Rand of Hard & Rand, who chartered steam trains to New Orleans for coffee trade upon realizing that steamer rates to New York from New Orleans were cost-efficient.

At the turn of the twentieth century, New Orleans was the second-most-prolific coffee port in the United States, right behind New York and significantly ahead of San Francisco. A 1903 article from the *Times-Picayune* attributed the success of the New Orleans coffee trade to the addition of the railroad, noting that the rates to ship coffee from New Orleans to the West were cheaper than the rates to ship coffee from New York to the West. The article goes on to say, "The cause for this wonderful growth had been the development of the natural advantages and better education of the trade to the fact that they can receive better service, quicker deliveries, and better freight rates from this port than any other port in the United States."

Coffee Trade Restrictions During World War I

In April 1918, World War I put a temporary hold on coffee importation into the United States. The Food Administration placed restrictions on the importation of green coffee, and dealers were required to notify the agency of the amount of Brazilian coffee they held. The restrictions stated that no buyer of green coffee would be allowed to import in excess of the percentage they imported in 1916 and 1917. The order was meant to ensure the equal distribution of green coffee based on past requirements of the trade. The reason for this restriction, as an article in the *Times-Picayune* from 1918 explains, was "to devote every available ton to the transportation of men and supplies to France to finish the fight."

During these restrictions, nearly all the coffee coming into the United States was through the Port Authority of New York. Consumers in the Mississippi Valley, Chicago, and San Francisco complained that because coffee importation was concentrated in New York, its port and railroads were becoming overcrowded and affecting other businesses. John M. Parker, food administrator for Louisiana, sent a complaint to Washington, DC, about New Orleans's limited share of the country's coffee importation and requested that the ships importing into New York and New Orleans be evenly split. The War Trade Board responded by agreeing to consider applications for coffee importation submitted to the Food Administration. However, applications had to be detailed and include the grade of coffee imported, the cost of licensees from whom the coffee was purchased, and the name of the vessel on which the coffee was being shipped. Licenses were issued at the discretion of the Sugar Equalization Board, an organization created during World War I to regulate sugar production and, later, coffee imports. The Board held the right to purchase or direct the distribution of licensed coffee over cost. If the coffee was offered for sale before its arrival to the United States, it had to first be offered to the Sugar Equalization Board.

When World War I ended on November 11, 1918, coffee importers were ready to return to business as usual. Six days after Armistice Day, the chairman of the Coffee Committee of the New Orleans Board of Trade recommended immediately reopening the New York Coffee Exchange for unrestricted trading in contracts for delivery by March 1919. The chairman also requested that all regulations and rules previously placed on coffee trade be lifted and new importations be immediately allowed to prevent a potential coffee famine. By December 22, 1918, all restrictions on food trade during the war were lifted.

The Port of New Orleans in the Twentieth Century

Charles S. Dittmann, a coffee importer and consul general of Brazil, is credited with successfully transporting coffee from Brazil following World War I. According to Ryen Stevens in "Caffeinating the Port of New Orleans," for nearly fifty years, Dittmann was one of the most renowned leading coffee commission merchants in the country, having entered the coffee business with Napier and Company, representing E. Johnston and Company, of Rio de Janeiro.

To export bags of coffee, Dittmann accessed a Lloyd Brasileiro steam merchant ship called *Campos,* which Brazil had seized at the start of World War I. On its trial run, *Campos* left Brazil on December 11, 1919, with a shipment of 35,000 bags of coffee and arrived in New Orleans on December 20. With that, a rapid shipping connection was established with Brazil, and Dittmann's efforts helped establish the Port of New Orleans as the second-largest importer of coffee after New York.

By 1920, most green coffee beans imported from Brazil were coming through the Poydras Wharf, which was now referred to as the "Coffee Wharf." The wharf was supported by a group of investors known as the Dock Commission, which not only built the railroad but improved warehouses and wharves, reduced port charges, and constructed navigational canals between the Mississippi River, Lake Pontchartrain, and the Gulf of Mexico. The Commission also constructed coffee sheds that acted as coffee facilities on the riverfront.

The wharf was equipped with steel-roof piers where coffee was stored until it was ready for shipment. A flag system, in which bags of coffee were marked with a shape, color, or pattern, made it easy for laborers to recognize where a bag of coffee would be stored on the pier after being unloaded from the ship. The marks such as a "red heart" or "green ball" were beneficial for laborers who were illiterate and otherwise wouldn't have been able to identify what type of coffee they were sorting. Today, the Riverwalk Marketplace is located where the Poydras Wharf once stood.

THE COFFEE DOCK FIRE OF 1925

On November 17, 1925, tragedy struck the New Orleans coffee industry when a major fire swept the coffee docks on the upper end of the Girod Street Wharf late at night, where new construction was taking place. According to the *Times-Picayune,* the flames, fanned by high winds, destroyed seven blocks of the docks in thirty minutes until it met the Canal Street firewall, leaving over $4.5 million worth of damage in its wake. The goods destroyed included between $2.75 million and $3.5 million worth of coffee, canned Hawaiian pineapple, ten Public Belt freight cars, cargo in the Girod Street shed, and the docks themselves. Other damages included fifteen Public Belt freight cars and electric lighting, power, telephone lines, and railroad tracks adjacent to the dock.

Also, at the time of the fire, the *Manila Marn,* a Japanese coffee ship, had just unloaded 75,000 sacks of coffee, and although the ship was saved, the coffee was destroyed. Another boat, *Parnahyba,* had been unloading at the dock before the fire but was towed downstream with 14,000 bags of coffee in its hold. Interestingly, *Parnahyba* was sunk during World War II on May 1, 1942, with 40,950 bags of coffee, 30,000 bags of cocoa, 27,155 bags of bran, 25,000 bales of leather, 17,585 of castor beans, and 15,108 volumes of miscellaneous cargo on board.

The *Times-Picayune* recounted the dock fire as an eventful scene, explaining that within ten minutes of the fire alarms being set off, every piece of firefighting equipment in the city was sent to battle the blaze. All available police were dispatched to the scene, some even commandeering citizen vehicles during the effort. As large crowds gathered at the foot of Canal Street to watch the fire stretch up to Julia Street, large drums of gasoline stored at the docks began exploding and adding to the inferno. The sound was described as similar to that of an artillery blast.

As the paper describes, "The flames licked heavenward, leaping hundreds of feet into the air, and illuminated all of New Orleans, their tremendous spread making it appear as if the entire city was in flames. Streets leading towards the river became congested with thousands of automobiles. So dense was the crowd of spectators at the fire that their automobiles lined the streets leading to the docks as far back as Tchoupitoulas Street from Canal and as far uptown as Julia."

Assessing the Damage and Planning to Rebuild

After the smoke cleared, the damage to the dock and the New Orleans coffee import business was significant but not earth-shattering. It was estimated that 100,000 bags of coffee, or 1 percent of the supply used annually in the United States, were destroyed in the blaze, leading to a half-cent increase in national coffee prices. F. W. Kuntz, president of the Green Coffee Association, assured the public that the coffee was insured, that there was still plenty of coffee on hand, and that there was no threat of any significant price increases in the future.

Immediately, the Dock Board got to work, planning to rebuild the damaged pier. Two days after the fire, the *Times-Picayune* outlined the work needed to clear the debris and begin designing a new facility, including building permanent concrete wharves. Other planned additions included fire gaps beneath the docks, adequate water connections, more fireboats, and a concrete driveway. Edward S. Butler, vice president of the Dock Board, promised to deliver plans for the new wharves just three days after the fire and noted that the Board was embarrassed that the fire happened in the first place. He insisted that rebuilding the docks would be beneficial in the long run; Butler and New Orleans Fire Commissioner Harry W. Fitzpatrick assured the public that safety measures would be implemented to prevent future dock disasters.

While plans for the new docks were being drawn, the Dock Board met with the Green Coffee Association to arrange for the reception of new coffee shipments until the dock was rebuilt. While the entire loss was covered by insurance, it was noted that the Dock Board would pay the first $100,000 out of its own insurance fund. Although the Chalmette Slip and other city railroads offered space for the coffee trade to resume, the Dock Board said that relocating coffee importation was unnecessary because the fire only destroyed 1,300 feet of the Board's six and a half miles of public wharves.

An Opportunity for Growth and a Bright Future for the New Orleans Coffee Trade

As plans for a new coffee terminal progressed, steamship operators and coffee importers seized the opportunity to design a state-of-the-art shipping complex fit for one of the country's largest coffee ports. Plans were made to create a facility that would double the efficiency of handling coffee shipments into New Orleans; the goal was to design a two-story plant, complete with conveyors, elevators, sorting capabilities, and rail facilities. As the *Times-Picayune* describes, Neal M. Leach, chairman of the Dock Board's Finance Committee, and W. H. de France, superintendent of the Dock Department, promised a coffee shed worthy of handling the nation's coffee supply. Veteran steamship agent M. J. Sanders was especially eager for a new complex, believing that a proper terminal would reduce freight costs by one-third. It was also noted that a more efficient terminal meant getting coffee off the ships faster and reducing delays.

The paper reported that many in the local coffee industry were concerned about New Orleans's place as one of the country's top coffee ports; New York quickly gained ground in the coffee importation industry partly due to its more adequate terminal. A plan came together for a multistoried facility where conveyors would move coffee from the ship to the upper floors. From there, the goods would be sorted and stored or dropped down to the first floor for shipment.

Sanders was emphatic in his plea that a new terminal be built quickly for the good of the city's coffee trade. He told Dock Board officials, "Don't let a matter of cost stand in your way. The coffee business is a matter of great importance to this port. One of the objections of foreign lines to sending ships here is that the coffee handling facilities have not been good. It is more important that you act on this matter right than to do it hastily."

Plans for the New Wharf Take Shape

By the summer of 1926, plans for the new two-storied Poydras Wharf had begun to take shape. The old landing, used exclusively by coffee vessels, allowed shipments to be stored for twenty days. The average time the cargo remained on the wharf was around fifteen days, even though only four days were required for unloading. This meant that for eleven days, this space was left occupied and unavailable for usage by another vessel.

The new wharf would double the cargo capacity of its section of the river and employ a two-story shed; the first floor would be reserved for coffee, while the second floor would be used for handling other commodities. One thousand feet of extra wharf front would be added to the harbor facilities, and the additional space would be permitted for continuous use by vessels. Furthermore, the new fireproof structure would be constructed from concrete with inclines so cargo could be easily moved between floors. Engineers noted that years prior, the Government Wharf was destroyed by fire and replaced with concrete, which proved to be fire-resistant and unaffected by the Mississippi River's waters.

A New Coffee Shed Means a New Beginning for New Orleans Coffee Trade

On October 3, 1928, nearly three years after a fire destroyed the Poydras Wharf, the new $2 million facility was dedicated when the first shipment of coffee was discharged and stored at the new shed. The *Times-Picayune* said the new coffee dock boasted a length of 1,360 feet and a width of 250 feet with a two-story fireproof shed constructed of steel and concrete. The new facility would store coffee, burlap, and canned goods.

The dedication ceremony for the new coffee shed was all business, with the steamship *Salvation Lass* carrying 16,642 sacks of coffee from Santos and Victoria, Brazil. The load was accepted by coffee importer Samuel Israel of Leon Israel and Brothers, Inc. As the first sack of coffee was placed on a wheelbarrow for handling, coffee broker Henry Young of Ruffner, McDowell, and Burch broke open a bottle of "near-beer" in celebration. Telegrams congratulating the Dock Board on the new shed came from as far as St. Louis, Kansas City, and Chicago. The momentous event was attended by Jay Well, chairman of the Foreign Trade Bureau of the Association of Commerce, and various other members of the United States Shipping Board and the Dock Board.

Dupuy Storage and Forwarding

John Dupuy was a World War I veteran who started in the coffee business as a Brazilian coffee importer. In July 1936, he opened the first location of his coffee warehouse, Dupuy Storage and Forwarding, in a three-story building on South Peters Street. He then expanded to Decatur Street in 1949, and the company moved to its current headquarters in 1989. Today, Dupuy Storage serves Charleston, Houston, Jacksonville, and New Orleans ports, run by fourth-generation Dupuy descendants Allan Colley and Janet Colley Morse.

Colley Morse explains that when the business started, coffee shipping was completely different, with loose coffee bags on ships and bags of coffee processed on the riverfront. Today, Dupuy Storage and Forwarding serves the coffee industry by processing and storing coffee and making the process of getting coffee from the farm to the roaster as easy as possible. As Colley Morse explains, an importer buys coffee from its origin sources, such as Brazil, Costa Rica, or Colombia, working on behalf of a roaster or buying coffee to send samples to roasters for a possible sale. Dupuy Storage and Forwarding stores the coffee until a sale is made or until the roaster arranges to pick up the coffee from the facility.

To revolutionize the way green coffee is handled, Dupuy opened the first green coffee silo in the United States and now owns two of the green coffee silos that are functioning in the country—one in New Orleans and one in Jacksonville, Florida. The system, which is popular in Europe, uses green coffee silos to protect and store raw green coffee beans before they are processed. Allan Colley was inspired to use green coffee silos for Dupuy's coffee storage when he saw them being used for coffee storage in Germany.

Services provided by Dupuy Storage and Forwarding include climate-controlled storage warehousing in which coffee beans are transported directly from the port to the storage facility, coffee blending that promotes the consistency and flavor of coffee associated with certain brands, coffee sampling to ensure that customers' orders are correct, and coffee upgrading. Coffee upgrading includes cleaners that sort and separate coffee beans by width and thickness for consistency; destoners that remove rocks, stones, or other items from the coffee beans; sizers that separate good coffee product from waste product; a gravity table that filters out coffee beans of an undesirable size; and a color sorter that separates defective coffee beans by color.

An advantage of having these additional services, Colley Morse says, is that an importer can buy a batch of coffee that is considered low quality for a low price—it might contain contaminants such as sticks and stones, or some of the beans might be black or misshapen. The importer can then send the coffee to Dupuy Storage and Forwarding, and they can "fix" it by sorting out any impurities and producing a marketable product that a roaster can use.

New Orleans Coffee Import Co. Imports Coffee from the Philippines to New Orleans

In modern-day New Orleans, New Orleans Coffee Import Co. is a small coffee importing company that specializes in introducing green specialty coffee from the Philippines to the United States. In 2017, founder Kellan Lyman was living in the rural Philippines and working with a development organization in small-holder producer communities when she saw an opportunity to bring Philippine coffee to the United States. She explains that the company came together through relationships with producers, farmers, coffee roasters, and coffee lovers. The company creates direct trade relationships between farmers and coffee buyers seeking to "do good."

Founded in 2021, New Orleans Coffee Import Co. began working with communities in the Philippines and, later, El Salvador to grow and harvest coffee and set an example of what a sustainable-trade coffee partnership looks like. Lyman wants to be the best partner to farmers and support growers by contributing to their share capital funds. She also supports farmers by buying their coffee at a higher industry price so they don't fall victim to predatory loan sharks who entice them with exploitative contracts to purchase coffee at lower than the market price. When farmers enter these contracts, often out of desperation, they don't profit significantly from the coffee they're growing. Lyman wants to break that cycle by offering an alternative.

She explains that most importers do not present coffee from the Philippines in their offer list because, for many years, the country's coffee offerings were limited. In the late nineteenth century, the Philippines was the world's second-largest coffee producer due to its high, mountainous elevation and volcanic soil. However, coffee rust, a fungus that affects coffee plants, practically destroyed the country's coffee trees, reducing the coffee industry in the Philippines to one-sixth of its total production from 1888 to 1891. With coffee plants under attack, many farmers opted to grow sugar instead. By the twenty-first century, coffee production had significantly increased but remained low compared to other coffee-growing nations. Today, specialty coffee production in the Philippines is limited, and much of the coffee produced there is commercial grade used in instant coffee for large brands such as Nestlé.

Because New Orleans Import Co. is small, the company's green coffee bean sampling, warehousing, and retail are handled in-house. Lyman sells green and roasted coffee beans on her company's website to connoisseurs nationwide and has noticed an increased interest in the Philippine coffee movement in Atlanta, Chicago, Los Angeles, and Seattle. Now that coffee is in its third wave, she says, small companies like hers are working to bring specialty coffee to the forefront and provide a more personalized experience to customers interested in their coffee's origin. Boutique importers help foster relationships between coffee buyers and coffee-growing countries that share a passion, and Lyman hopes to bring recognition to the Philippine coffee industry and introduce a new coffee origin to the specialty market.

Coffee Brokering: Buying and Selling Coffee on the Open Market

One of the pivotal roles in the coffee industry is the coffee broker. Brokers ensure quality control and create relationships between coffee buyers and farmers. The broker's most important job is guaranteeing quality coffee for the buyer and a fair price for the grower. The International Coffee Corporation was formed in New Orleans in September 1977, a day after J. Aron and Company relocated to New York. Founded by former employees of J. Aron and helmed by William G. Madary II, the International Coffee Corporation is one of the leading green coffee brokers in New Orleans. As a green coffee broker, the International Coffee Corporation, or ICC, buys coffee from the farmers themselves or conglomerations of producers running coffee mills in the coffee's country of origin.

When you're treating yourself to a bag of specialty coffee beans or a cup of coffee at a small coffee shop, you might wonder how the roaster arrived at the price you're paying at the register. A good way to think of green coffee buying is like the stock market; on some days, the price of coffee may be low, and on other days, it might be high. Many factors can affect the price of green coffee, which can vary by as much as fifteen cents depending on the day. One of these factors is origin-specific differentials, which encompasses the premium paid for a certain type of coffee. Drew Cambre, the sustainability manager for ICC and a twenty-year veteran of the coffee industry, explains that these differentials can depend on components such as equipment, fertilizer, or labor costs. Sometimes a crop is affected by a global recession, a drought, or an unseasonable frost—this could lead to coffee that is higher priced. Another factor that affects green coffee prices is transport. Expenses you don't immediately think of, like payment to steamship lines on which coffee is shipped, drayage fees that connect different points of origin during shipping, protection services that protect the product from potential interlopers, and customs fees, all dictate what coffee costs. Other expenditures like credit cards, pallets, and SCA certifications can also affect green coffee prices.

There are two options when a broker buys coffee: spot buying and forward buying. In spot buying, the standard type of small coffee buying, a broker buys green coffee directly from an importer or warehouse. In forward buying, used mainly by more prominent coffee companies, a broker commits to purchasing a specific type of green coffee in advance. The advantage of forward buying is locking in containers of coffee at a low price. This keeps the profit of the coffee predictable, and the coffee arrives fresh shortly after it has been harvested.

ICC mainly deals in forward coffee buying. When the coffee is ready to be shipped, the producer will send a preshipment sample, a fully processed representative sample of what to expect from the coffee when the complete shipment arrives. Cambre explains that the preshipment sample is saved. When the final sample, known as the arrival sample, lands, both the preshipment and arrival samples are cupped and tasted. If the quality is the same, ICC will notify the producer that they are willing to sell the coffee to its customers, which can range from large coffee companies to small coffee buyers.

Additionally, when working with large coffee corporations, the broker plays a large part in arranging sales between the producer and the buyer. When a coffee buyer enters a contract with ICC, the company negotiates everything from the shipping lines to arrangements with the port to ensure the transaction goes smoothly. When a customer is interested in buying coffee from a coffee broker, the broker will send coffee samples to the potential buyer so they can decide if they are interested in moving forward with the sale. Cambre says that ICC also creates an à la carte menu where they buy and store various coffee in coffee warehouses nationwide. This is specifically for smaller customers who want a wide variety of coffee options at their fingertips.

New Orleans Coffee Importation: Full Steam Ahead

By the mid-twentieth century, the United States was the largest importer of South American coffee, with most shipped through the Port of New Orleans. One-third, or 200 million pounds, of the imported coffee is from Brazil, while additional coffee comes from Colombia, Vietnam, Germany, Nicaragua, Mexico, Spain, Guatemala, Indonesia, and Australia.

Today, New Orleans is the number-one coffee port in the United States, importing an average of over 700,000 tons of green coffee beans annually from thirty-one different countries. According to data from the Port of New Orleans, the Port imported around 743 million pounds of coffee in 2020 and around 744 million pounds in 2021. That averages to around twenty billion cups of coffee per year! Dan Bolton explains in "Coffee Gateway to the USA" that the Port of New Orleans is the nation's premier coffee handling port, with fourteen warehouses and more than 5.5 million square feet of storage space. Also, New Orleans is home to Smucker Coffee Silo Operations, the world's largest automated coffee silo and fully computerized plant. This facility receives imported green coffee in bulk tankers, burlap bags, or super sacks and then weighs, samples, sorts, processes, blends, stores, and loads out in bulk to locations across North America. The plant produces more than two million pounds of coffee each day. If you are enjoying coffee roasted, ground, or sold in the United States, it is highly likely that it passed through the Port of New Orleans.

3

A Modern Exchange

The Role of Coffee in New Orleans Social Life

At the turn of the nineteenth century, New Orleans was on the cusp of change, and the city's population was on the verge of a boom. The landscape was evolving with the addition of settlers who brought their coffee practices to a new home. Coffee was a part of daily New Orleans life, and the practices of those emigrating to the city would become a part of the city's daily routine. Citizens found themselves gathering at exchanges to share ideas and get the news of the day, and coffee became a part of the social hour at home when entertaining guests. Some more creative citizens even developed better ways to enjoy coffee. There's no doubt about it: By the nineteenth century, New Orleans was a coffee town, and the drink was embedded in both the work and recreation of its citizens.

Saint-Domingue and the Revolt of the Enslaved

Jim Bradshaw explains in "Saint-Domingue Revolution" that the Saint-Domingue revolution of the West Indies, which took place between 1791 and 1804, led to the abolition of slavery in the former French colony. The revolution also affected how New Orleans looked as the city grew. Saint-Domingue was originally a part of Hispaniola, which Columbus claimed for Spain in 1492. When the

Spanish came in, the native Arawakan population was reduced to such an extent that enslaved people were imported from Africa for agricultural labor, beginning in 1502. In 1664, the French West Indies Company took control of the western portion of the islands of Hispaniola and Tortuga, and this change of power was formally recognized in 1697 in the Treaty of Ryswick.

From there, French immigrants settled in what was now called Saint-Domingue, working as sugar, indigo, and coffee planters. In the colony, the French established a tiered social structure. In *The Strange History of the American Quadroon: Free Women of Color in the Revolutionary Atlantic World,* Emily Clark writes that *grands blancs,* or the white elite, were mainly wealthy planters and colonial officials. *Petit blancs* consisted of small planters, overseers, artisans, merchants, and petty traders of French descent. Clark notes that whereas *grands blancs* felt confined by the rules of the French monarchy, the *petit blancs* were content for Saint-Domingue to remain a French colony. *Gens de couleur libres,* or free people of color, comprised the rest of Saint-Domingue's population and owned one-third of the colony's plantation property and one-fourth of those enslaved there.

By the 1730s, Saint-Domingue was responsible for 60 percent of the world's coffee. At this time, Saint-Domingue was the number-one supplier of sugar in the world, and the colony produced twice as much coffee as sugar, making it a significant player in the market for these commodities. Bradshaw explains that partly because Saint-Domingue was a substantial supplier of the world's coffee and sugar, it quickly became the wealthiest colonial possession in the West Indies and prospered due to enslaved laborers, who outnumbered the white population by over 460,000.

Richard A. Haggerty writes in *Haiti: A Country Study* that by 1791, Saint-Domingue boasted a population of 519,000 people. The enslaved comprised 87 percent of the population, of whom 8 percent were white, and 5 percent were freedmen. The French feared a slave revolt, and torture and violent beatings became a way of life for the enslaved. Even before the revolt of the enslaved, tensions were high in Saint-Domingue, and conflicts between the enslaved and landowners became frequent occurrences. C. L. R. James notes in *The Black Jacobins: Toussaint l'Ouverture and the San Domingo Revolution* that adding to this tension was the French National Assembly's approval of the Declaration of the Rights of Man and of the Citizen, which gave the colony's free people of color the same rights as any other citizen, including formal citizenship status for wealthy free people of color. White planters didn't recognize this decision, and a civil war between the formerly enslaved and landowners began on August 22, 1791.

Enraged after years of their enslavers' inhumane brutality and led by Henri Christophe, Jean-Jacques Dessalines, and Toussaint L'Ouverture, the enslaved and formerly enslaved led a revolution against the French colonizers. Two major cities, Léogâne and Jacmel, were burned, and plantations were destroyed, including nine hundred coffee plantations. After years of conflict and intercession from outside nations such as Great Britain and Spain, the last battle in Saint-Domingue, the Battle of Vertières, was fought on November 18, 1803. French forces were defeated, and the former colony gained independence.

On January 1, 1804, what was formerly Saint-Domingue was proclaimed Haiti. When it was established, it became the first Western nation governed by people of African descent and the second independent republic in the Western Hemisphere. Following the insurrection, thousands of refugees emigrated to the United States, including free people of color and white planters. Bradshaw explains that these immigrants, who settled in Louisiana between 1790 and the early 1800s, were planters and artisans with various skills.

Louisiana's Sale to the United States

Following the Saint-Domingue revolution, Napoleon Bonaparte, the first consul of France, was defeated. Between the crush of battle and disease, he lost tens of thousands of his army, including his brother-in-law, General Charles Victoire Emmanuel LeClerc, who died of yellow fever. Napoleon had hoped that he would be able to reclaim Saint-Domingue for his own purposes, specifically to cash in on the sugar trade and establish the island as an easy way to garner capital. Bradshaw explains that in 1800, Napoleon negotiated the Treaty of San Ildefonso with Spain for the French possession of Louisiana and took control of the colony in 1802. Due to France's defeat in the Saint-Domingue revolt, Napoleon decided he no longer needed the Louisiana colony. He hoped to make a quick sale to the United States and shake himself free of the territory once and for all.

In April 1803, Thomas Jefferson sent diplomats Robert Livingston and James Monroe to negotiate the sale of the Isle of Orleans with the French minister of finance, François Barbé-Marbois. At this point, Napoleon was desperate for money to fund his war with Great Britain, and Jefferson was eager to acquire the Louisiana territory because he saw the Port of New Orleans as a trade asset. The dictator sold the colony to the United States for $15 million, with money that was borrowed from Dutch banks and, ironically, Great Britain, and Louisiana was transferred to United States control on December 20, 1803. The purchase nearly doubled the size of the country and extended the United States' power over the Port of New Orleans and across the Mississippi River. The deal was made official on October 1, 1804, and the territory was divided into the District of Louisiana and the Orleans Territory, which would later become the State of Louisiana in 1812.

Creoles in New Orleans

In "What's the Difference Between Cajun and Creole—or Is There One?" Molly Cleaver explains that by the mid-eighteenth century, the term "Creole" was used to refer to someone, regardless of race, who was a native of a European colony, spoke French, and was Catholic. Nathalie Dessens writes, in *From Saint-Domingue to New Orleans,* that in New Orleans, "Creole" was used to describe both white people born in a French colony *and* people of color. Dessens goes on to describe this mixture of various cultures as "Creolization," the creation of a new cultural identity that expands outside of one rigid definition and includes African, French, Native American, and Spanish cultures.

According to Clark, following the Saint-Domingue revolution, many Dominguans migrated to Santiago, Cuba. They did well there, acquiring land and developing coffee plantations, a practice that exploded when Dominguan coffee farmers settled there. However, due to clashes between Napoleon and Spain, Cuba's colonial government swept the island, banishing any Frenchmen they believed to be dangerous. In 1809, Dominguans began pouring into Louisiana from Cuba, and New Orleans's population nearly tripled. Louisiana Creoles were enthusiastic at the prospect of an increase in the French-speaking population, and Louisiana proved to be a hospitable place for these refugees. Soon enough, they were integrating themselves into the city's already diverse population.

The Saint-Domingue Creoles settled into New Orleans life quickly, and their cultural practices and influences immediately began to change how the city operated. In the early nineteenth century, New Orleans's population consisted of French, Spanish, Germans, Italians, Africans, and Indians, and the city, with its mixing pot of cultures, languages, and races, was unlike any other in the country. In regard to the ever-expanding culture of New Orleans at the time, Richard Campanella notes in *Bienville's Dilemma: A Historical Geography of New Orleans* that William Darby, a Pennsylvania-born geographer, famously wrote, "No city perhaps on the globe, in an equal number of human beings, presents a greater contrast of national manners, language, and complexion, than does New Orleans."

Coffee Exchanges: A Hub of Social Discourse

With Louisiana was under American control, coffeehouses and exchanges began operating in New Orleans. These coffee exchanges were popular in Europe but new to the newly christened American territory. In "Brewed Awakening: Re-imagining Education in Three Nineteenth-Century New Orleans Coffee Houses," Robyn Andermann explains that, like their European counterparts, coffeehouses or exchanges became hubs where intellectual discussions and socialization occurred.

As mentioned in chapter 1, the coffeehouse originated in seventeenth-century London during the Age of Enlightenment, also known as the Age of Reason, when meaningful conversations about government, religion, science, and liberty often took place in coffeehouses and exchanges over cups of coffee. Here, businessmen, politicians, clergymen, and theologians could hold an audience while excited participants exchanged ideas. For lively debate in Europe, exchanges were much preferred over cafés, a popular European term for bars at the time. Introducing alcohol to such heated conversations wasn't preferred, and sipping coffee rather than ale allowed thoughts to be shared more respectfully and less volatilely. Emma Spary notes in *Eating the Enlightenment* that at this time, the coffeehouse fostered political conversations and intellectual exchange. While the coffeehouses and exchanges of London were places where people would receive the day's news, the exchanges in Paris were more literary-focused.

Although the terms "coffeehouse" and "coffee exchange" are often used interchangeably, it should be noted that the two are different. Coffeehouses were usually where socializing happened, and coffee exchanges were where socializing and *sales* occurred. However, in a change from its London counterparts, American coffeehouses and coffee exchanges served not only coffee within their walls but alcohol as well. However, alcohol service was restricted to nighttime hours. In nineteenth-century New Orleans, exchanges were a relatively new idea. Still, local exchanges quickly became social hubs where men, as they had in Europe, would chat about the day's news, argue politics, read the daily paper, and attend auctions. In the United States, these auctions included everything from the sale of ships to the auction of enslaved people.

One of the first exchanges was Café de la Bourse, or Exchange Coffee House, which operated from 1806 to 1837. Richard Campanella explains in "Gallier and Dakin's Merchants' Exchange," that one of the city's best-known exchanges, Tremoulet's New Exchange Coffee House, was opened at 501 Chartres Street. Tremoulet House holds a significant place in Louisiana history, as it was where forty-three delegates convened, in the winter of 1811–12, to vote Louisiana into statehood. It became La Bourse de Maspero, or Maspero's Exchange, in 1814.

The second floor of Maspero's Exchange is long-rumored to be where Andrew Jackson and Jean Lafitte planned the defense of New Orleans against the British in late 1814. Whether this is true or not is certainly up for debate. However, Stanley Clisby Arthur notes in *Old New Orleans: A History of the Vieux Carré, Its Ancient and Historical Buildings* that Maspero's Exchange was where a Committee of Public Safety met to discuss how they could rally citizens into throwing their support behind General Jackson's efforts to defend the city during the War of 1812. The committee was made up of an eclectic group that included attorney Edward Livingston; native Creole Pierre Foucher; a Frenchman of the ancien régime, Dussau de la Croix; American merchants Benjamin B. Morgan and George Ogden; a native of southern France, Jean Blanque; and members of distinguished Louisiana families Jean Noël d'Estrehan and Augustin de Macarty.

After Pierre Maspero died in 1822, the place became known as Elkin's Exchange. In 1826, John Hewlett renamed it Hewlett's Exchange, but locals referred to the establishment simply as "The Exchange." In his article, Campanella describes the Exchange as quite the sight, writing, "The two-story corner structure boasted, behind its Venetian privacy screens, a nineteen-foot-high ceiling, four chandeliers, framed maps, and oil paintings (described by one Northerner as 'licentious'), wood-and-marble finishing, an enormous bar with French glassware, and billiards and gambling tables upstairs."

After the success of the Exchange, American businessman and education activist Samuel Jarvis Peters saw a chance to make money in the exchange business. According to Campanella, Peters reasoned that an exchange built in the heart of this expanding commercial district, upriver from the Chartres-Royal corridor, would attract both a Creole and American clientele. Peters put his plan into motion to the tune of $100,000 he acquired through a joint-stock company and purchased a building on Royal Street. The investment became what would be known as the Merchants' Exchange.

The Merchants' Exchange began operating in 1836 at 26 Royal Street and quickly became a popular local hangout, hosting a shared space that featured auction areas, meeting rooms, trade floors, and day and night activities. On the second floor was a reading room where visitors could read the latest books and newspapers for only ten dollars a year. For a few years, the second floor boasted a federal district court. The U.S. Post Office was on the Exchange's ground floor, which aided the building in gaining popularity with the public. The third floor was for business, billiards, card games, chess games, and smoking. Of course, because this is New Orleans we're talking about, the Exchange was only a few steps away from a barroom, making it an even more favored hangout.

In 1838, Sewell Taylor began working as a bartender at the Merchants' Exchange, and within five years, he was running it. As the Sazerac company describes in the history of its brand, in 1849, when his lease to continue to run the Exchange wasn't renewed, Taylor switched gears and established a wholesale and retail liquor business selling Sazerac Forge et Fils Brandy. In the early 1850s, investor Aaron Bird opened the Sazerac Coffee House next to the Merchants' Exchange. While there was no proof that Taylor was involved in the business that bears the name of the product he had been selling, it's rumored that he was a financial backer of the establishment. The Sazerac cocktails made there, which included the all-important Peychaud's Bitters, invented by Antoine Amedie Peychaud, a Creole immigrant, quickly became popular. Not only would the cocktail put the Sazerac Coffee House on the map, but in 2008, the Sazerac would be named the official cocktail of New Orleans.

Another favored refuge was Gwathmey's Coffee House, located at 602 Conti Street in a building Stanley Clisby Arthur claims dates to when New Orleans was a Spanish territory. Founded by John Gwathmey, it isn't clear what year the building was constructed, though it's believed to be sometime after the Great New Orleans Fire of 1794. After its tenure as Gwathmey's Coffee House, it became the Merchants' Coffee House in 1822 and Phoenix Oyster and Beefsteak House two years later.

In the early nineteenth century, Café des Réfugiés was a coffeehouse between Dumaine and St. Philip Streets owned by Jean Baptiste Hyacinthe Thiot and frequented, as the name might suggest, by refugees of Saint-Domingue. Lyle Saxon explains in *Old Louisiana* that coffeehouse revelers spent evenings consuming a liquor called la petit Gonâve, named for their former home, and enjoying singing, dancing, and jubilation on a stage in the courtyard under orange trees. The café allowed the refugees to establish a community and network and socialize in their new home. Beyond the social aspect, the café served as a place where Saint-Domingue refugees met with others who had migrated to New Orleans and received assistance in finding homes and jobs. Unlike exchanges of the time, Café des Réfugiés was simply a place to enjoy each other's company—no business deals were made here, it had no designated political affiliation, and it wasn't an auction site. Robyn Andermann explains that the coffeehouse was open to everyone, including whites, travelers, free people of color, enslaved people, and the working class of both French and Spanish backgrounds. It served as a place where Saint-Domingue refugees could share their culture with others and discuss daily happenings.

Similarly, Café des Améliorations, located at the southwest corner of Rampart and Toulouse Streets, was a haven for French Creoles. *The Picayune's Guide to New Orleans* describes the place as where "Creole gentlemen discontented and alarmed at the growing power of the 'Americans' used to meet and discuss questions for the amelioration of their 'dear city' and its rescue from the hands of the invaders." Their concern was the Americanization of Creole culture, and weekly meetings were held on how Creoles could overthrow the government and arrest state officials.

New Orleans Exchanges and the Free Lunch

As the century progressed, New Orleans boasted hundreds of coffeehouses and exchanges. By this point, coffeehouses and exchanges weren't just for business affairs but were places where men gathered to enjoy food and drink during a busy workday. Meals were enjoyed in coffeehouses at all hours, especially by those unable to make it home for a home-cooked meal. A businessman named Alvarez, proprietor of the Old St. Louis Hotel and City Exchange, began offering a free noontime meal as the day's main meal in the 1830s. This "free lunch" became so popular that other coffeehouses adopted the practice, much to the delight of the city's workers. The owners of the exchanges knew what they were doing—offering a free lunch meant that people would stay at the exchange longer and spend their money on drinks. It was incredibly convenient when these free lunches coincided with the day's noon auctions.

Michael Mizell-Nelson noted, in his article "No Such Thing as a Free Lunch Anymore," that these midday meals changed how many New Orleanians ate. Workers would enjoy a large midday meal and work through what was traditionally considered dinnertime. As a result, dinner was served after the day's work was done entirely, and the workers' hunger returned. The New Orleans free lunch was a trendsetter as the practice spread to New York City and Ohio in the 1850s and elsewhere in the South throughout the rest of the century. However, it never garnered the same popularity as in New Orleans.

Coffee Innovators in New Orleans

While some New Orleanians were spending time at exchanges and enjoying their coffee in social settings, others were working behind the scenes to improve coffee preparation throughout the late nineteenth and twentieth centuries. A search of the United States Patent and Trademark Office reveals that quite a few New Orleans inventors received patents for better ways to prepare and brew coffee.

Cirilo Mingo was a Mexican who emigrated to New Orleans. In August 1893, he was granted a United States patent on a method of aging green coffee beans so they would take on the characteristics of beans aged for an extended time. In his patent filing, Mingo describes his method as layering green coffee beans between wet and dry burlap coffee bags. The coffee beans absorbed eight to ten times more moisture in six to sixteen hours by this method. The coffee berries, he says, are then laid out and dried by the sun. In this process, "the coffee berries are found to have developed the same flavor obtained by the process of nature, and to have increased in size, being in an expanded and brittle condition peculiarly adapted for roasting," Mingo writes.

Another New Orleanian, Orville Walter Chamberlain, was granted a United States patent in March 1916 for his improvement upon the automatic-drip coffeepot. In his patent filing, Chamberlain writes that his coffeepot is designed so that water will pass through coffee grounds only once during the brewing process. He achieved the feat by designing a coffeepot with a chamber where small quantities of water are pushed from one side of the pot to the other through percolation. During the process, water is evenly distributed over coffee grounds, and the coffee then drips into the chamber below, to be poured through the coffeepot's spout.

In November 1947, Lewis A. Scherck received a patent for his invention of a multiple-drip coffee urn, an improvement on an urn he had patented in 1931. The purpose of the urn was to brew a more robust and better-flavored coffee by introducing boiling water into the receptacle. Like Chamberlain's automatic-drip coffeepot, the system had multiple chambers and distributed water evenly over the coffee grounds. He explains that the urn is an all-encompassing brew system that eliminates the need for cloth bags and filters, which detract from the coffee's flavor.

CREOLE AND CAJUN COFFEE AT HOME IN THE NINETEENTH CENTURY

By the latter part of the nineteenth century, coffee had become a part of daily New Orleans life and was enjoyed at home by Creoles and Cajuns, whose at-home coffee practices were similar. *The Picayune's Creole Cook Book* describes Creole coffee, or café à la Creole, as a part of the typical morning routine. Café noir, coffee black, and Café au Lait, coffee with hot milk, were enjoyed throughout the day and evening. For a rich coffee experience, coffee with hot cream, or café a la crème, was a rare but decadent choice.

Café noir was often consumed at the start of the day, and Creoles believed their coffee to be the key to longevity. The book explains that when people reached the age of eighty and were asked the secret to their long life, they often attributed the achievement to their coffee consumption. Others believed that a hot cup of café noir after a heavy meal was the best way to relieve indigestion and help the stomach perform its functions properly.

Coffee was seen as medicinal, dating back to when it was first discovered, and Creole doctors added to this narrative by claiming that it was the best way to prevent infectious diseases. Coffee was also used as a deodorizer, and Creole physicians would pass grains of coffee burning in a chafing dish throughout a room. Some Creole physicians even considered coffee an antidote to poison.

Along with alcohol, coffee was served at Creole and Cajun social functions, such as house dances, in a practice called "high coffee." Marcelle Bienvenu describes the drink being brewed in the kitchen during high coffee and served in large bowls to guests in the living room. Children would often serve coffee to adult guests during a gathering, and the beverage was presented on a platter with a bowl of sugar and the utensils needed to prepare it the desired way. This special event could happen any time of day or evening, and guests enjoyed their coffee in the host's finest porcelain cups, complete with silverware and small cloth napkins, and were served a sweet accompaniment like cake.

The Picayune's Creole Cook Book describes the process of making a proper cup of Creole coffee in the nineteenth century. The best coffee beans came from Mocha, Yemen and Java, Indonesia, and coffee beans were roasted to a rich brown and never burned. After cooling in a covered dish, the beans were ground to a consistency that was neither too fine nor too coarse. Grounds that were too fine made the coffee muddy, and grounds that were too coarse produced coffee that lacked flavor. Boiling water was percolated slowly, most likely in a French drip, through the grounds and into a clean coffeepot. It should be noted that the water must be boiling or the quality of the coffee will suffer. If Creole coffee appeared muddy, some would drop an inch-thick piece of burnt wood into the water, settling the grounds to the bottom of the coffeepot. This could also be achieved by adding a few drops of cold water into the coffee. Food historian Elizabeth Williams explains that coffee was served in heated cups and, when served in the afternoon, contained only sugar and not milk as the morning coffee had. Café au lait is prepared in the same manner as café noir but with the addition of boiled milk. There seems to be a debate about whether the milk should be boiled, as my research has produced conflicting results, so please use your discretion when preparing your café au lait. *The Picayune's Creole Cook Book* also mentions that you should be sure not to boil your coffee to the point that it curdles.

William Ukers depicts New Orleans coffee preparation a bit differently, describing New Orleans's famous Creole coffee made from a concentrated coffee extract. As he explains, boiling water is poured over ground coffee until it is damp. Then, more boiling water is added, a tablespoon at a time, in five-minute intervals. The extract is stored in a bottle and used to make café au lait or café noir. Another approach is to brown three tablespoonfuls of sugar in a pan and simmer it in a cup of water until it dissolves. Combine the concoction with ground coffee, add boiling water, and serve black or with cream or milk.

Williams says that another way New Orleanians enjoyed their coffee was in demitasse cups, small cups that hold about half the amount of a regular cup of coffee. Demitasse originated in France and became a New Orleans coffee practice in the late nineteenth and early twentieth centuries. The coffee served in demitasse was brewed very strongly with sugar and was to be sipped. Williams adds that the practice became so commonplace that demitasse cups were included when you purchased a set of china.

Café Brûlot Diabolique

Coffee has been incorporated into several cocktails in the Crescent City; it should come as no surprise that New Orleanians quickly added a bit of boozy flair to their coffee consumption. A favorite of New Orleanians, especially during the holidays and celebratory events, is an after-dinner cocktail that combines coffee with a bit of liquor and finishes it with some flames. Invented in the nineteenth century, café brûlot diabolique, or "devilishly burnt coffee," combines cognac or brandy (sometimes both!) with strong French roast coffee. Sue Strachan explains in *The Café Brûlot* that the drink is said to have been invented at Antoine's Restaurant by Jules Alciatore, son of the restaurant's founder, Antoine Alciatore.

Although Antoine's is the accepted birthplace of the cocktail, William Ukers claims a variation of café brûlot diabolique originated in New Orleans coffeehouses, writing, "The old-time coffee houses of New Orleans were situated within the original area of the city, the section bounded by the river, Canal Street, Esplanade Avenue, and Rampart Street. In the early days, most of the city's big business was transacted in the coffee houses. The brûleau, coffee with orange juice, orange peel, and sugar, with cognac burned and mixed in it, originated in the New Orleans coffee house, and led to its gradual evolution into the saloon."

Café brûlot diabolique is traditionally prepared in a silver bowl with a tray and a long-handled ladle. While some restaurants choose to prepare their café brûlot with chicory coffee, Strachan explains that Antoine's version is prepared with coffee that doesn't contain chicory. What coffee you decide to use in your café brûlot preparation depends on your taste. She describes the steps in preparing the café brûlot: First, cloves, cinnamon, lemon peel, sugar, and brandy are combined in the bowl and heated over an open flame. When the brandy is hot, it is ignited with a match, and the liquid is stirred in the bowl. From there, the hot coffee is poured into the flaming brandy. One unique touch is when the waiter ladles the flaming mixture down a spiraled orange peel into the drink. The café brûlot is then scooped into special brûlot cups.

At restaurants like Antoine's, Arnaud's, Broussard's, and other New Orleans Creole restaurants that serve café brûlot, making the cocktail is a spectacle. The lights in the room are often dimmed, and the drink is prepared for large parties. The glow of the café brûlot's pageantry is part of the show and why many people enjoy ordering the drink, especially on special occasions.

Strachan writes that the café brûlot became so popular that it inspired a soft drink. At the turn of the twentieth century, Hotel Grunwald Caterers produced a drink called "Café-NOLA (Brulo)," a spicy, alcohol-free refresher marked with a devil on the packaging. The soft drink is thought to have captured the essence of the New Orleans favorite minus the danger of the booze and the flame.

FROZEN IRISH COFFEE

Another famous New Orleans coffee cocktail is the Frozen Irish Coffee, which has become a staple year-round, but especially during Mardi Gras and on St. Patrick's Day. Frozen Irish Coffee is a thick blend of coffee concentrate, ice cream mix, whole milk, brandy, whiskey, and coffee liqueur topped with a swirl of coffee grounds for a special touch. The concoction is premixed and pumped out via a frozen drink machine, giving it the consistency of a milkshake.

Jim Monaghan Sr. invented Frozen Irish Coffee at Molly's at the Market, an Irish bar that serves as the French Quarter's social hub in the 1100 block of Decatur Street. Founded in 1974, Molly's at the Market started serving the frozen cocktail to compete with other bars that were serving frozen daiquiris. Jim "Trey" Monaghan III, Jim Senior's grandson, explains that offering a frozen version of the classic Irish coffee was a no-brainer due to New Orleans's hot summers.

There is another place in New Orleans where you can get your Frozen Irish Coffee fix: Erin Rose on Conti Street. Erin Rose, previously known as Monaghan's Erin Rose, was owned by Monaghan Senior; he willed the bar to current owners Troy and Angie Koehlar upon his death. Monaghan III says that the Koehlars are responsible for expanding the international profile of Frozen Irish Coffee in the past twenty years; the frozen cocktail you get at Erin Rose is the same version served at Molly's. Although it recently closed, Junction Bar & Grill, owned by Lloyd Miller and the Monaghan family, also served Monaghan Sr.'s famous Frozen Irish Coffee alongside their delicious burgers.

Today, the frozen coffee cocktail has become as much a part of New Orleans history as Molly's at the Market itself. Monaghan III says that new versions of the drink include the addition of peanut butter whiskey, other flavors, and extra shots. However, the drink's base, coffee and ice cream, remains the same.

4

Heading to Market

Coffee Business and Customs of Early New Orleans

Over time, exchanges and the coffee culture therein gave way to open markets and coffee stands. Many of these stands were run by free people of color hoping to procure business from those who were out and about in the city and eager to spend their money. Rose Nicaud, an enslaved woman, bought her freedom with money she earned from selling coffee. While men frequented exchanges to socialize and conduct business, women went to markets to do their daily shopping. Some of these coffee stands still stand today. World-famous spots like Café du Monde and Morning Call have become a part of New Orleans tradition and draw in visitors from all over the world. The history within the walls of these landmarks tells a fascinating story that dates back hundreds of years. Café au lait, made with chicory coffee—the type of coffee most closely associated with New Orleans—is served at these coffee stands and other coffee shops throughout the city. However, the history of adding chicory to coffee extends beyond New Orleans and has international ties.

The French Market, a Crossroads in New Orleans

The French Market was one of the first markets in New Orleans and the only one predating the twentieth century that remains today. The roots of the French Market are deep; it's believed to date back to the seventeenth century. Charles L. Thompson explains in *Chronological History of the Old French Market* that the market originated in 1675 as an Indigenous trading post. He states that the end of the river was inhabited by Oumas Indians who had encampments along the river from Portage Road and extending for about a mile to what is now Julia Street. Canadian hunters and traders would stop at this settlement on their way down the Mississippi River to purchase fresh supplies, such as salt, wood, buffalo meat, and pottery, and hire guides to take them to their destinations. Other Indigenous groups such as the Chitimacha, Choctaw, Ishak, Tunica, and Natchez nations conducted trades here and called it Bulbancha, or "the place of many tongues."

This Portage Road, the river's end market, was well known to travelers to the area, such as French explorers Jean-Baptiste Le Moyne de Bienville and Pierre Le Moyne d'Iberville and their officers, Jean Barbason de Pailloux and Bernard de La Harpe. Thompson notes that Bienville's officers regularly traveled back and forth to Portage Road and were familiar with the route. As New Orleans grew, Portage Road became one of the main roads leading in and out of New Orleans.

Kalie Rhodes explains in "The Native Roots of the French Market," that the first formal market on the site where the French Market sits today was ordered in 1770 by General Alexander O'Reilly and built in accordance with the Compilation of the Laws of the Kingdoms of the Indies. This Spanish colonial law required that in all towns or cities near a body of water, the market house must be placed between the water's edge and the first row of houses. Thompson describes this first market as small and built entirely of cypress lumber produced in New Orleans. The market was forty feet wide and feet long with a pitched roof and mainly sold fish, meat, and poultry; vegetables and produce were sold on the levee.

As the market expanded, the structures became more extensive, and space was added to sell more goods. The second part of the market was one hundred feet in length and forty feet in width and divided with a partition, with the river side designated as a commodity warehouse with sections that were rented monthly. When a fire destroyed a large part of New Orleans in 1794, the commodity warehouse was made into a slaughterhouse, and a tax was placed on beef, veal, and mutton. A tax was also placed on barrels of flour used by local bakers.

In August 1812, a hurricane struck New Orleans, nearly demolishing the market. The Place de Armes was established as a temporary marketplace, and some merchants chose to sell their goods on the levee, as others had when the market was functional. Due to the hurricane, New Orleans lacked a proper market for one year, and when the market reopened, it was state-of-the-art for its time, with a street-level public square and corners marked with decorative wooden cannons made of cypress. The market was 302 feet in length and 47 feet in width. Its four sides had a walk made of flatboat gunnels laid three feet from the curb line, and its stands were made of cypress. The market was covered by a slate roof and paved with flagstones.

As time passed, the French Market settled into a routine and became a part of daily New Orleans life. Meat, fish, fruit, vegetables, and other goods were sold, and masses of people made their way in and out of the market as they ran their errands and socialized with neighbors. In addition to foodstuffs, household goods were vended at a bazaar in the market built in 1872. At this time, coffee was a commodity usually enjoyed at home or in exchanges; however, it was sold in many of the market's stands.

In *The Story of the Old French Market, New Orleans* (1916), Catherine Cole illustrates the importance of coffee in nineteenth-century daily life and describes her day at the market. As she walks in, she is greeted by a coffee stand and is immediately overtaken by the smell of fresh coffee radiating throughout the space. Cole considers coffee the keynote smell of the French Market and calls it the "aroma of the world."

As the nineteenth century progressed, so did the French Market's popularity. Like today's market, the nineteenth-century French Market became a spot that not only locals frequented but tourists as well. A statement that was commonplace at the time was that no trip to New Orleans was complete without a proper tour of the French Market. A New Orleans guidebook from 1893 describes the market selling everything from gumbo filé to "black coffee of superior flavor, made with a dripper in the Creole fashion." It was said that the coffee was so strong that "one cup, well-stirred into a tub of warm water, would make excellent boardinghouse coffee, sufficient for many days." Pralines were often sold with coffee, and vendors throughout the market spoke various languages, such as English, Spanish, French, German, and Indigenous tongues.

Regarding its aesthetic design, the French Market was advanced for its day. However, the late nineteenth century lacked what would now be considered modern amenities, which led to unhygienic conditions. In "The French Market at New Orleans," Paul Vargas explains that by the late 1890s and early 1900s, the market's condition was becoming more than just a passing problem. In 1897, journalist Orville T. Skillman stated, "The French Market is too horrible to mention further than to say it is the finest appetite destroyer imaginable." A few years later, another wrote, "One need not enquire of the whereabouts of the French Market: it makes itself known to you, without your seeing it, by its overpowering appeal to, and strenuous assault on, the degraded sense of smell." Not only that, but the area where the market was located was dangerous, and murders, robberies, and other altercations were regular occurrences.

The decline of the French Market was due, in part, to the proliferation of other markets throughout the city. The French Market attracted fewer customers, leading vendors to allow their stalls to fall into decline. However, by 1920, the French Market proved itself to be resilient; it had not only survived flooding due to issues with the nearby levee but also managed to stay operational during the yellow fever and bubonic plague outbreaks of the 1890s and early 1900s. Following these epidemics, the market began to get itself together. After a hurricane damaged it in 1915 and fire threatened it in 1919, the market was again back on the upswing, welcoming tourists and locals with regularity into the 1920s.

By 1931, a separate Division of Public Markets was established within the Department of Public Property, and in 1932, the city proposed, through ordinance 18693 CCS, to negotiate an agreement that would lead to the overall improvement of the market's conditions. On August 23, 1932, the French Market Business Men's Association organized the French Market Corporation. In 1934, the city passed an ordinance that put the French Market Corporation in control of the market. The corporation was put in charge of modernizing the market's facilities, and architectural plans were made to improve its overall look.

According to city archives, the project was financed by the corporation, area businessmen, the New Orleans government, the Orleans Levee Board, and the Public Works Administration. Construction on the new market began in 1936, with plans drawn by Sam Stone and Co. and executed by Gervais Favrot and Co. Construction. The plans included rehabilitating buildings that could be preserved, destroying the bazaar and Red Stone buildings, and constructing a new fruit and vegetable market as well as a fish market shed next to the meat market.

However, problems came when the nine-member board of directors carrying out the project could not budget the spending for the plan. In 1939, the city government bailed out the corporation and repaid its debts. From there, the city took over the French Market Corporation, becoming its sole stockholder. In 1943, a new lease was written, allowing the corporation to operate the market for fifty years. The corporation then subleased the market back to the city for twenty thousand dollars annually.

By 1971, the city had entered a new forty-year lease with the corporation in which the city would receive the corporation's profits.

Poydras Market

Poydras Market was another major open-air market located on Poydras Street and built in 1837. This market, ceded by the Carrollton Railroad Company, primarily sold goods transported by the city's rail system and ran through a two-block section of land on Poydras Street from Penn to South Rampart.

The market sold food, coffee, and household goods to prominent New Orleans families in hundreds of open stalls. Under the market's structure was a passageway where horse-drawn shipping containers and, later, streetcars could pass. According to Richard Campanella in "From Poydras Market to South Market District: Food Retail in New Orleans' Central Business District," antebellum markets of this era were city-owned. Stalls were sold, rather than leased, to vendors, controlled by ordinances, and managed by a market commissary. The commissary's job was to regulate the market's sanitation, suppliers, and general building maintenance.

Campanella explains that an 1858 *Daily Picayune* report states that Poydras Market's condition was less than desirable, noting that it was filthy, lacked water, and was sometimes impassable due to crowds. The area surrounding Poydras Market wasn't much better, attracting vagrants and loiterers in an area that gave way to a concentration of saloons and brothels, which fostered crime and scams. Infrastructure challenges and crime notwithstanding, Poydras Market managed remain operational until May 1866. The city purchased the neutral ground adjacent to Poydras Market from South Rampart to Basin Streets and established the Pilie Market, providing more space for crowds and a better vendor atmosphere.

In 1973, the corporation became a nonprofit with a twelve-member board appointed by the mayor. As a result, the French Market went through yet another renovation that included refurbishing existing structures, constructing two new buildings, and demolishing the fish market. In 1977, a parking lot was opened at the market, and in 1979, a flea market was opened to improve the market's profits.

THE CODE NOIR AND FREE PEOPLE OF COLOR

In nineteenth-century New Orleans, open-air markets were bustling with people purchasing the day's groceries, socializing, and going about their errands. At this time, the United States government had granted enslaved people a day of rest from servitude on Sunday, and enslaved people took this opportunity to spend the day working for themselves to earn money to buy their freedom, something that was a possibility due in part to the Code Noir.

The Code Noir, or Black Code, was a French law that first took shape in Louis XIV's edict of 1685. The Code Noir laid out a code of living for the enslaved until 1789. Some of its edicts included requiring the enslaved to be baptized into the Roman Catholic Church and only practicing Catholicism in public. Another stipulation was that Sundays and holidays were to be observed among both the enslaved and the free at risk of a fine or further punishment. The enslaved could only be wed with their master's permission, any children born to an enslaved person with a differing master would be considered the property of the mother's master, and if an enslaved male married a free woman, their children would be free.

The Code Noir was introduced to Louisiana in 1724. In 1763, when the Spanish gained control of Louisiana, the enslaved were allowed *coartación,* or self-purchase, in which an enslaved person could establish a fairly priced contract with two independent assessors, one representing the enslaved and one representing the enslaver, and purchase their freedom. Once the enslaved person had the money to buy their freedom, their enslaver could not deny the purchase, and the freed person could not be reenslaved. Even with *coartación* in place, saving enough money to buy freedom was difficult for an enslaved person. Often, the price set for freedom was high, and saving enough money to purchase emancipation took years of work during the little free time the enslaved were granted. Emily Clark writes that nearly two hundred enslaved people purchased their freedom due to this law between 1771 and 1779.

However, the introduction of the Black Code of 1806 limited the enslaved's minimal freedoms. This new code allowed only enslaved people over the age of thirty to be freed by *coartación,* and the newly freed were not permitted to remain in the territory. Clark explains that these rules were meant to restrict the benefits of manumission and preclude the freed population from quickly expanding. By 1827, when Louisiana was a state, the law was revised, allowing judges and police juries to decide if enslaved people under the age of thirty, born in Louisiana, could work for their freedom.

Most of those working to buy their freedom were enslaved women who sold food and other goods, such as coffee. These female street vendors of color, or *les vendeuses,* became a part of Sunday life in New Orleans, and citizens were more than happy to partake in their offerings, especially after mass or while doing the weekly shopping. Through their work, many *vendeuses* could purchase their own freedom and their family's freedom as well. Free *vendeuses* were required to wear a tignon, or head scarf, to distinguish themselves from enslaved women. The original tignon law was first put in place by Esteban Rodríguez Miró, who served as governor of the Louisiana province from 1785 to 1791. The head scarf was also meant to differentiate free women of color who otherwise might have been mistaken for white women. Free Black women of Louisiana embraced the tignon and made it their own, wrapping their heads in colorful scarfs and tying them with ornate knots. According to "Fashionable Rebellion," the head wraps became a mark of beauty among the free women of color and were often decorated with feathers and other adornments.

ROSE NICAUD PURCHASES HER FREEDOM WITH A COFFEE CART

One woman renowned for selling coffee to those in the French Market after Sunday mass was Rose Nicaud, or "Old Rose." According to the Historic New Orleans Collection, Nicaud was born an enslaved person around 1812 and learned to cook at the bakery owned by her enslavers, Nicaud's Bakery, on Dumaine Street. On Sundays, Nicaud worked for herself, providing hot coffee to churchgoers and those crowding around the busy French Market, first via a pushcart and later from her own stall in the market.

In *The Story of the Old French Market, New Orleans,* Catherine Cole describes the scene as citizens enjoyed their coffee as "all the small cuisiniers set up on the black, cozy flagstones their braziers of charcoal and brewed over them that all but immortal decoction, fit to be bottled and sold as perfume from Araby the blest—French Market Coffee."

Cole also describes a woman we assume is Nicaud in what may be the only firsthand description of her working at her coffee stand:

> Here, or hereabouts, "Old Rose," whose memory is embalmed in the amber of many a song and picture and story, kept the most famous coffee stall of the old French Market. She was a little negress who had earned the money to buy her freedom from slavery. Her coffee was like the benediction that follows after prayer; or if you prefer it, like the Benedictine after dinner.
>
> It was something to see that black "Old Rose" pile the golden powder of ground French Market coffee into her French strainer—a heaping tablespoonful for each cup—and then when the pot was well heated, pour in just two tablespoonfuls, no more, of boiling water.
>
> In ten minutes, this had soaked the coffee, and then, half a cup at a time, the boiling water was poured on and allowed to drip slowly. The result would be coffee, black, clear, and sparkling—ideal French Market coffee!

Cole's account checks out—by 1840, when she was twenty-eight years old, the city census recorded that Rose Nicaud was legally free and was the head of her household, comprised of three other women. The Historic New Orleans Collection explains that it was more difficult for enslaved men to buy their freedom than enslaved women because enslaved men were needed as laborers. Between 1822 and 1847, enslaved vendors made twenty to thirty dollars a month through their Sunday work, meaning that purchasing one's freedom would take years. After Nicaud purchased her freedom, she set up a permanent coffee stand in the French Market, which served coffee to people of all races and from all walks of life.

Nicaud likely bought coffee beans from the port next to the market, roasted them, and ground them by hand. Her days at the market were long, and she was likely working daily from midnight until noon to earn money to pay her business license and daily market fee. Nicaud came to be best known for her café au lait, hot milk mixed into coffee, that she originally served via her pushcart and now at her market stand. She surely sold calas with her coffee. These fritters were made of deep-fried rice, yeast, sugar, eggs, and flour. Nicaud died on September 13, 1880, at sixty-eight years old, but her stand, and other stands like hers, would inspire the creation of future French Market coffee stands such as Café du Monde and Morning Call Coffee Stand.

After Rose Nicaud, other enslaved women followed in her footsteps, earning money to purchase their freedom through coffee sales. Women known as Zabette, Manette, and Rose Glà operated their own coffee carts, selling their coffee mix like Nicaud did. Some free women of color held working-class jobs in other industries, such as housekeeping, while others held professional-class jobs, such as seamstress and nursing. Others were able to achieve high social status because they were half white.

However, as Louisiana headed into the mid-nineteenth century, the privileges of free people of color were significantly reduced. By 1845, the rights of enslaved people to purchase their freedom had diminished considerably, and such cases had to be approved by the district court. When the Union defeated the Confederacy in the Civil War, slavery ended in Louisiana and the rest of the Confederate States. As a result, former slave states began enacting stricter laws relating to now-freed, formerly enslaved people, considerably limiting the few rights that they had enjoyed under the Code Noir.

CAFÉ DU MONDE

In the mid-nineteenth century, coffee had woven itself into the everyday life of the people of New Orleans, and by the end of the century, the city had more than five hundred coffeehouses! While there were many coffee stands throughout the French Market, the one that remains to this day is Café du Monde. Even if you only have casual knowledge of New Orleans, you have undoubtedly heard of Café du Monde, the coffee stand famous for its café au lait made with coffee with chicory, and beignets.

Café du Monde, French Market.
Photo by David Rodrigue.

Legend says that Café du Monde, located at the corner of St. Ann and Decatur Streets in a building known as the Butcher's Hall, was founded by Fred Koeniger in 1862 and initially served only coffee with chicory. A few years later, beignets, a French-style, deep-fried pastry covered in powdered sugar, were added to the mix. However, the original coffee stand at this location did not bear the name Café du Monde; instead, it later took the name from Café du Monde–brand coffee. The timeline of when Café du Monde *became* Café du Monde is a bit complicated.

Café du Monde coffee was a product of Southern Coffee Mills, Ltd., founded by D. H. Hoffman in 1887, and located on Lafayette Street and, later, Tchoupitoulas Street. Interestingly, the company also sold a brand of tea simply marketed as "Du-Monde." As Paul Vargas explains in "French Market Coffee, New Orleans," it is possible that the original coffee served at what is now Café du Monde was French Market Coffee. Citing an advertisement from 1906, he suggests that the New Orleans Coffee Company, which owned the French Market brand, also owned what is now the current location of Café du Monde. This spot was marketed as serving the signature coffee of the French Market. It stands to reason that if you're in the French Market, you will want to enjoy coffee with the French Market name.

Vargas explains that "Café du Monde" is not mentioned in any advertising in the late 1800s or early 1900s. Also, throughout Catherine Cole's *The Story of the Old French Market, New Orleans,* published in 1916 and issued by the New Orleans Coffee Company, she makes multiple references to "French Market Coffee" but makes no mention of Café du Monde. Vargas suspects that Café du Monde didn't become the beloved coffee stand's name until the French Market was renovated in the 1930s.

Today, Café du Monde is owned by the Fernandez family. Hubert Fernandez owned Fernandez Wine Cellar across the street when he purchased the stand in 1942. After Hubert's death, his widow, June Fernandez, his sister Leonora Schwarz, and daughters

Sylvia Maher and Cynthia Roman took over the duties of running the stand. The fourth generation of the family now runs the stand, which, in addition to the French Market, boasts nine locations throughout the New Orleans metropolitan area, including two locations on the Northshore of Lake Pontchartrain.

COFFEE OF THE WORLD: CAFÉ DU MONDE IN JAPAN

Not only is Café du Monde a local institution, but the brand has gone international, opening a location in Japan in the early 1990s. The story of how a beloved New Orleans coffee stand arrived in Japan is fascinating. Jennifer Larino explains in "The Untold Story Behind How Café du Monde Stands Ended Up in Japan" that it all started in 1984, when New Orleans hosted the Louisiana World Exposition. During the fair, Japanese businessmen took an interest in the coffee stand.

A Japanese conglomerate called Duskin Co. Ltd. expressed interest in buying the rights to open Café du Monde stores in Japan. Lorino explains that there was interest because the Japanese greatly appreciated traditional American treats such as donuts, and Duskin Co. thought the beignets and a simple business model would be the perfect fit.

The risk was fairly low—Duskin Co. had already franchised Mister Donut, an American donut chain later acquired by Dunkin' Donuts, and made the brand famous in Japan; this licensing model allowed Café du Monde to expand into Japan without spending much money. Japan's very own Café du Monde debuted as a part of the world's fair in Osaka in 1990 and opened its first independent location in Ikebukuro, Japan, in 1992.

Lorino explains that there were a few bumps along the way; beignet and café au lait preparation isn't an exact science. Preparing the lightest beignet and the perfect cup of café au lait is a skill usually passed on casually from one employee to another. To ensure these skills were translated to Japanese employees, Café du Monde's managers wrote a company operations manual explaining how everything was perfectly prepared.

Japan now boasts more than twenty-one Café du Monde locations with the same aesthetic as their New Orleans counterpart. The color scheme is the same signature green and white, and the locations are designed in the style of French Quarter architecture. While the menu includes the stand's signature coffee with chicory, and beignets, other unique treats such as hot dogs, cinnamon beignets, frozen drinks, and soft-serve ice cream have been added.

MORNING CALL COFFEE STAND

Morning Call Coffee Stand is the other coffee stand closely associated with New Orleans coffee with chicory, and beignets. Joseph Jurisich, an immigrant from the Austro-Hungarian Empire, founded Morning Call in 1870, and it was operated by his immediate family until 2018, making the stand the second-most-extended family-run food operation in New Orleans; Antoine's Restaurant is the first. Carol Jurisich, the mother of current owner Robert "Bob" F. Hennessey, married Joseph Jurisich's grandson, Alvin "Al" P. Jurisich, and brought her children, Robert, David Michael Hennessey, and Karen Meyer, into the family business. When Al died, he left Morning Call to Carol, and when she died in 2017, at the age of ninety-one, Carol's children took over the store's daily operations.

When it first opened, Morning Call Coffee Stand was located at the opposite end of the French Market from Café du Monde and was known for serving boatmen and farmers late into the night or early in the morning. Not only was Morning Call popular among the merchants, but the stand, which sold about 1,500 cups of coffee a day, was a favorite stop for those attending a performance at the French Opera House. Located just a few blocks away on the corner of Bourbon and Toulouse Streets, it wasn't out of the ordinary to catch a musician at Morning Call between a show's rehearsals or a member of New Orleans society stopping in for a cup of coffee after a night at the theater. As the twentieth century progressed, parents would bring their children to Morning Call for a late-evening treat served car-side, and the stand became a popular date spot. Since the stand was open twenty-four hours a day, it became a late-night favorite of service industry workers who wanted a cup of coffee or a bite to eat before heading home.

Although Morning Call is known as the "other" coffee stand that serves beignets, the tasty pastries weren't always on the menu. Initially, the stand served a breakfast menu that included chicken, mutton chops, beefsteak, and soft-boiled eggs. It's believed that

Morning Call Coffee Stand postcard, French Market.
Wikimedia Commons.

Morning Call started serving beignets made with sourdough a few years after its inception.

Like Café du Monde, Morning Call was a staple in the French Quarter until February 1974, after renovations began on the French Market. Anxious about rent increases, lack of parking, and redevelopment of the French Market into a space geared more toward visitors than locals, Morning Call made what was a controversial move and relocated ten miles away to Metairie, a New Orleans suburb. The shop settled into a strip at 3325 Severn Avenue, where it would stay until that location closed in 2018 due to a saturation of coffee shops in the area and rising rent prices. By this time, Morning Call had expanded a bit, taking up residency in the Casino Building, also known as the Timken Center, in New Orleans City Park in 2012. However, a year after its Metairie location closed, Morning Call was pushed out of its City Park spot following a ten-month battle over the site's lease. Rather than renew Morning Call's lease, City Park chose to put the restaurant space up for bid. Seeing an opportunity for its own expansion, Café du Monde swooped in, submitted the highest bid, and was granted the lease to the City Park location in the summer of 2019, ending Morning Call's seven-year run there.

Morning Call might have been down, but they weren't out. In March 2021, the coffee stand made its triumphant return to the New Orleans coffee and beignet landscape, opening a location in a brand-new building just a few blocks away from City Park at 5101 Canal Blvd. The new location boasts Morning Call's famed archway and lights, a center bar, and plenty of seating inside and out. Today, the stand serves its proprietary blend of strong, dark-roast chicory coffee, iced coffee, frozen café au lait, and Irish coffee. Unlike Café du Monde, Morning Call has more on its menu than just coffee and beignets. Here, customers can enjoy local fare, such as red beans and rice, chicken andouille gumbo, jambalaya, and crawfish étouffée.

Horn and Hardart Automat and the New Orleans Coffee Connection

Those of a certain age might remember automats, the vending machine-style food vendors that served fresh meals in small windows. One would insert a coin, lift a window, and a freshly prepared meal wrapped in waxed paper would be there for the taking. The automat was fast and easy and eliminated the need for a waitstaff. The concept originated in Berlin, Germany, in 1895, and the first automat was opened in Philadelphia, Pennsylvania, by food services company Horn and Hardart on June 12, 1902. Soon, a Horn and Hardart Automat chain opened in New York City, expanding to one hundred locations throughout Philadelphia, New York, and Baltimore.

You may be surprised to learn that this nifty way to get a quick meal has a New Orleans coffee connection. Joseph Horn and Frank Hardart (né Franz Hardardt) were partners in the restaurant business, having opened their first restaurant in Philadelphia in 1888. Hardart was a German-born New Orleanian who learned how to prepare New Orleans–style French-drip coffee while working at one of the city's lunch counters at thirteen. After a brief attempt at moving to Philadelphia to sell New Orleans coffee in 1876, he was more successful in 1886, and the move stuck.

Carolyn Kolb explains in "The Orleanian at the Automat" that after Hardart settled in Philadelphia, he worked restaurant jobs before teaming up with Joseph Horn in the lunchroom business. Intrigued by the automats of his home country, Hardart purchased one of the food vending machines for $30,000, a tidy sum in 1900, and the pair opened the first American automat two years later. Not only did the Horn and Hardart Automat quickly become popular because of its fresh food, but, as Kolb describes, customers loved the "New Orleans–style" coffee that the duo promoted as "gilt-edge" brew. It was freshly brewed every twenty minutes and served properly dripped and dispensed from metal spouts for five cents a cup. In November 1950, the price of the automat's coffee increased to ten cents, and at the height of the automat's popularity, Horn and Hardart Automat sold ninety million cups of coffee a year! After the 1960s, the automats began to fall out of fashion, and the last remaining location closed in New York City in 1991.

DID NEW ORLEANS INVENT THE COFFEE BREAK?

The famed "coffee break," in which the monotony of the workday is broken by a cup of coffee and maybe something sweet, has become a part of American work culture. Was the coffee break, as we know it, invented in New Orleans? According to some historians, the answer is "yes," with most citing Lyle Saxon's description of a coffee break in his 1928 book *Fabulous New Orleans.* Saxon describes a businessman suggesting getting a cup of coffee before a visitor departs his office. Saxon writes, "It is a little thing perhaps, this drinking of coffee at odd times, but it is very characteristic of the city itself. Men in New Orleans give more thought to the business of living than men in other American cities." Buddy Stall credits the New Orleans coffee break coming into fashion two years after Saxon's description. In *Proud, Peculiar New Orleans: The Inside Story,* Stall writes that the first coffee break occurred on March 17, 1930, when managers of the Mississippi Shipping Company gathered the company's eighty employees in the Hibernia Bank Building in downtown New Orleans for a 3:30 p.m. coffee break. Stall explains that the managers got the idea from a similar Brazilian practice.

However, to give credit where it is due, the proper birthplace of the coffee break, as we know it, is possibly Stoughton, Wisconsin, where the coffee break dates to the late nineteenth century, when Norwegian immigrants migrated there to work in T. G. Mandt's Wagon Factory. Writer Lisa Frania explains that while workingmen built wagons, their wives were enlisted to harvest tobacco. They agreed to this if they could tend to their household duties in the morning and afternoon. This meant a cup of coffee would be enjoyed, thus the creation of the "coffee break." Stoughton is so dedicated to its position as the city that invented the coffee break that it holds the Stoughton Coffee Break Festival annually in August.

In the early 1900s, New York's Barcolo Manufacturing, a metal products manufacturer, laid claim to the creation of the coffee break when they offered their employees a break in their workday that included free coffee. During World War II, skilled weavers at a tiemaker company in Denver called Los Wigwam Weavers were called to serve their country. When older women were brought in to replace them, they tired quickly and requested two ten-minute breaks during the day so that they could relax with a cup of coffee. This coffee break increased production. The term "coffee break" was first seen in a 1952 Pan-American Coffee Bureau ad campaign with a slogan that read, "Give Yourself a Coffee-Break—and Get What Coffee Gives to You."

CHICORY

One of the most beloved ways to enjoy coffee in New Orleans is coffee with chicory, made with coffee grounds mixed with roasted chicory root. Café du Monde and Morning Call serve coffee with chicory but aren't the only coffee shops keeping the practice alive. What started as a way to supplement coffee has become a cherished tradition in New Orleans.

A member of the dandelion family, chicory is a woody, perennial herbaceous plant with bright-blue, pink, or white flowers. Consumption of chicory isn't a new concept; the practice dates back to ancient Egypt, where it was used as a medicine, and ancient Rome, where a salad dish called puntarelle was made with chicory sprouts. Chicory contains inulin, a prebiotic, and many health benefits are believed to be associated with the consumption of chicory root, such as a decrease in the risk of cancer and liver disorders, a lowering of blood sugar, and the stimulation of the growth of good bacteria in the stomach. Also, chicory root contains anti-inflammatory properties and stimulates the immune system. When used as an additive to coffee, the bitter-tasting chicory root is roasted and ground. When the chicory root is roasted, it takes on a caramelized taste. Coffee that contains chicory is thicker than coffee that doesn't because the sugars in the chicory root are more water-soluble than the oils in coffee beans.

COFFEE, CHICORY, AND CONSUMPTION

While many assume that adding chicory to coffee is a practice that originated in New Orleans, historians explain that the combination can be traced to Holland, where it was consumed for its health benefits. France then adopted the custom under Napoleon's Continental System, an embargo on trade with Great Britain that lasted from 1806 to 1814.

When traditional warfare failed, Napoleon decided to hit Great Britain in the pocketbook and destroy the British economy. Napoleon issued a series of orders called the Berlin Decree, which forbade all importation of nonessential British goods into any European countries allied with or dependent upon France. This included chocolate, tobacco, and coffee, among other goods. While some minor damage to the British economy was done, the Continental System didn't have the effect Napoleon hoped for and instead increased smuggling.

Due to Napoleon's Continental System limiting the importation of nonessential items, coffee importation was cut off, and coffee replacements became the next logical option. Chicory plantations have existed in France since the eighteenth century, and the French would consume their chicory coffee by roasting coffee beans very dark and combining the coffee grounds with one-third of ground chicory. While chicory didn't have the same smell or taste as traditional coffee, it was brown and could be brewed into a dark drink, and that was good enough for the French. According to P. L. Simmonds in *Coffee and Chicory,* when the Continental System ended, the French had developed such a taste for chicory that they continued to add it to their ground coffee. In 1825, France exported 1.25 million pounds of chicory, and by 1840, that number had surged to 16 million pounds.

This wasn't the first time that ground chicory root was used in place of coffee. According to *New Orleans Roast,* the use of chicory can be traced back even further to the Prussian Empire in the eighteenth century. Believing that coffee would lead to the downfall of German society, King Frederick the Great reduced the local supply of coffee by restricting imports and imposing massive taxes. Instead, he supported beer suppliers, citing beer as a core piece of German heritage. Frederick was so serious about his coffee restriction that he employed "coffee sniffers," a group of war veterans hired to sniff out the scent of illegally roasting coffee beans. No longer able to afford the highly taxed coffee, working-class citizens turned to the bitter taste of chicory to satiate their coffee cravings. Ironically, King Frederick's plan to push his beer agenda and topple the state's fascination with coffee backfired when chicory became the preferred drink, and Prussia soon became the world's top producer of chicory root powder.

Before Napoleon's Continental System, another pivotal moment in coffee and chicory's history includes Charles Giraud introducing chicory cultivation near Valenciennes in 1771. At the start of the nineteenth century, chicory was regularly used as a supplement to coffee, and in 1805, the first chicory roasting factory was established in Cambrai, France.

In "The History of the Chicory Coffee Mix That New Orleans Made Its Own," K. Annabelle Smith explains that because France influenced New Orleans culture in the nineteenth century and because of the part it played in establishing coffee plantations in the Caribbean, including Haiti and Cuba, it was only natural that the practice of combining coffee and chicory would extend to New Orleans.

When the French began to emigrate to New Orleans throughout the nineteenth century, they brought their homeland's traditions with them; one of these traditions may have been the inclusion of chicory in coffee, which had become standard practice in France. As in France during Napoleon's Continental System, chicory was added to coffee in New Orleans partly out of desperation. As we learned in chapter 2, during the Civil War, the Union blocked the Port of New Orleans, which limited Confederate access to coffee. When the Confederates got their hands on coffee, they had to augment it with something to make it last. Additives such as grains, ground nuts, and chicory were added to coffee to stretch the supply. However, it is essential to note that the practice of adding chicory to coffee predated the Civil War, and the conflict is not why New Orleanians embraced coffee and chicory.

According to Suzanne Stone, there could be another explanation for how chicory became a staple in New Orleans coffee. The Acadians, made up of French immigrants, emigrated from Canada to New Orleans in the eighteenth century. These people, who would come to be known as Cajuns, brought chicory with them on their journey and integrated it into their coffee consumption in New Orleans. Another story says that Germans brought chicory into the city in the early to mid-nineteenth century; they had been adding chicory to their coffee since the ban on coffee in Prussia. Whether these are facts is debatable, as many historians insist that chicory didn't appear in the city until the French introduced it. Of course, specific details can be expected to be lost in time when dealing with over two hundred years of history.

After the dust from the Civil War settled, the combination of coffee and chicory seemed to be the way New Orleanians preferred to drink their coffee. Chicory was used not only as an additive to coffee but also to boost poor-quality coffee, and coffee manufacturers were eager to capitalize on the trend, especially if it meant they could save a few bucks. Such long-forgotten New Orleans coffee and chicory brands produced in the late nineteenth and early twentieth centuries are French Opera, Honeymoon, Loyola, Marathon, Monteleone, Poydras Market, and Sum-Good. Another coffee and chicory brand, Suffragette, was produced in Shreveport.

THE SWILL MILK SCANDAL CHANGES FOOD REGULATIONS

In New York in the 1850s, the swill milk scandal changed food regulations as the United States knew them. During the scandal, distillers disposed of their spent mash by feeding it to old, sick cows to profit from their leftover grain. The cows, often diseased, too ill to stand, and held up by ropes, were milked, and water, rotten eggs, flour, plaster of Paris (you read that right), and burnt sugar, among other contaminants, were added to the milk. The junk was labeled "pure country milk" and distributed to the public. In one year, eight thousand infants died by drinking the concoction, and the scandal led to the first imposition of food safety laws in the country. The Board of Health exonerated the distillers, but public outcry led to the passage of the country's first food safety laws in 1862.

With the swill milk scandal fresh in the public's mind, some were understandably uneasy about the idea of chicory being added to coffee. However, because chicory was seen as a natural additive to coffee and not a substitute *for* coffee, the combination of the two was given a pass and permitted to be sold to the public. However, coffee packages had to be labeled with percentages showing how much product was actual coffee and how much was chicory.

While coffee with chicory was available in other areas throughout the country, especially in the South, it didn't fall into the tapestry of local tradition elsewhere as it did in New Orleans. As quickly as it was introduced, coffee with chicory became a way of life for New Orleans coffee drinkers.

COFFEE WITH CHICORY IN MODERN-DAY NEW ORLEANS

Elizabeth Williams explains that there was a time when coffee with chicory was what everyone in New Orleans was drinking in coffeehouses and offices. In the nineteenth century, New Orleanians served their café au lait from large bowls, just as their French counterparts had. Sure, you could get pure coffee that wasn't "adulterated" by chicory, but it was usually only served by request. Heading into the twentieth century, coffee consumption was a social affair. New Orleanians often drank three to four cups of dark-roast chicory coffee throughout the day while socializing and conducting business; coffee was even served with dinner. This might sound like a lot, but remember that the darker coffee is roasted, the less caffeine it contains, and chicory, of course, contains no caffeine. This meant it was easy to drink coffee throughout the day without getting the "jitters."

Although Louisiana had been a state since 1812, New Orleanians still held an unfailing loyalty to France and their French roots. When World War I erupted in 1914, that loyalty shifted into allegiance to the United States. Slowly, throughout the twentieth century, many New Orleans traditions intended to maintain the city's connection to France began to slip; one of these traditions was the inclusion of chicory in coffee. Williams explains that as New Orleanians became more Americanized, fewer enjoyed dark-roasted chicory coffee, instead choosing lighter-roasted pure coffee with more caffeine. As a result, some coffee shops established in New Orleans today don't serve a chicory coffee option. Additionally, the twenty-first century's first quarter has brought interest in specialty coffee trends that focus more on "pure," single-origin coffee rather than dark-roasted commodity coffee mixed with chicory. Ironically, chicory now costs more than coffee, which is likely another reason it isn't offered at some of the newer coffee shops throughout the city. However, Williams says that coffee with chicory is a part of New Orleans's coffee culture, and she believes the city's coffee shops should present at least one chicory coffee option on their menu to keep the traditional practice alive.

If you wish to add chicory to chicory-less coffee at home, the preparation is easy. Roasted and ground chicory can be found on market shelves in New Orleans or ordered online. Add one part chicory to three parts of coffee, or about 25 percent chicory, to your coffee mix.

5

Roast of the Town

Specialty Coffee and Roasters in Modern-Day New Orleans

In recent years, New Orleans's coffee scene has dramatically expanded to include boutique coffee shops, small roasters, a specialty coffee store that offers coffee education classes, a restaurant that boasts Ethiopian coffee traditions, and coffee specialists who add their own chapter to New Orleans's coffee story. A coffee festival featuring coffee roasters from all over the world has been added to the New Orleans coffee landscape, and specialty coffee has made its way onto the local coffee scene.

What Is Specialty Coffee?

Before coffee can be labeled "specialty," it must undergo a unique grading process. The Specialty Coffee Association of America (SCAA) defines specialty coffee as a coffee that scores eighty points or higher on the Association's one-hundred-point scale and has zero primary defects and five or fewer secondary defects. "Coffee Grades: Understand the Basics" explains that when graded, coffee is analyzed in three-hundred-gram samples. Primary defects in coffee beans include any damage to the coffee bean, such as severe insect damage or beans that have turned black due to lack of water. These defects can affect the taste of coffee made with the bean. Some secondary defects include broken or chipped beans due to machinery issues, beans that have suffered water damage, and withered or unripe beans. Unlike primary defects, secondary defects don't affect the coffee's taste. Points are also given when the coffee goes through the cupping process, as explained in chapter 1 of this book. Coffee quality is scored on a scale from one to ten based on fragrance and aroma; flavor, aftertaste, acidity, body, and balance; and sweetness, uniformity, and cleanliness. When these steps are complete, the points are calculated, and the final number determines if a coffee can be labeled as specialty grade.

Second-Wave Coffee and the New Orleans Coffeehouse Boom

Peter Giuliano, the chief research officer of the Specialty Coffee Association, has a career in the coffee industry that dates back to the late 1980s. Throughout his career, he's worked in every aspect of coffee, from running coffee shops to owning a coffee roasting company. He explains that the specialty coffee scene started in the 1960s, when the American coffee industry began focusing more on efficiency. He credits Alfred Peet, the founder of Peet's Coffee & Tea in Berkeley, California, with introducing a European coffee-roasting style to the United States and a more artisan approach to coffee, including sourcing and blending coffee beans from specific origin countries. Peet inspired imitators who wanted to try their own style of coffee roasting, and this period, known as the specialty coffee movement, marked the beginning of the second coffee wave. This wave started in the late 1960s but picked up steam in the 1970s and 1980s, with coffee roasters highlighting the flavor characteristics of coffee depending on its country of origin.

Giuliano says that in the late 1970s and 1980s, New Orleans was seen by those in the coffee industry as a cross between the old and new. During the early second wave, the city was best known for Café du Monde, the coffee stand that sells coffee with chicory.

and beignets, and PJ's Coffee, a coffee shop founded by Phyllis Jordan that marked the city's first run at specialty-style coffee. Coffee shops in the second coffee wave sought to serve better-quality coffee than what would typically be found at the grocery store or drunk at the office. Still, they had to make it accessible to casual coffee drinkers. Giuliano says that's why so many second-wave coffee shops served lattes, cappuccinos, and sugar-filled coffee drinks.

In the early 1990s, the second coffee wave fully hit New Orleans, with many coffeehouses serving lattes and other sweet coffee drinks in a social atmosphere that usually included live entertainment and poetry readings. Abstract Bookshop and Café on Magazine Street provided music, readings, food, and, as its name might suggest, books and flavored medium-roast coffee. Plantation Coffee House on Canal Boulevard served a rotating selection of one hundred varieties of coffee, including nine iced coffees, ten flavored cappuccinos, and café au lait. The Living Room Coffeehouse was a small café decorated with mismatched and well-worn sofas and chairs. Weekly live music and poetry readings drew customers in, with the owner admitting to the *Times-Picayune* in 1994 that the shop's atmosphere was a bigger draw than its coffee. Rhythm and Blues in Algiers Point served its coffee with brunch, pastries, and Brocato's gelato, and on Saturday nights, the café pulled in crowds with live acoustic shows. For over forty years, Neutral Ground Coffee House brought live music, open mics, poetry readings, and other cozy events to Daneel Street. Better known for its music events than its coffee, Neutral Ground shuttered its Daneel Street location in 2023, but owners Caroline "Phant" Williams and James Naylor hope to find a new location for the social spot soon.

In 1990, Rue de la Course was credited as one of the businesses responsible for revitalizing a long-stagnant Magazine Street. Owners Jerry Roppolo and Debra Dunn opened the café across the street from their home when the block was mostly abandoned. The shop eventually expanded into nine locations; however, only one location on S. Carrollton Avenue remains. True Brew Coffee House,

Coffee at French Truck Coffee.
Photo by David Rodrigue.

owned by Denise Austin, Mark Gonzalez, and Pat Wingerter, had two locations at 3133 Ponce De Leon Street and 200 Julia Street. The shop, best known for its frozen Mocha, served coffee from Coffee Roasters of New Orleans and hosted poetry readings, and stand-up and improv comedy nights. The Julia Street location boasted a small theater, dubbed True Brew Theater, that featured local productions. Wingerter and Gonzalez also operated a True Brew coffee cart at Canal Place in the early 1990s.

Ted Hood started managing and roasting coffee at Kaldi's Coffee House, an early third-wave–inspired coffee shop and coffee museum, named for the goat-herder responsible for the discovery of coffee, in 1991. Located on Decatur Street, the shop imported and roasted its coffee and featured a display of vintage coffee-making equipment, such as roasters and grinders, from 1990 to 2000. Kaldi's Coffee House is considered one of New Orleans's pioneer specialty coffee shops, and Hood describes Kaldi's as a hangout that featured live music and chess nights and acted as a gathering spot for young people, especially before a night out in the French Quarter. The shop served coffee from such countries as Colombia, Ethiopia, Guatemala, Mexico, and Yemen, that was freshly roasted weekly.

Hood, who has been roasting coffee since the late 1980s, describes roasting Kaldi's coffee on a vintage Gothot Coffee Roaster. "That machine ran off of hope," he jokes. "It was gas-fired and had a belt on it that always broke or slipped. They didn't make replacement belts for it, so we had to just make it work. I think we even had a couple of fires because it would get too hot inside."

The café was a gathering spot for the musicians of the French Quarter and featured shows from such Grammy-winning acts as Brian Blade, Nicholas Payton, and Wynton and Bradford Marsalis. Sunday featured Gospel music by the Friendly Travelers, who would play to what Hood describes as a standing-room-only crowd. "The place would be packed with people sitting on the floor and in windows to see the show," he says. "And it would be loud; you could hear the music all over the Quarter."

Over the years, writers and artists sat in Kaldi's, sipping coffee and working on their craft. In many ways, the space served as a modern-day coffee exchange where like-minded people met, swapped ideas, and inspired art in each other. Hood says everyone got along and appreciated what Kaldi's Coffee House stood for. Unfortunately, rent increases and the looming draw of the internet age led to Kaldi's closure in 2000, cementing the shop into the annals of New Orleans's "ain't there no more" history.

THE CITY'S FIRST STEPS INTO THIRD-WAVE COFFEE

Following Hurricane Katrina in August 2005, the coffee scene in New Orleans noticeably changed. Drew Cambre explains that before Katrina, twenty-four-hour coffee shops provided a place where people could study into the wee hours or grab coffee after working a late shift. Local coffee shop chains such as CC's Coffee House and

PJ's were some of the first businesses to reopen after the storm, serving the few locals who were able to return and first responders helping with recovery efforts. Smaller coffee shops like Z'otz Café on Oak Street and Rue de la Course on Magazine Street provided a sense of community for locals getting their bearings after the life-changing event.

It's possible that Katrina delayed New Orleans's entrance into third-wave coffee. After many local coffee shops were forced to close following the storm, the national coffee chain Starbucks, which opened its first Louisiana location on Maple St. in New Orleans in 1998, moved in and picked up where a lot of smaller shops had left off. In the three years following Katrina, Starbucks opened more than ten locations in the New Orleans area, including on the city's Westbank and the North Shore of Lake Pontchartrain.

The third coffee wave provided a more culinary approach to coffee, focusing heavily on roasting techniques and serving flavorful, sourced coffee. It began in the early to mid-2000s as New Orleans was dealing with the aftermath of Hurricane Katrina. In the twenty years since the storm, New Orleans has built a solid specialty coffee scene that boasts multiple roasters in neighborhoods throughout the city. Cambre got his start in the New Orleans coffee industry working at CC's Coffee House after the storm, where he became intrigued with the third-wave coffee movement, watching videos online about its science and technique. After CC's, he designed the coffee program at Sucré, a sweets and coffee shop.

Because few local coffee shops were embracing the trend, in 2008, a group of New Orleans baristas interested in third-wave coffee created the Society of New Orleans Baristas (SNOB). By then, Cambre had begun working with his friend and fellow coffee enthusiast John Knipmeyer at Dee's Coffee & Copy, a small coffee and copy shop combo in New Orleans's Central Business District. Together, they turned Dee's Coffee into a third-wave coffee shop that held monthly meetings with baristas interested in learning more about coffee, exchanging ideas, and holding competitions. A particular point of pride was in 2010, when Dee's won Gambit Magazine's "Best Coffee Shop in New Orleans" over PJ's Coffee and CC's Coffee House as a write-in vote. When Dee's closed, other coffee shops, such as Mojo Coffee House, began to fill in the city's third-wave coffee scene.

Although the city is slightly behind national coffee trends, Peter Giuliano thinks New Orleans is poised to be the country's next great specialty coffee mecca, explaining that combining new roasters with New Orleans's deep roots in coffee history will excite people about New Orleans coffee and make them eager to add it to their rotation. The confidence in New Orleans's place in the national specialty coffee scene is so high that the Specialty Coffee Association hosted its Specialty Coffee Expo in New Orleans in 2021.

The New Orleans coffee scene has never been more prosperous than it is today. The city is leaning into its coffee legacy and becoming a destination for specialty roasters and professionals who want to be on the cutting edge of national coffee trends. People in New Orleans are excited about coffee now more than ever, and enthusiasts attend coffee education classes and festivals, grind their beans at home, and experiment with brewing techniques. New coffee roasters are regularly being added to the New Orleans coffee landscape, and as the community grows, so does local interest in specialty coffee and its origins.

Current Crop Roasting Shop

If there's one spot that's leading New Orleans's charge into the next wave of specialty coffee, it's Current Crop Roasting Shop, an all-purpose coffee supply and education hub on Magazine Street that opened in 2023. Here, customers find specialty green coffee beans and learn to roast them with the help of the shop's skilled staff. Current Crop stems from Coffee Bean Corral, an online coffee supply store in Jackson, Mississippi, specializing in wholesale raw coffee, home roasting and grinding equipment, and coffee brewers. John Puckett, the owner Coffee Bean Corral, wanted to create a space where anyone who wanted to learn about coffee roasting and tasting could gather in an educational space with coffee professionals. Puckett chose New Orleans as Current Crop Roasting Shop's home because of the city's history with coffee and the coffee culture ingrained in the city.

Director of Product and Programs Catherine Mansell runs Current Crop, where customers explore over seventy varieties of green coffee beans available from regions such as the Congo, Ethiopia, Kenya, Rwanda, and Central and South America, to name a few. A certified Q Grader, Mansell walks customers through the process of discovering the type of coffee they might be interested in based on their personal tastes. Once a customer finds the coffee they are interested in purchasing, they can roast it to their preference in one of the shop's small air roasters. When Current Crop opened, the coffee inventory was the same as that of Coffee Bean Corral. However, Mansell has cultivated Current Crop's coffee selection and has introduced microlot coffee from smaller farms worldwide to give her customers a taste of different types of coffee from various regions.

In addition to its incredible coffee selection, Current Crop offers classes that teach skills such as intro to coffee roasting, cupping and tasting, and brew method. Mansell has noticed an increased desire for coffee education in the city, and her coffee classes regularly sell out. In the roasting class, students roast coffee in light, medium, and dark roasts. Using a small Fresh Roast SR800 air roaster, participants can watch the changes in the progression of the roasting coffee beans, learn what sounds to listen for when the coffee is roasting, and understand how to use their sense of smell to detect different points in the roasting process. In the cupping class, students learn to decipher varying tasting notes and engage in discussions about scent differences in types of coffee. The class I took paired coffee with four French pastries containing flavors that coincided with the different coffees we were sampling. The class is approachable for coffee cupping novices like me, and Mansell is happy to answer questions and guide participants through the roasting and tasting process. She says that no matter a person's experience with coffee, she wants to create coffee education classes that anyone can enjoy.

In Current Crop's "Coffee Cocktail Creation" class, hosted by mixologist Craig Seaman and Current Crop coffee expert Savannah Timmerman, coffee education blends with mixology to create signature cocktails using specialty coffee. The classes focus on the balance between the flavors of coffee and spirits and how the nuances of coffee elevate the notes of a cocktail. Seaman explains that the classes' cocktail styles vary from light, like a tropical punch, to more robust, like an Irish coffee.

TRY-ME COFFEE ROASTERS

Try-Me Coffee Roasters is a New Orleans coffee roaster that has existed for one hundred years, but you may have never heard of it. Even though Try-Me supplies well-known spots such as Angelo Brocato's and the Court of Two Sisters with coffee, the company still seems to fly under the local coffee radar, especially compared to larger companies like Community Coffee and French Market. Founded in 1925 by Henry Kepler, a nineteen-year-old teller and errand-runner at Whitney Bank, Try-Me Coffee Mills started in a small, unassuming building on France Street in New Orleans's Bywater neighborhood. The company operates in the same building to this day.

As former owner Bob Lutz greeted me on a hot morning in August, I was taken at how the roaster blended into the rest of the block. If I hadn't noticed the sign on the door declaring that Try-Me Coffee operates here, I might have assumed this was just another house on a relatively quiet street. Lutz explains that his maternal grandfather, Kepler, started his business by walking down Franklin Avenue and knocking on doors, asking people to try his coffee—

that's how the company got the Try-Me name. In the 1970s, Kepler passed the company to his son-in-law and daughter, John Patrick "J. P." Lutz Jr. and Carolyn Lutz. When J. P. died in 1997, Carolyn took over daily operations at Try-Me Coffee until 2000, when her son Bob assumed ownership.

When Bob took the reins at Try-Me Coffee, the business was nothing new to him. He had practically grown up in the building on France Street, watching his grandfather and then his father roast and sell coffee to neighbors who dropped in to make their weekly coffee purchases. When Bob was old enough to drive, he started delivering Try-Me Coffee to customers throughout the city. Bob is quick to call Try-Me Coffee more of a family than a business. Nothing makes this more obvious than Try-Me's small staff. Jerico Cyres has worked here since 1991, when he first knocked on the door and asked J. P. for a job. Today, he takes care of the company's daily operations such as taking and processing orders, organizing roasting, packing coffee, invoicing, and coordinating coffee orders locally and nationwide, ensuring that Try-Me customers get their coffee as quickly as possible. Willie Butler has been Try-Me's coffee roaster since 1993, logging long hours and roasting coffee fresh to order.

Try-Me Coffee gets its single-origin green coffee from Antigua, Brazil, Colombia, Costa Rica, Ethiopia, Guatemala, Java, Kenya, and Sumatra, and roasts on multiple antique coffee roasters, including a Jabez Burns & Sons Roaster that was patented in 1915. The company's roasters are maintained by Lutz, a skilled mechanic, and operate as well as they did when they were first manufactured. Try-Me offers whole bean and ground coffee, including espresso, and flavored coffee, introduced by Bob, such as Bavarian Chocolate, French Vanilla, Irish Cream, and Pralines & Cream.

One of Bob's most significant challenges came during Hurricane Katrina, when Try-Me's building on France Street flooded. With the help of the National Guard, he gutted the entire building, disposed of nine thousand pounds of waterlogged coffee beans, and temporarily relocated Try-Me's operations, including three antique thirty-pound roasters, to Mississippi. Thankfully, the business was able to return to its original location by Christmas of 2005.

When Bob was ready to retire in October 2023, he reached out to his Bywater neighbors, Abby King and Lauren "Mermaid" McCabe. King is an entrepreneur and lifelong coffee lover who has been roasting coffee for twelve years. King and McCabe were eager to enter the coffee business, and Try-Me Coffee, a company rich in history and with ties to the community, seemed like the perfect fit for the couple who bought the company on their son's first birthday. The couple plans to raise their son, Marlin, in the coffee business so that Try-Me Coffee will be enjoyed for generations to come.

While Try-Me's wholesale business is thriving, the couple hopes to increase branding and make more people aware of the roaster's history. King lovingly refers to Try-Me Coffee as "The oldest roaster in the city that nobody has heard of" but wants that to change. As new owners, King and McCabe plan to make more people aware of Try-Me Coffee by using social media such as Facebook and Instagram to engage potential customers and participate in local events. For example, in conjunction with the Krewe of the Rolling Elvi, a social organization that participates in parades, fundraisers, and other philanthropic activities, Try-Me Coffee participated in a blood drive to address the critical shortage in New Orleans's blood supply. The event featured live entertainment, and Try-Me served coffee to attendees.

Cherry Coffee Roasters

Cherry Coffee started as a pop-up at Stein's Deli in New Orleans in 2013. In 2016, owner Lauren Fink opened a brick-and-mortar location of Cherry Coffee Roasters on Laurel Street, but it wasn't until 2019 that she began roasting and selling her own coffee. Fink went from roasting coffee on a 1.5-kilogram roaster, which produces under three pounds a batch, to a twelve-kilogram roaster, which produces about 18.5 pounds of coffee that she sells retail.

Coffee Assortment at Cherry Coffee.
Photo by the author.

When speaking with Fink, I was eager to learn the process of modern-day coffee from seed to cup. She explains that when curating the coffee for Cherry, she bases her selections on unique flavors that excite the palate rather than coffee from specific countries of origin. She trusts importers such as Red Fox Coffee Merchants and Royal Coffee in Oakland to provide her with coffee that contains the flavor profiles that fit Cherry's model. "You get to know the person that you're working with in the company, and they get to know the flavor profiles you're looking for, and they send samples of coffee that they think you'd be interested in," Fink explains.

The importers that Fink works with find small coffee producers unfamiliar with marketing their coffee and help the producers source their product to the masses, ensuring they can continue growing coffee. She says that many of these coffee growers wouldn't be seen if it weren't for these importers. When searching for the beans that will produce the best cup of coffee, Fink leans toward acidity, explaining that coffee with acidity produces a ripe fruit flavor balanced by sweetness.

"We look for coffee that's a little more unique in the sense of 'Can we find any fruit flavors in this coffee from Peru, because it's really rare?'" she explains. "The fruit flavor isn't at the forefront, but the acidity reminds you of fruit. Then there's African coffee that is interesting but some might note that its flavor is closer to tea because it's floral or fruity."

Fink says that the palate for different types of coffee can change over time, especially when someone knows what type of coffee flavor profile they're looking for. She notes that the type of coffee you prefer could depend on where you were raised. Those on the West Coast tend to favor African coffee with a fruity and floral flavor whereas those on the East Coast, which has a colder climate, prefer coffee from Latin America with a savory taste with chocolate and nutty notes. As with food or wine, the flavors you enjoy today might not be what you enjoy years from now.

When Fink is roasting her coffee, her goal is to bring out the beans' best flavors without over-roasting them. As she explains, coffee resembles wine in its delicacy; everything affects it, from where it grows to the rainfall the trees receive in a particular year. These different elements contribute to the flavor components of the coffee, and you don't want those roasted away; you want the roasting process to enhance the flavors locked into the beans. Furthermore, every time you roast coffee, the flavor profiles differ, and no two batches of coffee are the same. Part of the science of coffee roasting is getting to know the personality of each coffee and how it reacts when it's in the roasting drum.

In addition to coffee roasting, Fink wants Cherry Coffee to make a difference in the coffee industry by providing education for those who want to learn how to taste coffee and what flavors to look for in different batches of coffee. She wants to teach people what to look for when choosing their perfect coffee, how to enjoy black coffee, and how to appreciate all the flavors in various types of coffee. Before the COVID-19 pandemic, Fink hosted cupping classes where people tasted different coffee side-by-side to learn what flavors make up various types of coffee. She recently relaunched her cupping courses and plans to teach skills like making the ideal pour-over and other brewing techniques.

HEY COFFEE CO.

At HEY Coffee Co. on St. Louis Street, co-owner Greg Rodrigue curates his company's coffee from Honduras, Guatemala, Colombia, Brazil, Ethiopia, Rwanda, and Peru. HEY works with coffee importers Sucafina Specialty in New York, the Coffee Quest in Austin, and Red Fox Coffee Merchants in Oakland to get coffee from farms worldwide to stores' shelves and customers' cups. He also works with Juan Hipp in Honduras, a well-known coffee farmer who runs Monte Vista Coffee, a coffee farm that has been in operation for generations. Rodrigue is a passionate coffee roaster whose love of coffee shows in his description of the roasting process and his relationship with the farms that grow HEY's coffee.

HEY Coffee Co. began roasting its coffee on a two-kilogram roaster in 2013 before graduating to a twelve-kilogram Diedrich Roaster in 2018 that roasts coffee in a rotating drum that uses a ceramic heating element. Because it's a smaller roaster, it allows for control in gauging how roasted the final product will be and the person roasting the coffee can make any necessary adjustments throughout the process. Rodrigue explains that different factors such as country of origin, age of the beans, and even moisture in the coffee beans affect how the coffee responds to roasting.

When researching various coffee companies, I was curious about what type of flavors each roaster looks for when choosing the coffee they will sell to their customers. Rodrigue told me that different coffees work better in different styles. For example, he says he primarily uses Colombian and Guatemalan coffee in the company's cold brew because it's a rich coffee with a chocolate, caramel, nutty flavor that can withstand more heat in the roasting process.

The Colombian coffee that HEY Coffee Co. uses is a washed-process coffee. Washed-process coffee means that fruit is stripped off of the coffee bean when picked and washed with water before it's dried, giving the coffee a clean taste. Most coffee that you buy at the supermarket is washed-process coffee. The alternative to washed-process coffee is natural-process coffee. In the natural process, the coffee fruit is harvested and dried with the fruit's skin intact. During this process, the coffee bean absorbs sugar from the fruit pulp. The result is a coffee with a fruity, sweet flavor.

HEY uses washed Peruvian or Mexican coffee as the base for its espresso and balances it with Ethiopian coffee as the "high note" in the blend. Rodrigue says the washed coffee adds a sweeter, brighter, lighter flavor to the blend with floral and citrus notes. He considers the espresso less like traditional Italian espresso and closer to a modern third-wave espresso profile.

HEY's Honduran coffee is a natural-process coffee with notes of pineapple that leans to the fruitier side, and its Ethiopian coffee is a natural-process coffee that is light and sweet. Another washed Colombian coffee is a single-origin coffee that is fruit-forward with strawberry notes and good textures. When a coffee is single-origin, it comes from one place and isn't a blend. HEY sells its single-origin coffees in retail bags for customers to enjoy at home, and the café sometimes serves them as drip coffee. "When I'm sourcing coffee, I'm looking for something exciting or a microlot coffee with a limited amount," Rodrigue says.

MOJO COFFEE ROASTERS

Angela Jackson opened Mojo Coffee in 2006, following Hurricane Katrina, in a building on a corner of Magazine Street. After the storm, a location of Rue de la Course closed, and the landlord of the building asked Jackson and a former business partner if they would like to buy it and open their own coffee shop. They jumped at the opportunity to sell coffee in a neighborhood they loved.

Like other coffee roasters in the city, Jackson and co-owner and roastmaster Matt Cronin source much of their coffee from Guatemala, Peru, Honduras, Nicaragua, Costa Rica, Ethiopia, and Kenya, giving extra attention to coffee grown by women farmers. What first attracted Jackson to coffee and the roasting business was her enjoyment of watching things evolve. When she opened Mojo, New Orleans coffee was in its second wave. Now in its third wave, the local coffee scene is rich, with more roasters sourcing their coffee from small farms. In this "next generation" of coffee professionals, solid roasting knowledge is a significant part of the process.

When Jackson began her third-wave journey, many local roasters served quick and consumable coffee that appealed to a mass audience. These darker roasts served in cafés focused on a "vibe" rather than selling high-quality coffee. Jackson, a pioneer of the third-wave coffee movement in New Orleans, honed her skills at the Specialty Coffee Expo, which she attends annually. Attending the expo opened Jackson's eyes to the importance and influence of the coffee industry not only worldwide but in New Orleans. She explains that New Orleans was underrepresented in the specialty coffee scene when she first began attending the expo, but that has slowly changed throughout the years. Jackson brings as many members of her leadership team to the expo as possible, encouraging them to meet coffee farmers, experience cuppings, and sample coffee from all over the world.

Jackson has watched the national coffee industry evolve and is happy to see farms converting to better practices and consumers caring more about the farmers' quality of life, noting that if you're going to be a part of something like the coffee industry, it should be something you feel good about. On the national coffee scene, women-owned farms and co-ops are becoming a more significant part of the industry, and Mojo and other New Orleans roasters are keeping pace with that trend.

In addition to good coffee practices, Jackson takes pride in selling her coffee at various coffee shops throughout the city. She recognizes that New Orleans needs proper educational opportunities for coffee professionals, and an essential part of serving her coffee at other shops is training baristas to brew coffee properly. When a coffee shop begins selling Mojo's coffee, a staff member trains the shop's barista step-by-step on preparing the coffee. Crafting a proper cup of coffee is more complex than loading it into a machine. To avoid cross-contamination, the machine should be cleaned thoroughly before coffee is put into it. It seems like common sense—coffee leaves behind oils that contain a particular flavor profile. If you are brewing a new coffee without cleaning the machine, cross-contamination could create an unpleasant coffee experience.

While other coffee roasters I've researched prefer not to serve traditional New Orleans coffee with chicory and keep the coffee they serve "pure," Jackson, who isn't from New Orleans originally but takes pride in local traditions, explains that including coffee with chicory on her menu was a cultural acknowledgment of its significance in the New Orleans coffee story. She serves coffee with chicory in an iced coffee drink made with a chicory extract that Mojo created. The extract ensures that the chicory stays fresh, doesn't go to waste, and is available for customers who enjoy a bit of New Orleans tradition mixed into their coffee. Jackson explains that New Orleans changed her life, and coffee with chicory is a cultural practice that she is happy to acknowledge. She admits that as the years have passed, she has noticed that fewer customers ask for chicory coffee, perhaps because the younger generation didn't grow up drinking it with the enthusiasm their parents and grandparents did.

ORLEANS COFFEE

Orleans Coffee's roots go back forty years, making it one of the oldest coffee roasters in New Orleans. The company started as Coffee Roasters of New Orleans, a wholesale roaster, in 1983. When Coffee Roasters of New Orleans came along, many smaller coffee shops were taking shape in the city. Coffee Roasters of New Orleans was happy to serve their coffee roasted on a 1905 perforated drum Royal Roaster. Sandy Cutner opened the Orleans Coffee Exchange on Orleans Avenue in the French Quarter two years later, in 1985. In the mid-1990s, Bill and Kathy Siemers purchased Orleans Coffee Exchange and later Coffee Roasters of New Orleans and consolidated both businesses into a wholesale and retail brand, becoming one of the first specialty coffee companies to offer coffee via mail order and later via website. The business quickly expanded outside of coffee, selling brewers, espresso machines, grinders, flavored syrups, and milk for coffee.

Bob Arceneaux started in the coffee business in 1988, working for PJ's Coffee and Covington Coffee Works. In 1996, he teamed up with Bill and Kathy Siemers to work in the roasting department of Orleans Coffee Exchange in the Warehouse District on S. Peters Street. Arceneaux explains that although the New Orleans coffee scene was very small, the few locally owned coffee shops in the city bought specialty coffee from the Orleans Coffee Exchange.

In 2000, the business moved to Rendon Street, and Bill Siemers expanded the company's production with larger coffee roasters. When Hurricane Katrina hit New Orleans in 2005, the roasting facility on Rendon took on six feet of water. At the time, Orleans Coffee Exchange's only competitor in the city was another specialty coffee company called New Orleans Coffee Works, which operated in a facility on Industry Road in Kenner. Following the storm, Siemers purchased New Orleans Coffee Works and moved Orleans Coffee Exchange into the Industry Road space, which made it through

Hurricane Katrina unscathed. In 2007, Siemers sold Orleans Coffee Exchange to Bob Arceneaux and Tom Oliver. The business dropped the "Exchange" and became Orleans Coffee in 2012, and in 2014, Arceneaux bought out Oliver, who went on to own Coffee Science, a small coffee roaster on S. Broad Street in New Orleans.

When developing his coffee for Orleans Coffee, Arceneaux experimented with coffee from different importers until he found the perfect formula. He also began a relationship with the Specialty Coffee Association, which serves many purposes, including fostering a relationship between coffee roasters and those in the green coffee importation business. He explains that finding the right balance of coffee that will appeal to customers is a practice in trial and error, and, like other coffee roasters I met, he works with importers who are acquainted with the type of coffee he prefers to sell. When Arceneaux is curious about a particular coffee, he'll ask one of his importers to send him a sample to roast and cup. From there, he and his roaster, Greg Hill, decide if it's a coffee they want to buy and sell to their customers.

When Arceneaux talks about New Orleans coffee he comes alive; coffee is clearly his life's calling. When I visited the Orleans Coffee roasting facility he took me around to every machine, delicately explaining in detail what they do. He walked me around and showed me the large burlap coffee bags packed with beans that would be roasted, bagged, and sold to eager customers. He even showed me the facility's bagging stations, where coffee is lovingly packed by dedicated employees. Arceneaux's appreciation for the New Orleans coffee legacy goes a step further when he walks those new to coffee roasting through the process and lets them use his roasters to roast their coffee.

When it comes to roasting coffee, Orleans Coffee employs two large roasters—a twenty-five-pound-capacity San Franciscan Roaster and a seventy-five-pound-capacity San Franciscan Roaster. Other smaller roasters are used for sample roasting small batches. Arceneaux explains that inventory is kept tight, gauging as closely as

Seventy-five-pound San Franciscan Coffee Roaster, Orleans Coffee.
Photo by the author.

possible how much coffee will be roasted that week. The goal, he says, is to end the week with coffee barrels that are close to empty.

Orleans Coffee sells its traditional New Orleans coffee in stores and at the brand's storefront on Prytania Street. The company also specializes in specialty branded coffee for hotels, gift shops, gift sets, and coffee shops. Orleans Coffee can be found at multiple Café Beignet locations and is the coffee used in the coffee ice cream at Creole Creamery, an ice cream shop on Prytania Street. Parish Coffee, produced by Orleans Coffee, is a lower-price-point coffee meant to compete with other similarly priced brands and can be found on local grocery store shelves.

Coffee Science

Tom Oliver is a New Orleans coffee expert who has been in the coffee scene since the 1980s. Unassuming, with snow-white hair and a casual style, he cut his teeth in the industry in Ann Arbor, Michigan, at a shop called Espresso Royale. He acquired his barista skills there and learned the ins and outs of coffee grinding and brewing mechanics. He explains that when he started in coffee, coffee shops were in their second wave, and although baristas timed their shots and were judicious about ratios, careful measuring with scales and weighing coffee was rare.

When he moved to New Orleans in 1991, specialty coffee shops in the city were few and far between. Still, Oliver quickly found a place in the industry fixing espresso machines and teaching baristas how to make espresso and latte art. Soon, he found himself sharing his coffee knowledge with others rather than just fixing coffee equipment. His first steady job in New Orleans coffee was as a barista at CC's Coffee House's first location at the corner of Jefferson Avenue and Magazine Street. From there, he moved on to Kaldi's Coffee House on Decatur Street.

Oliver explains that the coffee scene in New Orleans in the 1990s was limited. In addition to CC's Coffee House and Kaldi's Coffee House, there was PJ's Coffee, a chain of shops founded by Phyllis Jordan, and Rue de la Course, a string of cozy neighborhood coffee shops that offered a variety of coffee drinks. A few other smaller shops dotted New Orleans's coffee landscape, and Oliver notes that your best chance of getting a decent espresso in those days was at an Italian restaurant or one of the city's finer hotels. Still, even that depended on who made it and how they were trained.

After his time at Kaldi's ended, Oliver was approached by Orleans Coffee Exchange to join the team there, providing coffee to specialty shops around town, such as Coffee Chateau, Fair Grinds, and Royal Blend. Oliver was working for the company with Bob Arceneaux in 2007 when the owner sold it to the pair. Arceneaux bought out Oliver's share in 2014 and continues to operate Orleans Coffee today.

In 2018, Oliver opened Coffee Science, a specialty coffee shop on S. Broad Street that employs a zero-emission approach to its coffee roasting. A year after opening the shop, Oliver partnered with Artemis Pebdani, Scott Perry, and Leah Vautrot in the endeavor. Not one to shy away from putting the "science" in Coffee Science, Oliver reworked a drip coffee maker to make coffee with the same flavor profile as pour-over coffee, achieving the feat by "tweaking" a Curtis D500 Brewer. The exact details of the project are a secret, but he tells me it involved drilling and modifying the brewer's system to shorten the machine's brew time—I'll take his word for it. The result, he says, is "Golden Cup" coffee from a machine that produces the equivalent of a half gallon of pour-over coffee, or eight, eight-ounce cups of coffee that can be brewed in three minutes. According to the Specialty Coffee Association, the Golden Cup Standard for coffee is, "Coffee shall exhibit a brew strength, measured in Total Dissolved Solids, of 11.5 to 13.5 grams per liter, corresponding to 1.15 to 1.35 'percent' on the SCA Brewing Control Chart, resulting from a soluble's extraction yield of 18 to 22 percent."

Oliver initially had no interest in roasting coffee when his business partner Artemis Pebdani introduced him to fluid bed coffee roasting. In this process, the roaster drum is heated by air rather than a flame, as in a traditional roaster. This method uses convection heat, much like an oven, that heats the coffee beans from the bottom during the roast. The airflow keeps the coffee moving constantly and the force of the air causes the beans to float, which is how "fluid bed roaster" got its name. Oliver liked the idea of roasting coffee without filling the neighborhood with the smoke that a conventional roaster produces. When he added the machines to his shop, Coffee Science became the city's first zero-emission coffee roaster, and he began selling bags of roasted coffee beans in-store and online. Oliver says the advantage of the fluid bed roaster is an even roast that doesn't produce hot spots in the drum that could burn coffee beans and change the coffee's taste.

At Coffee Science, Oliver and his team roast their beans on a Bellwether Coffee Roaster. Scott Perry explained that this roaster

Bellwether Coffee Roaster at Coffee Science.
Photo by the author.

is entirely electric and doesn't require a gas line and flame to heat its roasting drum. The roast profile is selected on a digital screen to begin the roast. As the drum preheats, six pounds of green coffee beans are loaded into the hopper like a traditional coffee roaster. From there, the beans enter the roasting drum and roast for eight to fourteen minutes, depending on the preferred roast level. When the roast ends, the beans drop into the cooling tray. After the beans are completely cooled, they drop into a bucket below.

There are some learning curves when it comes to using an electric roaster. For example, Oliver explains, you don't smell the coffee as it roasts because the system is completely enclosed. To gauge where you are in the roast process, you can watch the beans change color through the machine's window, but you don't hear first crack, the sound that marks the beginning of the light-roast stage. Instead, you learn to roast using data points on the machine's digital screen. Oliver says that mastering the machine takes some trial and error but, in his experience, produces a more consistent roast than a gas roaster. Additionally, an advantage of the Bellwether system is the sustainable green market it offers and the company's focus on women's co-ops.

It's possible that fluid bed coffee roasting is set to be the latest addition to the third-wave coffee movement. Oliver notes that the shift into third-wave coffee in New Orleans accelerated after Hurricane Katrina, with the influx of people from other cities moving into town. Today, he considers the third wave to have had the most positive impact of any movement on coffee in his lifetime. As for Coffee Science, Oliver plans to continue improving New Orleans's coffee with fresh ideas, including an espresso concentrate "super shot" soluble that contains 22 percent coffee meant to replace freeze-dried instant coffee. He also produces Coffee Science canned cold brew in multiple flavors.

CONGREGATION COFFEE

In 2015, Eliot Guthrie and Ian Barrilleaux opened Congregation Coffee, a small coffee shop and roaster in Algiers Point on the Westbank of New Orleans. After eight years, the business was taken over by Patrick Brennan, a member of the Brennan family known for its plethora of New Orleans restaurants. Brennan kept Congregation Coffee's skilled staff upon the sale, including roaster Zoe Underhill and Director of Operations Grace Murphy. In 2018, Congregation Coffee was named the best coffee roaster in Louisiana by *Food & Wine,* and in 2023, the magazine named it one of the country's ten best coffee brands.

Brennan was familiar with Congregation Coffee long before he was its owner. While working for his family's company, the Ralph Brennan Restaurant Group, he served Congregation Coffee for years at the famed Brennan's Restaurant and considered it quintessential New Orleans coffee. He takes pride in the fact that Brennan's Restaurant was Congregation's second business account, and when Guthrie was ready to sell the company, Brennan jumped at the opportunity to keep his favorite coffee brand alive.

Underhill has been in the coffee industry for ten years, working as a barista in small cafes before starting her roasting career as an apprentice at Congregation Coffee. She has been the company's roaster and green coffee buyer for five years. When looking for the perfect coffee to sell at Congregation, Underhill chooses approachable, high-quality coffee that customers will enjoy. She roasts her coffee on a twenty-five-pound-capacity San Franciscan Coffee Roaster to fit flavor profiles that appeal to customers, including blends and more intricate flavors. Underhill also keeps a coffee with chicory on her coffee menu as a nod to local tastes and traditions. Murphy balances the operations between Congregation Coffee's roasting facility, the company's café, and elsewhere in the city where the coffee is served. She is also responsible for managing retail and vendor orders, acquiring new accounts, and distributing coffee to grocery stores like Whole Foods. Soon, the team will expand Congregation Coffee's brick-and-mortar shops and rebuild its wholesale coffee business.

PRETTY COFFEE

South Alabama native and Pretty Coffee founder Sarah K. Lambeth moved to New Orleans in 2015 when she saw the specialty coffee scene exploding in the city. Experienced in the coffee competition world as both a participant and a judge, Lambeth got her start in the New Orleans coffee scene like so many—by working as a barista at various coffee shops throughout the city. While living in Alabama, Lambeth learned to roast coffee, often spending time at shops to learn the ins and outs of the business. When she got to New Orleans, she used her coffee knowledge to buy, roast, and profile green coffee for Congregation Coffee in Algiers Point.

In June 2019, Lambeth founded Pretty Coffee, focusing heavily on women-owned farms and sources in the coffee industry. She recognizes that women in the coffee industry are often underserved, and with Pretty Coffee, she works to ensure that women can build careers in the trade. Lambeth has developed relationships with coffee women in Costa Rica, El Salvador, and Guatemala but doesn't limit her options to specific countries when buying her coffee; instead, she prefers a product that exudes high quality and cleanliness. A certified Q Grader, Lambeth wants her coffee to be a palate-driven experience. She sometimes chooses coffee with fruity or chocolate flavors but doesn't have an exact preference for one specific taste and adjusts her coffee roasting techniques to develop each coffee to its highest potential. Though she gravitates toward medium roast, she acknowledges, as other roasters have, that different coffee requires different roasting techniques.

When she isn't roasting her own coffee, Lambeth can be found at Whatever Coffee, her pop-up coffee shop in Stein's Market and Deli on Magazine Street. In just a few years, Pretty Coffee has become one of the city's major specialty coffee roasters thanks to word of mouth and is served at coffee shops throughout the city, such as Pond Coffee on Chartres Street, Church Alley Coffee Bar on Canal Street, and Bakery Bar on Annunciation Street.

Lambeth thinks the New Orleans specialty coffee scene is impressive, considering the relatively new and small market. As a barista competition judge, she believes New Orleans's specialty coffee stands out from other coffee-famous places like Seattle and Portland. She explains that specialty coffee has been around for a long time in the Pacific Northwest and is considered the "norm" there. In New Orleans, the ideas surrounding specialty coffee roasting are fresh, and people in the industry have a lot to bring to the table.

Cora's Girls Coffee

Since 2021, founders of Cora's Girls Coffee and sisters Mia Patterson and Kiara Smith have been roasting coffee and selling it wholesale at local farmer's markets. Kiara Smith has worked in the local coffee industry since she was sixteen. When she was diagnosed with end-stage renal disease and received a kidney transplant, she and Patterson decided to create a business that they could work on together. Named for their late mother, Cora's Girls Coffee was a learning experience for the pair who bought a coffee roaster and taught themselves about roasting coffee and the coffee business. As New Orleans's first Black woman–owned coffee roaster, Cora's Girls wants to make an impression on the New Orleans coffee scene and add its own chapter to the New Orleans coffee story.

Patterson and Smith get their coffee beans from a coffee broker in Mississippi who works in fair trade and provides them with beans from Brazil, Colombia, Costa Rica, Ethiopia, Guatemala, Nicaragua, and Papua New Guinea. Smith creates unique blends with a New Orleans flair. Da Kwarters is Cora's Girls New Orleans blend made with chicory, the Uptown Wind-down is a Brazilian decaf with dark chocolate notes and a hint of cinnamon, and Throw Me Somethin' Sista is a low acidity seasonal blend of Colombian, Guatemalan, and Papua New Guinea beans with caramel and cane syrup flavors, and a smooth finish. Cora's Girls coffee is served at Old Road Coffee Shop in the Tremé neighborhood and Mae's Bakeshop in the Milan neighborhood and is sold on the company's website.

Delicious Sips

Andrew Madary comes from a family with deep roots in the New Orleans coffee business, so it's no surprise that he founded a coffee roaster, Delicious Sips, in 2016. Madary is the grandson of William G. Madary II, who began working for J. Aron and Company in 1946 and was elected vice president of the company in 1963. William founded the International Coffee Corporation (ICC) when J. Aron and Company relocated to New York in 1977. He served as president of the New Orleans Green Coffee Association, president of the Southern Coffee Association, and director of the National Coffee Association. Many of William's children still work for ICC.

Following in his family's footsteps, Andrew Madary took an interest in coffee roasting after graduating from LSU, spending time at ICC learning about roasting, cupping, and the intricacies of the coffee business. He and his father purchased a warehouse in New Orleans East and spent a year restoring an antique Burns Jubilee Coffee Roaster. Madary explains that the cast-iron roaster produces a coffee with a flavor that customers find appealing, likening the machine to a seasoned cast-iron skillet. To keep his business as New Orleans–centered as possible, Madary works with ICC and Westfeldt Brothers Inc. to import his coffee from Central America, Ethiopia, and Indonesia. Staying true to his New Orleans roots, Madary also sells coffee with chicory, which is popular among his customers. He explains that despite being small, Delicious Sips has built its reputation on word of mouth, selling coffee wholesale and producing private-label coffee for companies interested in branding it for their business.

Madary is excited about the future of New Orleans specialty coffee and says that the influx of small coffee roasters, coffee shops, and general interest in coffee from customers has boosted the local industry. Delicious Sips was featured at the inaugural NOLA Coffee Festival, and Madary notes that the attendance shows New Orleanians interest in a wide variety of coffee. He hopes to see more attendees at the next event as the appreciation for local coffee increases.

FRENCH TRUCK COFFEE

French Truck Coffee began as a small door-to-door coffee delivery venture and has expanded into twelve locations and counting in New Orleans, Baton Rouge, and Tennessee. Owner Geoffrey Meeker has a background in the food industry and worked as a food and beverage consultant for W New Orleans before entering the coffee business. It was a sunny Wednesday morning when I pulled up to the unassuming warehouse on South Telemachus Street where French Truck's magic, meaning its roasting and packaging, happens. I was promptly greeted by Meeker, a tall gentleman with bright-blue eyes.

French Truck's roots are interesting—Meeker and his wife were living in the Caribbean when his cousin visited with a package of Blue Bottle Coffee, a specialty coffee brand out of Oakland. Meeker, who had made a career working in five-star restaurants, had never tasted coffee that was so enjoyable. After researching specialty coffee roasting, he took out a fifty-thousand-dollar loan and invested in a small coffee roaster. He called his business French Truck Coffee, after the company's quirky delivery truck, and quickly created a system in which people could order fresh-roasted coffee and have it delivered the same day. French Truck Coffee took off and soon expanded, opening a warehouse on Erato Street and its first coffee bar at the corner of 1200 Magazine Street.

Meeker imports French Truck's green coffee beans from Brazil, Colombia, Ethiopia, Honduras, Guatemala, and Peru, and whenever able, works to create long-term relationships with coffee growers. Because French Truck buys from the same farmers year after year, they can depend on a steady income that allows them to build a better quality of life. Unlike other specialty coffee roasters in the city, Meeker stores most of his coffee in his own warehouse located next to his roastery, and most of French Truck's coffee is shipped through the Port of New Orleans. He finds this beneficial because he doesn't have to pay high warehousing prices or pay to have the coffee shipped to New Orleans from another port. The result is money returning to the farmers who grow his company's coffee.

Meeker roasts French Truck's coffee on a Loring Coffee Roaster, a state-of-the-art air roaster that, similar to the Bellwether Roaster,

Loring Coffee Roaster, French Truck Coffee.
Photo by the author.

roasts coffee by recirculating hot air through a static drum rather than heating a rotating drum with a flame. According to the company website, Loring Roasters use a single gas-burner system that provides heat for roasting coffee and incinerates chaff and smoke from the roast chamber thus reducing emissions. Because hot air is circulated, the roaster doesn't need to keep reheating cool air; the heated air cycles through the roasting process.

Meeker likes working with the Loring Roaster because it uses less gas, and the machine's screen is all digital; he can easily profile-roast consistent batches of coffee across the company's roasteries in New Orleans, Baton Rouge, and Memphis. When working with multiple store locations across two states, consistency in quality is essential. Meeker's eyes light up as he explains that it's important that the cup of French Truck Coffee you might drink in Tennessee is of the same quality that you would enjoy in New Orleans. Just as when the company started, to keep the coffee as fresh as possible from roast to cup, it isn't roasted until it's been ordered. Looking to the future, Meeker hopes to expand French Truck Coffee into more locations and provide opportunities to the over two hundred employees who work within the company and add to the French Truck family.

Del Alto Valle Coffee

Del Alto Valle Coffee is a micro coffee roaster in New Orleans specializing in single-origin Colombian coffee. Founded by Paola Barona in 2021, Del Alto Valle uses coffee to support Colombian children in need.

Growing up in Colombia, Barona spent her youth around the country's coffee farms. Colombia is the world's third-largest coffee producer after Brazil and Vietnam. In 2011, the United Nations Educational, Scientific and Cultural Organization (UNESCO) added Colombia's Coffee-Growing Landscape to the World Heritage List. This included the departments (Colombia's equivalent of states) of Risaralda, Quindio, Caldas, and Valle del Cauca.

Barona's brother worked in the region and supported schools in the village of Ulloa by providing school supplies and donating other things needed for their education. She explains that there isn't enough money for government assistance in Colombia, so those struggling depend on each other for support. During the COVID-19 pandemic, hard times worsened, and Barona wanted to find a way to help. Since Barona had moved to New Orleans in 2002, she had difficulty finding the Colombian coffee she enjoyed in her home country. Taking matters into her own hands, she connected with a coffee farmer in Colombia and asked him to sell her raw coffee so that she could experiment with coffee roasting. She planned to use her love of Colombian coffee to do good for the people of Colombia. In 2021, Barona found a facility to start roasting coffee when Hurricane Ida damaged the building, making it uninhabitable.

Finding herself in a bind, Barona contacted Bob Arceneaux at Orleans Coffee, who was happy to let her roast coffee at his roasting facility. He walked her through the process of coffee roasting on Saturdays, trying different blends, and experimenting with various roasting techniques. In the meantime, Barona brought her coffee to local grocery stores to make connections to sell her product. When Rouses agreed to sell Del Alto Valle Coffee at their stores, she knew she was ready to move forward in the coffee business. Barona sources the coffee for Del Alto Valle from a single farm in Colombia, so the quality of her coffee is consistent. Now that her coffee is available in multiple markets statewide, like Breaux Mart, Dorignac's Food Center, Langenstein's, Robért Fresh Market, and Rouses Supermarket, her next step will be to move into her own roasting facility.

With the profits she made from Del Alto Valle Coffee, Barona accompanied her brother to Colombia and donated school supplies to children in need in the region where she buys her company's coffee. In 2022, through Del Alto Valle Coffee's success and donations from supporters, Barona donated school supplies, Christmas presents, and essential food items, such as flour, rice, beans, and lentils, to children in three villages. What's most important to Barona is using Del Alto Valle Coffee to make a difference. Because she is single-handedly running the company, she wants to use its profits to give back to the country that has given so much to her.

Del Alto Valle's flagship coffee is honey-processed. When the beans are collected, their sticky mucilage covering remains intact after the coffee cherry has been depulped. Leaving this honey "coating" on the beans results in sweeter coffee with chocolate and brown sugar notes. The honey-processed coffee uses less water than traditionally washed coffee. At the inaugural NOLA Coffee Festival in 2023, Del Alto Valle Coffee's Geisha coffee, with floral and tea-like aromatics characterized by its vibrant acidity, nuanced sweetness, and clean, silky body, won Best Brewed Coffee. Barona explains Geisha coffee is made from a temperamental coffee tree with unpredictable bean production. It's these qualities that Barona says make her Geisha coffee exceptional. Del Alto Valle Coffee's packaging reflects Colombian biodiversity and features a poison dart frog, a jaguar, and a hummingbird; it was awarded "Best Coffee Packaging" at the festival.

APPLIED ARTS COFFEE

Baruch Rabasa and Melissa Stewart founded Applied Arts Coffee during the COVID-19 pandemic. Rabasa first had the idea to roast coffee when his mother and brothers bought a coffee farm in Colombia. Inspired by the family purchase, Rabasa and Stewart, who are from the DC area but have lived in New Orleans for years, temporarily relocated to Portland to hone their roasting skills on a Loring Roaster, consult with coffee experts, and network with specialty coffee importers. Rabasa likens the time in Portland to attending a coffee school.

When they perfected their craft, they returned to New Orleans, opening their roastery in a building in the Bywater neighborhood. Although Rabasa and Stewart sell the coffee the family coffee farm produces, which inspired their business, they quickly realized that the farm was too small to maintain their venture full-time. As a result, they work with importers that focus on ethically sourced coffee, such as Sustainable Harvest, Catalyst Trade, and Genuine

Origin, which provide Applied Arts with sustainable coffee from Burundi, Colombia, Ethiopia, Guatemala, Honduras, Indonesia, Mexico, and Rwanda. Applied Arts offers coffee from light to French roast and various blends, and the roaster employs a Ground Control Coffee Brewer that uses a vacuum pump to produce cold brew concentrate and batch espresso with no bitterness in about eight minutes.

When deciding to open their roastery, New Orleans was a natural choice for Rabasa and Stewart. A trained chef, Rabasa has worked at lauded local eateries like The Franklin and observed how New Orleans keeps pace with national culinary trends. He sees the city's third-wave coffee industry similarly—a bit behind what other specialty markets produce but a robust addition to the scene. Because so many small specialty roasters are emerging in the city, the potential to be the next big destination spot for specialty coffee is significant. With the addition of smaller roasters, New Orleanians' interest in specialty and single-origin coffee is increasing. The fascination seems to be more than a passing trend, with customer demand for single-origin coffee extending past traditional coffee shops. Although Applied Arts is a relatively new roaster, its coffee can be enjoyed at local restaurants such as Café Degas, Emeril's, Gautreau's Restaurant, and Zasu.

CR Coffee Shop

CR Coffee Shop is a coffee shop and roaster that boasts three locations, including in the famed St. Roch Market, a bustling food hall encompassing multiple vendors. Owner Kevin Pedeaux entered the coffee business full-time in 2009 after getting his feet wet as a teenager delivering king cakes for Randazzo's Bakery. One of Randazzo's clients was PJ's Coffee, and when Pedeaux would stop into one of the shops, he was offered a cup of coffee. He developed his coffee palate, tasting blends from different regions and learning what made individual coffees unique. After Hurricane Katrina,

Coffee at CR Coffee Shop.
Photo by David Rodrigue.

Pedeaux spent time on the Gulf Coast, where he met Shawn Montella, the owner of Coast Roast Coffee and Tea. A friendship blossomed, and Pedeaux began selling Coast Roast's coffee to make some extra money. Eager to absorb all he could about the business, he learned how to roast coffee from coffee-roasting expert Bruce Walle, whom he met through Montella.

When Pedeaux had the idea to sell his coffee at the Covington Farmer's Market, he connected with one of the market's sponsors, Coffee Rani, and began selling them coffee. From there, Pedeaux's coffee career grew as he began selling wholesale; he opened his first CR Coffee Shop location at St. Roch Market in 2015. The current St. Roch Market building, located in the center of St. Claude Avenue, was initially constructed in 1875 and served as an integral part of the St. Roch neighborhood in the late nineteenth and early twentieth centuries. The original market sold fresh produce, meat, and plated meals. However, following Hurricane Katrina, the market closed and sat vacant until 2012, when federal funding was used to restore the building. St. Roch Market reopened in 2014 as a food hall, and CR Coffee Shop was one of the hall's first vendors.

Pedeaux is passionate not only about New Orleans's coffee history but also about New Orleans's history as a whole. This passion motivated him to assume responsibility as the market's operator after the COVID-19 pandemic, and a slow summer caused the market's vendor selection to dwindle. Pedeaux is now responsible for day-to-day business and hiring vendors to fill out the market's food stands.

Pivoting back to his coffee business, Pedeaux expanded CR Coffee Shop to Magazine Street in 2019 and Metairie Road in 2023, roasting his coffee on two antique Royal #6 seventy-pound capacity roasters. The roasters are equipped with a thin, perforated drum, allowing the roasting flame to go through the drum. This allows the drum to retain less heat, resulting in fewer hot spots during the roasting process. Pedeaux likes the antique roasters because they enable him to replicate antique-style coffee flavors and produce a historically accurate New Orleans–style French roast that contains smoky flavor notes. Along with a classic French roast, Pedeaux has framed CR Coffee Shop around serving a good medium roast and a coffee with chicory to keep with New Orleans coffee traditions. He also sells a selection of single-origin coffee. As for future coffee trends in the city, Pedeaux has found that while people do appreciate single-origin coffee, what keeps them coming back is their old favorites done well. For example, he has focused heavily on perfecting his medium roast and cold brew, right down to the filtration techniques in the water used to brew the coffee and the blends used to bring out the coffee's best flavors.

MAMMOTH COFFEE COMPANY

Mammoth Coffee Company is a boutique specialty roaster owned by Jonathan and Darlene Riethmaier. What started as a simple coffee bar in 2016 has expanded into a roastery in New Orleans's Warehouse District and another coffee shop in the works. Jonathan Riethmaier's road to coffee is an interesting one. He was working in public relations in Atlanta, and one of his company's business accounts was a paper goods manufacturer that made paper hot cups for beverages. Because the paper goods company was interested in providing hot cups for coffee shops, Riethmaier began networking in the independent coffee market and working on sponsorship agreements. While networking and attending coffee festivals, he met others in the industry and began learning the coffee business from the inside. In 2006, he met with some executive council members of the Barista Guild of America, the global trade guild of the Specialty Coffee Association, and learned that it was possible to make a career out of his love of coffee. Some years later, while living in Washington, DC, Riethmaier began moonlighting as a barista to learn the science of coffee, master commercial coffee equipment, and work with high-level specialty coffee roasters. After working closely with a coffee café manager, Riethmaier planned to open his own coffee shop.

When Riethmaier opened Mammoth Espresso, he opened it from a barista's perspective, working behind the bar seven days a week for the first years it was in operation. From there, he began training baristas, allowing his staff to expand their knowledge of the coffee business and learn on the job. As the business became successful, Riethmaier began exploring other ways to generate revenue. Rather than immediately expanding to another location, Riethmaier began roasting coffee in 2022 and selling it wholesale to restaurants, bars, and cafés. In 2022, *Food & Wine* named Mammoth Espresso the best coffee shop in Louisiana.

When sourcing coffee for Mammoth Coffee Company, Riethmaier buys vibrant washed-process coffee from Brazil, Colombia, Ethiopia, Guatemala, and Kenya. He chooses his coffee based on cleanness and nuance, and prioritizes agricultural cycles and the quality of the coffee from seed to cup. Rather than roast coffee from every region, he keeps his coffee consistent with specific classical profiles. Moreover, his business focuses on equity, working with companies aware of what is happening in different areas where his coffee is being sourced, the quality of livelihood, and the economic impact of the coffee business.

One way to ensure that his company's coffee is being harvested ethically and the farmers are earning a fair wage is by working with companies like Shared Source in Colombia and Guatemala. Shared Source facilitates robust, transparent, and equitable trade between roasters and small-scale producers and employs practices that empower producers to make a living from coffee. The company makes the Farm Gate price available, which is the price paid to the farmer for the coffee being purchased. It's important for Riethmaier to know what is happening at the farm level of the coffee he is buying and how the farmers are being compensated. He appreciates transparency and values building relationships with small groups of coffee importers and exporters so that his company can be knowledgeable about its impact on the communities that make his coffee special. Ensuring that farmers are being adequately compensated for their work adds value to their livelihood so that these farmers' children will want to take over the family farm in the future rather than seek work elsewhere. Taking care of farmers today means a legacy for families and more coffee for years to come. Drinking ethically sourced quality coffee is a way for consumers and coffee sellers like Riethmaier to feel good about themselves, even if it costs a bit more than a cup of coffee you might grab at the gas station.

Compared to other cities' specialty coffee scenes, Riethmaier thinks that New Orleans offers a lot of diversity and says that the biggest thing that can be done as a local coffee community is to excel differentially. New Orleans is good at not following trends, so while roasters in other cities might see a company like Starbucks and want to emulate that business model to reach that level of success, local roasters are creating their own niches in the coffee world and standing out from the crowd with different roasting techniques and coffee sourcing methods. Riethmaier notes that coffee captures enthusiasm from both a producer and consumer perspective. As a coffee business owner, he finds joy in training and mentoring people excited about being surrounded by coffee.

Michael Matthews is a coffee expert and the founder of Alinea Coffee Roasters. A passionate roaster, when I spoke with Matthews, he had just returned from the 2024 U.S. Coffee Championships, where he placed fifth out of thirty-two roasters and advanced to the nationals in the "Roaster" and "Cup Tasting" categories. In May 2024 he placed third in the U.S. Roaster Nationals and first in the Big Shoulders Coffee Chicago Roaster Workshop Competition. The U.S. Coffee Championships is one of many national competitions celebrating specialty coffee professionals.

Matthews attends these coffee competitions to test his skills as a roaster and share knowledge with those who care about coffee as much as he does. His first foray into the specialty coffee world was in Charleston, where he tasted a natural-process Ethiopian coffee. A touring musician at the time, he was blown away by the coffee's flavor notes. Soon, he began tasting coffee all over the country and buying beans to roast at home. As he began networking with others in the coffee industry, he appreciated the camaraderie and willingness of seasoned roasters to educate new roasters.

Matthews has only been a part of national coffee competitions for a year, but one of his favorite parts is tasting other roasters' coffee. Every competing roaster is given the same coffee to roast. After each competitor roasts their coffee, it's batch-brewed, and every competitor tastes the other's coffee. It's a process that Matthews says gives a glimpse into other roasters' palates and how they think the roasted coffee should taste. Anyone with any coffee experience knows how flavors vary depending on the roasting technique. A roaster's interpretation of how a coffee should be roasted is as different as they are. No two specialty coffees are roasted the same way by any two roasters. Furthermore, roasters are working with a machine they aren't familiar with, adding another component to the competition; a skilled roaster applies their roasting knowledge to the machine they are using.

MORE ABOUT COFFEE COMPETITIONS

The U.S. Coffee Championship is a three-level competition that celebrates specialty coffee. The levels are the U.S. Coffee Championships Preliminaries, the U.S. Coffee Championships Qualifying Competitions, and the U.S. Coffee Championships National Competitions. The competitions include the U.S. Barista Competition, U.S. Brewers Competition, U.S. Coffee in Good Spirits Competition, U.S. Cup Tasters Competition, U.S. Latte Art Competition, and the U.S. Roasters Competition. Those who receive top placement in the National Competition then compete in the World Coffee Championships in North America, Asia, and Europe.

Although the World Coffee Championship is the biggest coffee competition, it is far from the only one. Other competitions are hosted throughout the year. For example, the NOLA Coffee Festival hosts a barista competition, and Coffee Fest, a traveling coffee trade show, hosts a latte art competition. Coffee professionals consider competitions a great way to network and learn skills from other pros.

How a roaster decides to roast their coffee also depends on who will be drinking it. For Bearcat Café in New Orleans, a café that Matthews owns, he sources and roasts coffee that can stand up to a customer's cream and sugar. Although he offers high-end coffee at the café, he wants to supply his customers with approachable coffee that can be enjoyed black. With his coffee brand, Alinea, he gets to shine, carrying a variety of coffee for everyone from the casual coffee drinker to those obsessed with specialty rarities. For Matthews, learning to roast coffee was a trial-and-error process. When he first started roasting, he attended the Coffee Roasters Guild Retreat, a three-day event in which coffee professionals from all over the world attend classes, hold competitions, and hone their roasting skills. Attending the retreat was a turning point for Matthews, who met his first group of importers at the event.

From there, Alinea Coffee took off, with Matthews roasting a pound and a half of coffee at a time on a small roaster. When he started getting up to forty orders for coffee a day, he knew he had to expand. He now roasts two hundred pounds of coffee a week at HEY Coffee Roasters, a roastery that he says has been pivotal in his company's growth. He plans to open his own roastery in the near future.

When sourcing his coffee, Matthews gravitates toward Ethiopian, Mexican, Salvadorean, Nicaraguan, Colombian, and Brazilian farms. The coffee he buys depends on region, elevation, season, and market price, and he enjoys sampling coffee from different countries and unlocking its specific flavor profiles. Circling back to the roasting style, he explains that different regions of coffee have different roasting requirements. While one coffee may need more heat to release its full flavor potential, another may need less heat to produce the same effect. Working as a well-rounded coffee roaster means knowing how to bring the best out of any coffee and produce a product that customers will enjoy.

Concerning the specialty coffee scene in New Orleans, Matthews sees the city as a few years behind the curve compared to other cities, such as Seattle and Portland, which he attributes to certain coffee practices ingrained in the city's DNA. He notes that most people raised in New Orleans grew up drinking dark-roasted coffee, and when tourists visit the city, they tend to gravitate toward the coffee that New Orleans is known for—coffee with chicory and café au lait. He also thinks that because New Orleans produces a large amount of commodity coffee, such as Folgers and even PJ's Coffee and Community Coffee, people tend to be less experimental regarding the type of coffee they drink. When Matthews encounters people in his café who prefer dark-roast coffee, he'll give them a solid medium roast with some of the same characteristics as a traditional New Orleans dark roast. From there, he starts the coffee conversation and finds the customer is more likely to try different types of coffee when they return.

Moving forward, Matthews says one of the most important parts of working in specialty coffee is working personally with farmers to ensure they are treated fairly because raising and harvesting specialty-grade coffee is laborious. Matthews's devotion to coffee and the fair treatment of coffee farmers was obvious in his tone when he described the farmers' lives. Sometimes, buyers will approach farmers and offer to buy their coffee at a lower market price, and because the farmers need the money, they oblige. The result is that farmers can no longer afford to maintain their farms and the labor the farms require. Matthews likes to buy his coffee directly from farmers to ensure they are paid a fair wage, often cutting importers out of the process. That way, all the profit from the coffee sale can return to the farm. In the end, he notes that coffee resale will be more expensive, but farmers will earn a more sustainable living and cultivate farms that will grow coffee for years to come. An indisputable benefit is that when farms do well, importers reinvest in them, and farmers can purchase better farming equipment. In turn, the farm can produce better coffee season after season. Matthews says it's a cycle that benefits everyone in the coffee business, including the casual coffee drinker.

UNDERGROWTH COFFEE

Tucked into a cozy corner on Magazine Street is Undergrowth Coffee, an LGBTQ-owned coffee shop dedicating itself to sustainability and producing coffee that doesn't just taste good but does good. Owners Alyssa Johnson and Zack Rescoe opened Undergrowth Coffee in 2020, planning to operate their shop and roastery on a smaller scale. Johnson is from New York, and Roscoe is from New Jersey; Johnson explains that she knew that Undergrowth Coffee would thrive in New Orleans because the city celebrates the obscure and does business a little differently.

The first batches of coffee that Johnson got for Undergrowth Coffee came from Dupuy Storage in New Orleans East. When Undergrowth Coffee started, Johnson chose to get the shop's coffee directly from the warehouse rather than contribute to carbon emissions or use coffee that had to be shipped nationally. Johnson describes this as "working with what we have" in a process as simple as getting into her car, driving to the warehouse, and picking up the bags of coffee she needs for her business. Undergrowth Coffee roasts its coffee in four-pound batches on a two-kilo coffee roaster in the shop's courtyard and sells its coffee by the bag to locals eager to take home Undergrowth Coffee's sustainable beans.

In the years that Undergrowth Coffee has been in operation, Johnson has begun purchasing her coffee from other importers around the country in large batches to reduce the travel and labor needed to obtain the product. She also works with other businesses that share her passion for sustainability, whether social or ecological. This includes working with Mercon Specialty, a Seattle-based company committed to sustainability and empowering independent coffee roasters. Johnson enjoys working with Mercon Specialty because of their Seeds for Progress and LIFT program. According to the company's website, Seeds for Progress is a nonprofit organization committed to transforming lives in Central America's coffee communities through quality education. LIFT is a sustainable production platform providing valuable tools, training, and services to coffee farmers and communities. Through its LIFT program, Mercon Specialty works directly with coffee producers to raise their quality of life and help them improve their well-being in a socially and environmentally conscious manner. In addition to working with companies that put sustainability at the forefront, Undergrowth Coffee extends the mission into its shop with compostable and recyclable plates and cups.

Johnson sources most of her coffee from women-owned coffee farms, and most of Undergrowth's coffee comes from Ethiopia,

Guatemala, Honduras, and Rwanda. One of the shop's most beloved coffees comes from the first woman-owned co-op in Rwanda; the co-op's owner inherited it when she was widowed. In the brief time the co-op has been in operation, Johnson explains, its coffee production has exploded.

RIVERBOAT COFFEE COMPANY

Riverboat Coffee Company is dedicated to sustainability and is out to change how people enjoy coffee. Founded by Evan Golden, Brady Horn, and Brice Sanderford in 2018, Riverboat Coffee Company serves cold brew coffee at its cold brew bar on Magazine Street and delivers growlers and kegs full of the stuff to customers who want the convenience of cold brew coffee at their doorstep.

Golden approached Sanderford, a New Orleanian, and asked him to help create a business that would put cold brew into kegs and deliver it to local businesses like restaurants, hotels, and law offices. When Riverboat Coffee Company started, it focused on cold brew coffee kegs, but it quickly pivoted to cold brew growler delivery, in half gallons, to homes during the COVID-19 pandemic. Sanderford describes the growler delivery as a "milkman" method in which customers sign up for a regular delivery and simply leave empty glass growlers outside for pickup.

Sanderford explains that sustainability impacts every aspect of Riverboat Coffee Company. The company's coffee vessels are reusable, compostable, or recyclable. Kegs are reused, and when they are no longer usable, they are repurposed. Glass growlers are reused, and when they break, the team brings them to Glass Half Full, a local recycling company that recycles glass waste into sand and gravel for coastal restoration and eco-construction. Riverboat's cold brew bar uses Eco-Products cups that can be recycled or composted and offers discounts to customers who bring in their own cups for their coffee. Even Riverboat's coffee grounds are reused; local farms repurpose grounds as fertilizer or a natural deterrent for pests. Sanderford says Riverboat's goal is to ensure that the least amount of waste ends up in landfills.

Serving freshly roasted coffee from Colombia and Nicaragua, Riverboat's cold brew bar on Magazine Street is where customers can purchase growlers and enjoy nitro cold brew coffee served on tap from eight draft lines, in the same way draft beer is served. Nitro coffee, coffee infused with nitrogen gas, is a specialty of the cold brew bar and available to anyone who orders a keg of Riverboat's cold brew. Nitrogen gas gives coffee a creamy texture and eliminates some bitterness found in typical cold brew coffee. Although Riverboat's coffee is best served cold, Sanderford says they can heat it for customers who prefer hot coffee.

Sanderford finds that the interest in coffee consumption has increased, especially with some people choosing to forgo alcohol. He also notes that office coffee culture is changing from the typical countertop drip coffee brewer to other coffee options like cold brew coffee kegs. Riverboat's coffee kegs, equipped with a kegerator to keep them cold, are the next step toward approachable coffee consumption. Sanderford explains that because the kegs are filled with nitrogen gas instead of oxygen, the coffee stays fresh longer and doesn't have to be consumed immediately upon delivery. He also asserts that a superior coffee station provides a more enjoyable experience to those in the workplace.

Junk Drawer Coffee

One of New Orleans's newest coffee roasters, Junk Drawer Coffee, is nestled in the Uptown neighborhood on Broadway Street. What first started as a small shop owned by David Privat-Gilman has since expanded into a roaster and coffee shop that serves a variety of single-origin and blended washed- and natural-process coffee from Burundi, Colombia, Ethiopia, Guatemala, Indonesia, Peru, and Rwanda. Like other roasters, Privat-Gilman uses specific coffee for different purposes. For example, he likes to employ coffee from Central America in his espresso blends because he feels beans from that region have a strong flavor profile that stands out.

At Junk Drawer, Privat-Gilman's focuses on what he calls old-school, bold New Orleans coffee, specifically, the chicory coffee and dark-roast coffee he feels many roasters have abandoned for lighter roasts. He argues that most people enjoy dark-roast coffee, even if it's not the coffee they usually reach for. Privat-Gilman explains that when he first started Junk Drawer, his customers enjoyed the cappuccino he made with dark-roast coffee.

Like Coffee Science, Junk Drawer roasts coffee on an electric Bellwether Coffee Roaster. Although Privat-Gilman learned to roast on a traditional roaster, he wanted to transpose the skills he honed on a gas coffee roaster onto an electric one for a cleaner roasting process. As a conscious coffee roaster, Privat-Gilman ethically sources his roaster's green coffee beans; the coffee used at Junk Drawer comes from specialty green coffee importers rather than commodity distributors.

As for the shop itself, Junk Drawer isn't a sleepy little coffee shop. Privat-Gilman serves coffee in a fun atmosphere to open-minded, curious, and social coffee drinkers who are more interested in good coffee than the latest coffee fads. The shop boasts one hundred seats, and with the motto "Take a Break and Rejuvenate," the space offers great-tasting coffee in an upbeat, social environment that encourages customers to interact with one another.

TURGAY AND AMY YILDIZLI AND TURKISH COFFEE

Turgay Yildizli is a certified Q Grader, roaster, and barista from Istanbul who studied hotel management before discovering his passion for coffee. After he met and married his wife, Amy, a New Orleanian living in Istanbul, the pair embarked on a sixteen-month backpacking trip around Central America. While in Guatemala, they visited a coffee farm and got to know the family there. As their journey continued, they visited Asia and Africa, stopping at coffee farms and learning about coffee culture along the way. This education ignited their interest in coffee brewing and the coffee industry.

Upon returning to Istanbul, Turgay began taking barista classes and networking in the coffee community. He attended the coffee professionals' World Brewers Cup competition, and he won some events there. In 2011, he participated in the World Coffee Events competition in the Turkish coffee category, better known as the Cezve/Ibrik Championship. Turgay also competed again that year in the World Brewers Cup, as well as in Coffee in Good Spirits, a contest in preparing cocktails. In 2013, the Cezve/Ibrik Championship was held in Istanbul, where both Turgay and Amy competed, with Turgay representing Turkey and Amy representing the United States. Turgay won the championship, and Amy placed third. Turgay is a three-time Cezve/Ibrik champion representing Turkey.

Turgay explains that low-grade, commercial coffee from Brazil is most often used in preparing Turkish coffee because it's cheap. Turkish coffee is overextracted, making it very bitter, so adding sugar, cinnamon, and cardamom to make it more palatable has become a common practice. When Turgay brews Turkish coffee, he uses natural-process coffee from Ethiopia, which he finds more flavorful because it grows at a higher altitude. Although many Turks still enjoy coffee, in the 1940s, tea became the drink of choice in Turkey due to the rise in coffee prices.

Now retired from coffee competitions, Turgay and Amy live in New Orleans. The couple initially planned to open a specialty coffee shop in the city but instead chose to design and sell equipment used to prepare Turkish coffee. Their company, Specialty Turkish Coffee, sells everything needed to brew the perfect cup of Turkish coffee, such as cezve/ibrik, brewing stands, coffee grinders, and Turkish coffee cups. Yildizli has noticed an increased interest in Turkish coffee in the West, although it remains a niche concept, and he hopes that more specialty coffee shops begin adding Turkish coffee to their menus. Two New Orleans restaurants where you can enjoy Turkish coffee are Fatma's Cozy Corner and Jamila's Café.

THE ETHIOPIAN COFFEE CEREMONY AT ADDIS NOLA

At Addis NOLA, in New Orleans's Seventh Ward, Dr. Biruk Alemayehu and her son Prince Lobo are keeping the traditions of Ethiopian coffee alive. At their restaurant, which honors Ethiopian food and culture, Lobo performs an Ethiopian coffee ceremony by request, paying tribute to his family's Ethiopian roots and the roots of coffee itself. The Ethiopian coffee ceremony has been conducted in Ethiopia for thousands of years, allowing people to socialize with their friends and family while celebrating their culture and blessing their guests.

Lobo is an electric figure whose presence fills the room as he conducts this ancient ceremony. His hands are busy as he readies everything needed for his process, and his voice is booming as he transfixes the audience with the demonstration. Lobo begins his ceremony by burning frankincense and myrrh, filling the room with a sweet aroma. He likens it to giving a gift to those watching the ceremony in the same way that Jesus received gifts of frankincense and myrrh at his birth. Lobo explains that someone's mother or grandmother typically performs the coffee ceremony, but because he grew up watching his mother perform the ceremony, he has taken over the honor at Addis NOLA.

Lobo does a beautiful job of starting the ceremony by telling the story of Kaldi and how coffee was initially discovered. From there, he roasts green coffee beans from Yirgacheffe, one of the biggest producers of coffee beans in Ethiopia, in a pan. Although coffee originated in Ethiopia, the country is eighth in coffee production today. However, Lobo explains that the natural harvest process sets Ethiopian coffee apart; in Ethiopia, the coffee fruit is allowed to ferment before harvesting, adding a fruitier profile to the coffee.

As Lobo roasts the green coffee beans, you hear them popping as they begin to smoke. This aromatic haze fills the entire space, and Lobo explains that when coffee trees were thrown into the fire, filling the churches with smoke, people fell in love with its toasty aroma. The people of ancient Ethiopia took the roasted beans and put them in water. The beans would then ferment, creating a wine-like coffee beverage, one of the first iterations of making a drink with coffee beans.

In Ethiopian homes, the coffee ceremony is considered a saging ceremony, or a spiritual blessing; the smoke from the roasting coffee beans is an essential part of the ritual. Lobo encourages all who watch his coffee ceremony to wash and bless themselves in the smoke of the roasted beans, a process traditionally done three times as a representation of the trinity and to allow the experience of the ceremony to wash over their senses.

Once the green coffee beans are roasted until they are shiny and black, the person performing the ceremony grinds the roasted beans by hand in a mortar, a heavy wooden bowl called *mukecha,* and a pestle, a cylinder with a blunt end called a *zenezena.* The coffee is then brewed in a large ceramic pot with a neck, a pouring spout, and a handle called a *jebena.* Handleless cups called *sini* are placed on a table called a *rekebot* after the coffee is brewed. The coffee is poured into the *sini* from about one foot up; the idea is to fill each cup equally in an uninterrupted endless pour—a skill that can take years to master.

Guests typically enjoy three cups of coffee in a full Ethiopian coffee ceremony. The first cup is *Abol,* which is for pleasure; the second is *Tona,* which provokes contemplation; and the third is *Baraka,* which bestows a blessing for all. Snacks such as fresh fruit, candies, peanuts, and popcorn are often served with the coffee.

NOLA COFFEE FESTIVAL

In 2023, New Orleans hosted its first NOLA Coffee Festival, an event founded by businessmen Jim Currie and Kevin Richards celebrating the joy of coffee and the people who serve in the industry. The two-day festival hosted a trade and industry day where coffee professionals discussed brewing techniques and equipment and attended special skill classes. It also featured a consumer day in which coffee lovers were invited to experience a day of coffee sophistication and culture, learn home-brewing techniques, attend coffee education talks, and sample coffee from all over the country.

The event was open to coffee lovers who wanted to sample various coffees and participate in educational seminars to further their coffee knowledge. The goal of the NOLA Coffee Festival is to highlight the Port of New Orleans as a national leader in coffee importation, feature coffee professionals from New Orleans and the Gulf South region, and foster a coffee education that will serve as a backbone to growth in the industry. This work includes educational classes and programs for regional coffee professionals and consumers.

Currie and Richards were inspired to create the NOLA Coffee Festival to raise New Orleans's profile in modern specialty coffee. While cities like Portland and Seattle are established in the specialty coffee scene, Currie and Richards believe that New Orleans's specialty coffee scene has earned its place in the national coffee conversation. Richards, who previously worked for the Sazerac Company, explains he wants to do for the New Orleans coffee story what has been done for the New Orleans cocktail story. With the opening of the Sazerac House, a cocktail educational center on Magazine Street, and the inception of Tales of the Cocktail, a cocktail conference that draws bar and cocktail professionals from all over the country annually, New Orleans has become a destination city for cocktail lovers. He believes the same method can be applied to coffee to raise national interest in New Orleans's coffee roasters and baristas.

When building the festival, Currie and Richards started by meeting with local roasters and learning about the city's specialty coffee scene. Richards explains that he realized that although New Orleans is a relatively small city, roasters wanted opportunities to gather and talk about the coffee business. The pair wanted to create a centralized coffee event to facilitate discussions between people making the New Orleans coffee industry run. From there, they began adding roasters from other cities into the conversation, discussing new coffee trends and how these small groups of roasters can learn from each other.

The Specialty Coffee Association of America (SCCA) holds coffee education seminars and networking opportunities for coffee professionals throughout the year. As Currie and Richards began speaking with local coffee experts, they discovered that roasters wanted to attend the educational courses offered by the SCAA but couldn't due to a lack of time or funds. The duo began planning a local coffee trade show that was accessible and affordable for both the average coffee professional and the casual coffee drinker.

"If we are really going to change coffee in the South and accelerate skills and quality, education is the backbone," Currie says. "We framed the NOLA Coffee Festival to these coffee professionals as a trade show where they could come and network and take advantage of various classes. It's tricky to try to create educational programs for both professionals and consumers because it isn't the same topics and speakers. But we felt it was important to offer education for the consumer if we want to grow the high-end side of coffee in the South."

The result was two thousand attendees at the inaugural NOLA Coffee Festival in 2023. Currie and Richards see this event as the foundation for what it can represent not only in the New Orleans coffee industry but also throughout the South. Currie says that the secret to the trade show is bringing the right industry people together and allowing them to collaborate. When these professionals come together, they inspire great things.

The Future of Specialty Coffee in New Orleans

Beyond the festival, Currie wants to work with local roasters to get specialty coffee typically only available to their counterparts in the

Northeast. He's discovered that it's difficult for roasters in New Orleans to import certain types of specialty coffee because the coffee that comes through the Port of New Orleans is mostly in commodity volume. To obtain coffee from smaller farms, in the way that Cherry Coffee Roasters and HEY Coffee Co. do, unique relationships must be built between coffee brokers who work with farmers and the roasters who are eager to sell their coffee in New Orleans's coffee shops. Currie's long-term goal is to create a relationship with the Port of New Orleans and specialty coffee growers and establish the Port as one of the "stops" when this coffee is shipped to the United States. This will make it more accessible to local roasters and reduce shipping costs by shipping directly to the city. He also sees the importance in developing lasting relationships between specialty coffee growers and coffee professionals in New Orleans. Coffee farms such as Agua Fresca Coffee, Monte Vista Coffee, Nica-

Bagged coffee beans, French Truck Coffee.
Photo by the author.

Nola Coffee, and Rebirth Coffee have already established direct-trade relationships with New Orleans.

"We are working on developing better relationships with countries of origin, farmers, and co-ops in those places and making sure that New Orleans is on the list of ports that they'll ship.," Currie explains. "A lot of these countries, such as Colombia, want to ship [specialty coffee] directly to New Orleans but there are procedures and processes in the Coffee Federation of Colombia, for example, that are working against us. It's easier for some of these coffee growers to ship to Miami than to ship to New Orleans, at least for now."

Currie and Richards think that steps should be taken to put the Port of New Orleans on the radar of smaller coffee growers. He explains that it is a systematic process that could take five to ten years, but creating an even better coffee scene here in New Orleans is worth the time. Richards adds that it takes repetition and hiring the right people in the New Orleans coffee space to make the city a significant part of the national coffee business as it was in the nineteenth century. Also, Currie and Richards want the Port of New Orleans to update its equipment to be more receptive to specialty coffee shipped in from these growers. Although the Port hits big coffee import numbers annually, some smaller growers cannot ship to the city because of logistical issues.

While interviewing various New Orleans roasters, I kept hearing that many smaller roasters don't receive their specialty-grade coffee through the Port of New Orleans and that the Port was for more prominent names that call New Orleans home, like Folgers. Bob Arceneaux explains that many specialty-grade coffees in the United States are shipped to Continental Terminals, a coffee warehouse in Carteret, New Jersey, and the Annex Warehouse in San Leandro, California. He says that importers send their coffee to these facilities because they are more equipped to handle specialty-grade coffee that is shipped in smaller batches. New Orleans's specialty coffee market is small, so it makes more sense to ship to a city with a larger market and arrange to ship any desired coffee from those ports to New Orleans.

However, Arceneaux says that one importer he does business with, InterAmerican, is dedicated to shipping coffee to the Dupuy Storage facility in New Orleans, creating a connection between the city and specialty coffee importers. He notes that a relationship with a company like InterAmerican makes it easier for roasters to place orders and access their coffee inventory in a city like New Orleans that only gets a few direct shipments of specialty coffee. Janet Colley Morse says that her company, Dupuy Storage and Forwarding, handles a good amount of specialty coffee in New Orleans. Still, she notes that the company's facility in Houston handles the most, adding that Dupuy's most significant accounts are Louisiana-based national retail brands Reily Foods and Community Coffee.

Colley Morse asserts that the specialty coffee business in New Orleans is complex because it is a smaller market, especially when specialty coffee shops are competing with more prominent names like PJ's Coffee and CC's Coffee House. Shelby Westfeldt Mills adds that specialty coffee doesn't often come through the Port of New Orleans because the port handles a lot of Brazilian coffee. Much of the specialty coffee that comes from places like Africa isn't mass-produced in big bulk and doesn't warrant coming through a small specialty market like New Orleans.

Drew Cambre of the International Coffee Corporation agrees that the Port of New Orleans is best equipped for commodity coffee because it's cheaper, and the system for that type of coffee shipping is faster in New Orleans than in other ports. It also comes down to geography; New Orleans is close to and receives most of its commodity coffee shipments from Colombia and Brazil, and the coffee produced in these nations is frequently used in more prominent coffee brands. Although New Orleans receives coffee shipments from other countries such as El Salvador, Honduras, Nicaragua, and Panama, the amount of specialty coffee in these countries is low. In contrast, ports on the West Coast are more likely to handle specialty coffee from countries like Indonesia, Ghana, Ethiopia, and Rwanda because they are in closer proximity to those countries. Shipping directly to the Pacific Ocean ports is cheaper than shipping to New Orleans.

6

VIETNAM TO VERSAILLES

Vietnamese Coffee and Culture in New Orleans

In the latter part of the twentieth century, New Orleans was transforming due, in part, to immigration. The Vietnam War led many Vietnamese to flee their home country and settle in the city. New Orleans's coffee practices would change how these new Americans enjoyed their coffee, and the Vietnamese would add their own traditions to the fabric of New Orleans's food and coffee culture.

One type of coffee that New Orleanians love is Vietnamese iced coffee, which is brewed very strong and sweetened with condensed milk. The city is peppered with many Vietnamese restaurants, and Vietnamese iced coffee is a staple, especially during the hot summer months. This drink is steeped in history and tells a story that began fifty years ago.

THE VIETNAMESE FLEE SOUTH VIETNAM

On April 30, 1975, the Vietnam War ended when South Vietnam's capital, Saigon, fell to the Communist-ruled North. The residents of South Vietnam, a United States ally, faced hardships like prison, forced relocation, and death. President Gerald Ford acknowledged the crisis and arranged for the refugees to seek asylum in the United States. Ford summoned help from church groups, the

American Jewish Congress, Democratic governors, and labor leaders to secure housing and jobs for those fleeing the war-torn country. Although only 36 percent of Americans favored Vietnamese immigration, the United States government stated that the country had a moral obligation to help those evacuating.

On May 23, 1975, President Ford passed the Indochina Migration and Refugee Assistance Act, which granted Vietnamese refugees a special status and provided funding of $305 million for the Department of State and $100 million for the Department of Health, Education, and Welfare for the resettlement of Vietnamese and Cambodian refugees. The act financed the resettlement costs of 130,000 Vietnamese who were evacuated from Vietnam; the transfer of these people was nicknamed Operation New Life. Most refugees settled in California, while the rest were spread out between Arkansas, Florida, Illinois, Louisiana, New York, Pennsylvania, and Washington. Of these refugees, 2,100 settled in New Orleans.

Vietnamese Refugees Settle in New Orleans

In May 1975, New Orleans Archbishop Philip M. Hannan visited the Vietnamese refugees in Fort Chaffee, Arkansas. Realizing they needed help and feeling responsible because he had previously successfully helped settle Cuban immigrants in America, he agreed to sponsor one hundred families through Catholic Charities. According to "History of Vietnamese Immigration to New Orleans" in the *Clarion Herald,* Hannan failed to realize that in Vietnamese culture, "family" means not only direct descendants such as parents and children but everyone who lives in a Vietnamese village, including grandparents, cousins, and extended family. Once this was understood, Hannan responded to the need and agreed to sponsor one thousand families in New Orleans. Half of these families settled in the Kingstown Marrero Apartments in Marrero, Louisiana, a suburb of New Orleans, and half settled in the Versailles Apartments in

New Orleans East. The latter became the largest group of Vietnamese settlers in Louisiana, and today, this community is called Village de L'Est. The Vietnamese also put down roots outside the city in the Louisiana parishes of Lafourche, St. Mary, and Terrebonne.

New Orleans's newest citizens quickly settled into their new home. The city's subtropical climate was familiar, and many residents, especially those who worked as farmers in Vietnam, planted vegetables along the bayous and in their backyards. Fishermen fished and shrimped in the surrounding waters of Lake Pontchartrain and the Gulf of Mexico, just as they had in the waters at home. The Vietnamese were also drawn to New Orleans for religious reasons; most were Catholic and attended mass weekly at Mary Queen of Vietnam Church. The church, built in 1983 and consecrated in 1986, was the first Catholic Vietnamese-centered church in the country. It added an education center in 1987, and a community vegetable garden sits across the street from the church. Mary Queen of Vietnam Church quickly became an important place for religious gatherings and acted as a social hub for New Orleans's Vietnamese citizens.

Because of cultural differences, finding work was difficult for the Vietnamese, with some taking jobs in factories or as waitstaff at local restaurants. Upon arriving in New Orleans, many of them were employed by Café du Monde, the famed coffee and beignet spot in the French Quarter. In 1975, owner Jay Roman was asked by Catholic Charities to give employment to Vietnamese refugees in need of work, and those who worked there were comfortable as it reminded them of the coffeehouses of their home country. As time passed, the Vietnamese opened businesses, such as restaurants, bakeries, and nail salons, and joined labor professions, such as shrimping enterprises.

Carl L. Bankston III explains in "Vietnamese in Louisiana" that by the early 1990s, the Vietnamese had become the largest Asian group in Louisiana, and by 2018, twenty-nine thousand people of Vietnamese ancestry lived in the state. Although these groups were heavily concentrated in Orleans and Jefferson Parishes, they also called other parts of the state home, such as East Baton Rouge and parts of Shreveport.

French Colonialism and the Changes to Vietnam

When the Vietnamese migrated to New Orleans, they brought traditions from their home country. Many of these Vietnamese traditions are rooted in French influence, and to understand these practices, we first must learn some basic Vietnamese cultural history.

French-Vietnamese relations began in the early seventeenth century. Europe was involved in Vietnamese trade, and the arrival of Jesuit missionaries Girolamo Maiorica and Alexandre de Rhodes triggered an influx of French-Catholic influence into the country. By the nineteenth century, the French colonial empire was heavily involved in Vietnam, and the Nguyễn dynasty saw Catholic missionaries as a political threat. In 1858, fourteen French gunships with 3,300 men on board, led by French Admiral Charles Rigault de Genouilly, attacked the port of Tourane and occupied the city. De Genouilly then attacked and captured Saigon in 1859.

According to Bill Hayton in *A Brief History of Vietnam,* The Nguyễn dynasty expanded into what is now southern Vietnam, Cambodia, and Laos due to the centuries-long Nam tiến and Siamese–Vietnamese wars. However, by 1862, it had relinquished control over parts of Southern Vietnam to France. On June 5, 1862, representatives of the French Empire and Emperor Tự Đức, the fourth and final precolonial emperor of the Nguyễn dynasty, signed the Treaty of Saigon, which legalized the practice of Catholicism and opened trade in the Mekong Delta and three ports at the mouth of the Red River in Northern Vietnam. This treaty was confirmed on April 14, 1863, by signing the Treaty of Huế. The provinces of Biên Hòa, Gia Định, and Định Tường were ceded to France, as well as the island of Poulo Condore.

French colonialism in Vietnam lasted more than six decades. Vietnam, Laos, and Cambodia were entirely controlled by France by the late nineteenth century and were known as French Indochina. France was motivated to push into Vietnam for a few reasons. First, they saw a financial opportunity in two of Vietnam's significant crops: rice and rubber. Jennifer Llewellyn and Steve Thompson explain in "French Colonialism in Vietnam" that the land used for growing rice had quadrupled in the first twenty years since France colonized the country, and Southern Vietnam boasted twenty-five large rubber plantations.

Hayton explains that toward the end of World War II, Japanese forces were facing a threat of Allied invasion of Indochina and feared a revolt against them by French colonial forces. On March 9, 1945, the Japanese overthrew France's colonial regime during Meigō Sakusen, or Operation Bright Moon, and France's power in Vietnam fell. After the Japanese surrendered later that year, the Việt Minh, a national independence coalition formed at Pác Bó by Hồ Chí Minh and declared Vietnamese independence. When France regained control of French Indochina, it led to the start of the First Indochina War. The State of Vietnam was proclaimed by the French in 1949, and France was defeated at the Battle of Điện Biên Phủ in May 1954. The Kingdom of Laos and the Kingdom of Cambodia proclaimed their respective independences, and, when the Geneva Accord of 1954 was passed, Vietnam was declared independent from France and split into North Vietnam and South Vietnam.

FRENCH INFLUENCE ON VIETNAMESE CUISINE

Even though the Geneva Accord of 1954 emancipated Vietnam from French control, the heavy French influence reflected in Vietnamese practices and cuisine remained. Before French colonialism, Vietnamese cuisine was greatly influenced by its neighboring country, China. As Emily Monaco explains in "The French Influence on Vietnamese Cuisine," this Chinese influence is reflected in wontons, wheat noodles, and vegetables like chili peppers and corn, which are prevalent in Vietnamese dishes.

The Vietnamese also constructed their meals like the Chinese, with dishes containing the five taste elements: spice, sour, bitter, salty, and sweet. Chinese medicine suggests that these elements correspond with the five major digestive organs: the gall bladder, small intestine, large intestine, stomach, and bladder. When the French came in, they brought new produce to the region, such as potatoes, green onions, and asparagus, and the Vietnamese began integrating them into their meals.

One food that became primarily associated with the Vietnamese-French influence, widespread in New Orleans Vietnamese restaurants, is the bánh mì, a sandwich made with a short baguette, split lengthwise and packed with grilled meat and raw vegetables. In New Orleans, its closest relative would be the po'boy, a sandwich consisting of a loaf of French bread typically filled with meat or seafood. The French introduced the baguette to Vietnam in the 1860s. Due to the price of wheat, baguettes were considered a luxury; however, when wheat imports were interrupted during World War I, bakers began mixing rice flour into the grain. The combination made the bread fluffier and the baguettes themselves less expensive.

In 1954, people began migrating from North Vietnam to South Vietnam, bringing traditional Vietnamese food practices with them. According to food writer Paul Kristoff, two of these migrants, Lê Minh Ngọc and Nguyễn Thị Tịnh, are responsible for first selling the bánh mì in their bakery, Hòa Mã, in District 3, Saigon. They filled their sandwiches with grilled meat, cilantro, pickled vegetables, and pâté, a blend of meats and seasonings. When the Vietnamese settled in the United States, bánh mì became a favorite of family-owned restaurants. In New Orleans, bánh mì is a staple enjoyed at various Vietnamese restaurants and is served at the city's annual Oak Street Po-Boy Festival.

Vietnamese Coffee and the New Orleans Connection

One of the most influential changes the French brought to Vietnam was the inclusion of coffee. Before French colonialism, the Vietnamese drank tea, like those in the surrounding Asian nations. The French introduced arabica coffee to Vietnam in 1857, and the Vietnamese took to it immediately, consuming it with gusto and growing coffee crops on plantations by 1888. The subtropical Vietnamese climate offers the perfect environment for coffee cultivation, and coffee is one of the country's most plentiful crops. Today, Vietnam is the second-largest coffee exporter in the world after Brazil, and coffee is second only to rice as Vietnam's most exported product.

The most common type of Vietnamese coffee is cà phê sữa đá, or Vietnamese iced coffee. Considered the standard for Vietnamese coffee, cà phê sữa đá is prepared very strongly with a layer of sweetened condensed milk at the bottom of a glass. Shelf-stable condensed milk has been used in cà phê sữa đá since the 1850s, when fresh milk wasn't readily available in Vietnam due to the country's tropical climate and limited storage capabilities. Longevity Brand's full-cream sweetened condensed milk is traditionally the brand that purists use in their cà phê sữa đá. When the coffee is brewed, it is mixed with the condensed milk and poured over ice. Cà phê đá is black iced coffee made in the same way as cà phê sữa đá, minus the condensed milk. Other types of Vietnamese coffee include cà phê dừa, or coconut coffee, cà phê trứng, or egg coffee, and sữa chua cà phê, or yoghurt coffee.

When the Vietnamese settled in New Orleans in the 1970s, they brought food and coffee traditions with them. As mentioned, many Vietnamese who settled in New Orleans got jobs serving coffee and beignets at Café du Monde. Today, many people working at the coffee and beignet stand are descended from those who worked there nearly fifty years ago. When the Vietnamese came to New Orleans, they had to adapt; the coffee they were familiar with wasn't readily available. Instead, they made their cà phê sữa đá and cà phê đá with dark and rich Café du Monde coffee.

In "How Café du Monde Became a Vietnamese American Staple," Sahra Nguyen explains that the Vietnamese appreciated the deep, rich flavor of Café du Monde coffee. For many, it reminded them of the coffee they had enjoyed in Vietnam, and introducing chicory to the coffee added a bitterness that the Vietnamese found familiar. The appreciation for Café du Monde coffee isn't just a phenomenon among New Orleans's Vietnamese citizens; it's enjoyed in Vietnamese communities nationwide. Although the Vietnamese community is large, the network itself is small. Word traveled quickly among the newly American Vietnamese that Café du Monde was the coffee to drink if you were looking for the flavors of home. As a result, Café du Monde coffee and its market brand, CDM, in the bright-yellow airtight pack or can, are the top coffees drunk nationwide by Vietnamese Americans. Although Vietnam-grown coffee is now readily available in the United States and enjoyed in drinks

Café du Monde Coffee and CDM Coffee,
used in Vietnamese-American coffee drinks.
Photo by the author.

such as cà phê sừa, Café du Monde coffee has become a beloved part of Vietnamese-American communities and can be found in most Asian markets throughout the country.

According to Alfred La Nassa, the vice president of restaurant operations for Luzianne Café in New Orleans, a restaurant owned by Reily Foods, which also owns Café du Monde coffee and CDM, there is a difference between Café du Monde coffee served at the famed coffee stand and the CDM coffee you can buy in the yellow package. Café du Monde coffee is made with robusta coffee beans, whereas CDM is made with a combination of robusta and arabica beans. In Vietnam, the main variety of coffee grown and consumed is robusta, with a distinct bitter flavor and a peanutty aftertaste. Because Café du Monde and CDM are made with robusta beans and chicory, it makes sense that it would appeal to the palate of Vietnamese Americans who missed the intense flavors of the robusta coffee they enjoyed in Vietnam.

Vietnamese coffee such as cà phê sữa đá and cà phê đá is made with a device called a phin filter that consists of four parts: the filter plate, the brew chamber, the gravity press, and the cap. When I enjoy cà phê sữa đá, it's usually at one of my favorite Vietnamese restaurants in New Orleans. The preparation for the drink is so simple that most restaurants will bring the phin filter, filled with brewing coffee, to your table, and let you mix the concoction yourself. If you are interested in preparing cà phê sữa đá at home, the process is easy.

Here are the steps in preparing Vietnamese coffee:

- When brewing cà phê sữa đá or cà phê đá, first place the filter plate and brew chamber on top of a coffee mug containing two tablespoons of sweetened condensed milk (if desired), fill the brew chamber with two scoops of coffee and drop the gravity press on top.
- Then, fill one-third of the brew chamber with hot water and let it sit for forty-five seconds, allowing the coffee to bloom.

- Fill the rest of the brew chamber with hot water, cover the phin filter with the cap, and allow the coffee to brew for five minutes.
- When making cà phê sữa đá, stir the coffee into the condensed milk, pour the coffee over ice, and enjoy.

Vietnamese coffee preparation with a phin filter.
Photo by the author.

Along with their cuisine, the Vietnamese brought another piece of their culture to New Orleans with the celebration of Tet Festival, Mary Queen of Vietnam Church's annual three-day Lunar New Year celebration that features home-cooked food, games, and performances every January or February. The festival has become a centerpiece of Village de l'Est and invites people from all over the city to celebrate Vietnamese culture.

Today, approximately fourteen thousand Vietnamese people live in New Orleans, and it is impossible to deny their impact on the city's culture. Although the community has been affected by disasters like Hurricane Katrina and the BP Oil Spill, homes and businesses have been rebuilt with little help from outside communities. The word "resilient" is often used to describe those who overcome such hardships, but New Orleans's Vietnamese population was left with few options when faced with economic and infrastructural adversity. For a small community, New Orleans's Vietnamese citizens have indisputably influenced the city, and all who live here are richer for it.

7

Beyond the Big Easy

New Orleans Coffee Makes a National Name for Itself

One of the best parts of being a coffee drinker is going to the coffee aisle of the grocery store and picking out an old favorite or trying something new. New Orleans has established itself in coffee importation, and the city has made an impression on the national coffee stage through various brands. A few of my favorite local coffees are CDM, Community, and French Market. While researching this book and tasting different coffees, I developed a taste for medium-roast coffee, but my first urge is always to go for a delicious dark roast. No matter your taste, however, there is sure to be a New Orleans coffee brand that pleases your palate. From a household name that helped make New Orleans the top modern-day coffee city to homegrown New Orleans coffee companies enjoyed nationwide, making a cup of the Crescent City a part of your morning routine is easier than ever.

Folgers and the New Orleans Connection

One of the most recognizable brand names in national coffee is Folgers. In 1850, when a fire destroyed his family's livelihood in Nantucket, Massachusetts, fourteen-year-old James Folger and his brothers Henry and Edward set out for the West in search of gold. When they arrived, James's older brothers headed out to the mines, but he stayed in San Francisco and took a job with the Pioneer Steam Coffee and Spice Mills. Folger was a skilled carpenter and built a coffee mill for William H. Bovee, the owner of the Pioneer Steam Coffee and Spice Mills.

After he built the mill, James became a business partner with Bovee. However, the Civil War led to the economy's collapse, and the Pioneer Steam Coffee and Spice Mills went bankrupt. According to the Folgers brand story, James Folger convinced creditors to pay off the company's debts, and he used the money to buy out the rest of the company's partners. He renamed the company J. A. Folger & Co. Under James Folger, J. A. Folger & Co. quickly became a heavy hitter in the coffee industry. Rather than focus on the appearance of coffee beans, as other brands had, Folger & Co. emphasized how the coffee tasted. Folger implemented a cup-tasting technique, began testing batches of coffee beans, and developed a taste standard for his coffee. He quickly discovered that mountain-grown coffee beans had the best taste and aroma and produced the best cup of coffee.

When James Folger passed away in 1889, his son, James Folger II, inherited the business. He took it national with the help of Frank P. Atha, who assisted grocers with coffee sales and handed out coffee samples. By the early 1900s, the company, now known simply as Folgers, boasted roasting and packaging plants in Texas and Kansas City. In the early 1950s, the demand for instant coffee increased, and Folgers was more than happy to oblige its customers' thirst for a fast coffee fix. While the company's first attempt at instant coffee in 1953 wasn't a success, the instant coffee the company released in 1958 helped solidify Folgers as America's favorite coffee brand.

After World War II, New Orleans was one of the largest green coffee markets in the United States, and Folgers wanted to take advantage. Because of its proximity to Central America, where Folgers gets its coffee beans, the company began building its newest roasting plant in New Orleans East in 1960. In the early 1990s, Silocaf of New Orleans Inc. set out to revolutionize coffee importation into New Orleans. Silocaf refurbished 203 former grain silos at the Nashville Street Wharf, converting them for use in storing and processing coffee. At the same time, Silocaf partnered with Folgers to process millions of pounds of its green coffee beans that arrived in New Orleans via ship in twenty-foot steel containers that held the equivalent of 350 bags of green coffee and weighed 132 pounds each.

From there, the coffee beans entered a computerized system in which they were cleaned, blended, sorted, and stored. The process reduced labor costs and produced coffee faster and more efficiently. According to the *Times-Picayune,* Folgers also used Silocaf to import coffee for two roasting plants in Texas and Missouri in the 1990s; those plants have since closed, and all of Folgers' coffee operations are now located in New Orleans.

The introduction of Silocaf made a significant impression on New Orleans's coffee imports. In 1991, the city imported 321,977 tons of coffee; in 1992, it imported 349,025 tons—an increase of 8.4 percent. Immediately, Silocaf of New Orleans Inc. became the world's largest coffee silo operation shipping millions of pounds of coffee annually.

In 2005, following Hurricane Katrina, Folgers was one of the first businesses in the city to return to operation. "Folgers Continues to Grow New Orleans East's Economy" in *Biz New Orleans* reports that 90 percent of the company's workforce had returned a month after Hurricane Katrina. Brenda Toepfer, an employee at Folgers' whole-bean plant during Katrina, explains that following the storm, the company set up trailers in the parking lot of its main plant to ensure that employees who lost their homes had a place to stay. Furthermore, she says the company did everything possible to keep their workers employed during that unpredictable time.

Folgers has also done good for the community. Mark Ricard, a retired HR senior coordinator for Folgers, explains that when the company was owned by Procter & Gamble, it had a $120,000 annual budget for charity projects. In keeping with the spirit of giving back to the city it calls home, Folgers hosts yearly charity employee events such as basketball games to help raise money for organizations most in need, like Children's Hospital of New Orleans. Folgers' employees have also participated in other charity events, such as Susan G. Komen's Race for a Cure and Rebuilding Together New Orleans. Ricard also explains that, under his guidance, Folgers organized volunteer efforts to rebuild houses affected by various storms around the state. In 2020, during the COVID-19 pandemic, Folgers partnered with United Way of Southeast Louisiana to provide 2,500 meals to EMS workers across seven Louisiana parishes.

Today, Folgers is owned by the J. M. Smucker Company and employs thousands of New Orleanians at two facilities in New Orleans East and two warehouses in metropolitan New Orleans. These employees handle the facility's daily operations, from packing and processing to shipping and distribution. The company also maintains its silo facility on the Mississippi River and a warehouse in Lacombe, Louisiana. Folgers is the largest producer of ground coffee products in the United States.

PJ'S COFFEE AND THE COLD BREW REVOLUTION

On September 5, 1978, Phyllis Jordan opened a coffee shop on Maple Street in New Orleans that would change how New Orleanians consumed coffee. A Des Moines native, Jordan wanted to create a neighborhood specialty coffee shop where everyone would feel welcome. PJ's Coffee and Tea Co., as it was originally named, started as a retail shop, but Jordan quickly pivoted when she found a coffee maker for sale for seventy-five dollars. Within a year and a half of opening her shop, she was serving her customers freshly made coffee.

In 1982, a friend of Jordan's sold her a roaster for one hundred dollars a month, and she began roasting her own green coffee beans. She rented a warehouse and learned how to use her new roaster;

the rest is New Orleans coffee history. PJ's Coffee became a beloved Uptown destination, and within ten years, Jordan had opened three PJ's Coffee locations.

With neighborhood success under her belt, Jordan wanted to create a coffee drink that would appeal to a younger crowd. While PJ's Coffee was a local hit, coffee consumption on the national scale declined in the 1980s. In the 1960s, the average person drank around three cups of coffee daily. That number dropped to two cups daily in the 1980s due, in part, to the younger generation gravitating toward cold soft drinks rather than the hot coffee their parents drank to start their day. Furthermore, the 1980s coffee industry didn't cater to the younger crowd, but Jordan hoped to change that with a simple idea.

Mike Buckley, one of Jordan's coffee suppliers, introduced her to the Toddy Coffee Maker. Invented by Todd Simpson in 1964, the cold-brew system created a coffee concentrate that, when mixed with hot water, would produce a low-acidity alternative to hot-brewed coffee. Jordan was familiar with the idea of iced coffee—her mother had a habit of putting leftover coffee on ice when Jordan was a child. However, she initially rejected the idea of cold coffee until Buckley encouraged her to try it with a bit of vanilla extract. From there, PJ's signature iced coffee began to take shape.

The concept of cold brew and iced coffee was far from new when Jordan began experimenting with it; the Pan-American Coffee Bureau encouraged coffee drinkers to brew double-strength coffee and pour it over ice in an advertisement in the *Times-Picayune* in 1944, and Folgers encouraged customers to enjoy its coffee iced as early as 1949. The cold brew process, in which coffee grounds are steeped in cool water for an extended period, originated in Japan and is believed to have been introduced by Dutch traders in the 1600s. The Japanese cold brew method often achieves this process with a glass Oji Tower, or Yama Tower, that consists of three chambers. Ice is placed in the top chamber, and coarse-ground coffee is placed in the second chamber. A paper or fine metal filter is placed at the bottom of the second chamber holding the grounds. As the ice in the top chamber melts, the cold water filters through the grounds in the second chamber. The cold-brewed coffee then collects in the bottom chamber. What is left is a coffee concentrate served diluted with water or milk. This method has been practiced

Oji Tower producing cold brew coffee, French Truck Coffee.
Photo by the author.

in Japan for centuries, and the coffee produced is often referred to as Kyoto-style or Dutch-style coffee.

While New Orleanians loved cold-brew coffee, the rest of the country took more time to get on board. Poppy Tooker notes in "The Mother of All Iced Coffee" that Jordan pushed iced coffee at a meeting of the National Coffee Association. However, the meeting attendees didn't share Jordan's enthusiasm for her concoction. It took some time, but eventually, iced coffee took off in coffee shops nationwide. While it is hard to say definitively that Phyllis Jordan invented the type of iced coffee we enjoy today, she *did* develop the cold brew process that is used at all PJ's Coffee locations. Her innovative approach to cold brewing protects the coffee's flavor and strength while producing coffee that is two-thirds less acidic than hot coffee.

The first PJ's Coffee franchise opened in 1989 in Mandeville, and its first out-of-state franchise opened in Houston in 1993. The brand has expanded rapidly since. In 1998, Jordan was eager to pursue other interests and stepped down as the company's CEO. In 2002, PJ's Coffee was sold to Raving Brands, and in 2008, PJ's was purchased by Ballard Brands, a Covington-based hospitality company formed by New Orleans natives and brothers Paul, Steven, and Scott Ballard, which also owns New Orleans Roast Coffee and Tea. Since then, PJ's Coffee locations have expanded nationwide, including to Iowa, Kentucky, Maryland, New Jersey, South Carolina, and Tennessee. Additionally, Ballard Brands opened its one-hundredth PJ's Coffee location in Pearland, Texas, just in time for the company's fortieth anniversary in 2018. Today, there are nearly 200 PJ's Coffee locations nationwide.

PJ'S COFFEE'S ROASTMASTER AND BRAND AMBASSADOR FELTON JONES JR.

The chief roastmaster and brand ambassador for PJ's Coffee and New Orleans Roast, LLC, is New Orleanian Felton Jones Jr. As a student at St Augustine High School, he was a member of the Marching 100, the high school's famed marching band known nationally for its incredible talent. From there, he pursued engineering at Xavier University. For Jones, PJ's Coffee started as a part-time job. The idea of making coffee a career wasn't at the forefront of Jones's mind back in 1993 when he was working a warehouse job brewing cold-brew coffee for corporate stores. From there, he became a delivery driver for the company and, under the guidance of Phyllis Jordan and former green coffee buyer for PJ's Coffee Scott Reed, Jones began learning more about coffee production and the inner workings of the business. After two years of honing his skills at another commercial coffee company, he returned to PJ's Coffee, at Jordan's behest, and took over as warehouse manager in charge of quality control. When Scott Reed left PJ's to focus on green coffee trading, Jones took over Reed's role as chief roastmaster.

As roastmaster, Jones's responsibilities include selecting green coffee for PJ's and deciding how it will be roasted, creating coffee blends for the brand, and securing futures contracts. In his futures buying role, Jones chooses the best time to purchase specific coffee and travels to the coffee's countries of origin, establishing relationships with farmers and exporters. As brand ambassador, Jones provides marketing, operational, and sales support to PJ's Coffee franchises. He also travels to PJ's Coffee locations nationwide, conducting on-site coffee classes and tastings for customers so they can learn about PJ's Coffee from seed to cup.

Certified by the Specialty Coffee Association of America in green coffee purchasing and contracts, Jones sources the world's top 1 percent of arabica beans from Brazil, Colombia, Ethiopia, Guatemala, Honduras, Nicaragua, Papua New Guinea, and Sumatra. Throughout his career, Jones has worked to build relationships with not only the people who consume PJ's Coffee but importers and farmers. Through Jones's expertise and a direct trade agreement, PJ's Coffee adopted two farms—one in Nicaragua and one in Honduras, which Jones visits annually. Through the agreement, PJ's

Coffee commits to purchasing all the coffee these farms can produce that meets PJ's quality standards, which is about 95 percent. Supporting these farms ensures that PJ's Coffee will have quality coffee for years to come and that the farmers will continue to be able to make a living and pass their farms down for generations.

Moving forward, Jones's goal is to buy 100 percent responsibly and ethically sourced coffee for PJ's, guaranteeing that the company does business with farms that offer workers a good quality of life and maintain sustainable practices. For example, Jones explains that the Honduran farm he does business with is a woman-owned farm that is vertically integrated, meaning they control every aspect of coffee production, from growing coffee to the milling process. Furthermore, the farm gives back to its community by providing medical care and education for neighboring farmers. Jones works with local importer Westfeldt Bros., which is committed to helping PJ's Coffee create an ethical coffee regime, and he has solidified personal relationships with farmers in Brazil, Colombia, and Honduras. The other countries from which PJ's buys coffee will soon follow.

Jones's proficiency in the coffee industry recently earned him a proclamation from the New Orleans City Council, which honored him as the only known African American roastmaster for a major coffee brand representing New Orleans. Jones says the honor was significant to him because, in a billion-dollar industry like coffee, you don't see many people who look like him in critical positions. Jones sees himself as an advocate in the coffee industry and wants to bring awareness to the opportunities that exist for everyone, beyond sales or working as a barista. He explains that there are so many positions in the coffee business that need to be filled, and often, skills that a person already possesses can translate into a job in coffee. Jones says that coffee jobs are frequently overlooked by young people when deciding on a career, and he hopes that coffee will be a consideration for those looking for job opportunities in a field that offers a lot of room for advancement.

PJ'S COFFEE'S PACKAGING AND FRESHNESS

Ashlee Voss, the director of roaster operations for PJ's Coffee, is also involved in the company's green coffee sourcing, roasting, flavoring, and packaging. For over twenty years, Voss has built a career in the coffee industry, with a background that includes a focus on product innovation, creating specialty drinks, and procurement. In her role at PJ's Coffee, she uses her experience in green coffee to run the company's roasting facility. She also works with Jones to secure green coffee contracts and decide how green coffee will be roasted, flavored, ground, packaged, and shipped. Voss ensures coffee quality through cuppings and checks coffee beans for qualities that can affect the coffee's taste, like moisture level and coffee bean roast level.

PJ's Coffee is packaged immediately when roasting facility manager Brian Beck roasts it, ensuring maximum freshness. Voss explains that a one-way valve stamped into the company's bags allows the coffee to de-gas after roasting while preserving the coffee's freshness and protecting it from oxygen. This process guarantees that PJ's customers get the freshest coffee possible, upholding PJ's Coffee's high-quality standards.

LUZIANNE COFFEE AND REILY FOODS

William B. Reily worked as a wholesale grocery clerk in Monroe, Louisiana, when he began roasting coffee for his customers. After noticing the high demand for coffee, Reily moved to New Orleans in 1902 and started roasting, grinding, packaging, and selling canned coffee. He called his company Luzianne. However, Reily's plan to work in the coffee business was almost derailed when, two years into his venture, a fire at his coffee factory nearly destroyed the facility. At the same time, a portion of the Brazilian coffee crops that Reily used for his product were wiped out in a freeze. In 1906, coffee importer Jacob Aron saved Reily Foods when he joined the

Reily board of directors, and Aron's expertise in coffee made the brand take off.

Reily began selling tea products in 1903, although his focus remained on the roasting and distribution of coffee. In 1932, due to the rising national popularity of iced tea, Reily began brewing a type of tea blend made specifically for the company's iced tea brand, Luzianne Iced Tea. Luzianne products were sold all over the South in Alabama, Florida, Georgia, Louisiana, Mississippi, the Carolinas, and Virginia. From there, Reily and his son William B. Reily Jr. started Standard Coffee Company, delivering coffee products directly to consumers' homes. Today, Luzianne is more closely associated with its tea than coffee, although the Reily Foods Company continues to sell not only Luzianne coffee but other coffee and food brands as well.

CDM: A Historic Connection

CDM is another coffee brand owned by the Reily Foods Company. In chapter 6, we touched on a bit of the history of CDM, its distinctive yellow packaging, and how it has become an integral part of Vietnamese-American culture. CDM stands for Café du Monde, but the coffee in the package differs slightly from the coffee served at Café du Monde coffee stands worldwide. While Café du Monde coffee is made with robusta coffee beans, CDM is made with a combination of robusta and arabica beans. Of course, both Café du Monde coffee and CDM contain chicory.

CDM coffee is one of the Reily Foods–owned coffees served at Luzianne Café in New Orleans, a café owned by Reily Foods that specializes in serving a menu featuring the various products produced under the Reily umbrella. Luzianne Café's vice president of restaurant operations, Alfred La Nassa, explains that due to Reily's contract with Café du Monde in the 1940s, the coffee served and sold at Café du Monde and the coffee sold with the CDM label must be different. As a result, when you order coffee at Café du Monde, you are enjoying coffee exclusively served at Café du Monde locations.

French Market Coffee: A Taste of the Past

A brand of coffee regularly seen on grocery shelves is French Market Coffee. As discussed in chapter 4, French Market Coffee was the "official" coffee of the French Market, likely until the 1930s, when Café du Monde became the famous coffee stand with which we are familiar.

The French Market Coffee that we know today was marketed by the Bartlett and Dodge families in 1890 for French Market Mills under the umbrella of the New Orleans Coffee Company. Although French Market Coffee dates to the mid-nineteenth century, when it was sold at the French Market, 1890 was likely the first year it was canned. In my research, I discovered that the application for an official trademark of "French Market Coffee" was filed in December 1890 and secured on January 27, 1891. A 1915 ad in the *Times-Picayune* for French Market Coffee notes that the brand has been a New Orleans favorite for "fifty years" and was enjoyed by the likes of Henry Clay and Andrew Jackson. Who knows if that's true or not, but it sure looks good in an advertisement!

Early 1900s ads for French Market Coffee boasted that the coffee came from Bogota, Caracas, Guatemala, and Jamaica and was sold in a sealed, airtight can. The ad also encouraged customers to drink *a lot* of the coffee, writing, "Like the coffee of Paris, you can drink it at midnight. Old habitues of the French Market drank it all day long—ten to fifteen cups a day—and were noted for good health and a long life." In 1920, French Market Coffee was located at 800 Magazine Street.

Since 2008, the Reily Foods Company has owned French Market Coffee, which also owns Luzianne and CDM. Bruna Iljazi, the senior director of commodities for Reily Foods, offers some insight into the history of French Market, stating that since Reily Foods bought French Market Coffee, the company has kept the coffee's beloved recipe the same. So, when you drink French Market Coffee, you're drinking the same coffee enjoyed by those who once strolled the French Market doing their weekly shopping and, maybe, by Andrew Jackson.

Along with French Market Coffee, CDM, and Luzianne Coffee, Reily Foods also owns RT Coffee and Union Coffee, two other famous New Orleans coffee and chicory brands. Union Coffee was previously owned by Merchants Coffee Co. of New Orleans, Inc., until the company merged with the American Coffee Company in 1986. Reily Foods acquired the American Coffee Company in 2008.

COMMUNITY COFFEE: LOUISIANA COFFEE ON A NATIONAL STAGE

Community Coffee is the largest family-owned coffee company in the United States. While the company's home base is in Baton Rouge, it has a New Orleans connection. In the early 1900s, grocer Norman "Cap" Saurage took regular trips to New Orleans to buy fresh coffee beans for his grocery store, Full Weight Grocery. In 1919, he began roasting beans for his company, which he named Community Coffee. He delivered his coffee to retailers via horse-drawn wagon, and the company quickly grew. On March 1, 1924, Saurage closed his grocery store and turned his barn into a coffee mill to focus on selling Community Coffee full-time. In 1946, Community built a modern roasting plant overlooking the Mississippi River, and by 1957, the company was importing its coffee beans directly from Brazil. Community Coffee was also one of the first brands to grind and bag coffee with chicory, which has become so associated with New Orleans coffee culture. Saurage notes that Community began adding chicory to its ground coffee in the 1930s. In 1980, the company became the first in the North America to market vacuum-sealed "firm packs" of coffee. It was also the first to

Bagged Community Coffee.
Photo by the author.

stamp its coffee packages with a "best by" date for recommended brewing.

Matt Saurage is the fourth generation of the Saurage family to lead the company as chairman. In the more than one hundred years that Community Coffee has been in operation, the company has grown to employ eight hundred people and sell coffee in twenty-six states, with half of the sales coming from grocery stores and half from sales to offices and restaurants. In 2018, Community purchased an 87,000-square-foot coffee manufacturing facility in Harahan, Louisiana, just a little over ten miles from New Orleans. The building, previously used by Folgers to roast coffee beans, is a centerpiece for the company's roasting and packaging and joins Community's other roasting plant in Port Allen, Louisiana.

Since 2016, Community Coffee has been the coffee served on most Southwest Airlines flights. As part of the agreement with Southwest, Community provides funding to the ECOM Foundation, a public charity committed to ensuring a better life for origin producers. During the first year of this partnership, internet-connected classrooms and online curriculums were constructed in Unión Buenavista and Tierra y Libertad in Chiapas, Mexico, to provide education and access to academic, agricultural, and technological training. This education will ensure that coffee growers in Chiapas will continue to thrive for generations.

Community Coffee's beans are imported from Brazil, Colombia, El Salvador, Ethiopia, Guatemala, Honduras, Kenya, Mexico, Peru, Rwanda, and Sumatra through New Orleans and Houston ports. When choosing coffee for Community, Saurage says it is essential to work with brokers who buy ethically sourced coffee and employ fair business practices that adhere to the company's code of conduct. Depending on volume demands, Community also buys coffee directly from select farms. Community's green coffee buyer, Mark Howell, maintains relationships with farmers and brokers in the countries that produce the company's coffee and the exporters Community works with are familiar with the company's desired flavor profile and choose the quality of coffee they know customers expect. Howell, who is also responsible for managing Community Coffee's taste, flavor, and consistency, visits the countries where Community buys coffee, meets with exporters, and cups coffee samples that they believe will be a good fit for the company.

Community Coffee gets its Colombian coffee from southern Norte de Santander, in towns that include Chitagá, Labateca, and Toledo. These areas are incredibly fertile and produce high-quality coffee beans for rich-tasting coffee. The economy in these areas depends largely on coffee farming, and the family-owned farms here provide a living for multiple generations. Community Coffee has established a contract with these farmers to ensure that the company will purchase the coffee they grow. In 2016, a local school, Hogar Juvenil Campesino Toledito–Henry Norman Saurage III, adopted the Saurage name to honor Community Coffee's commitment to the hardworking people of the area. Community Coffee also initiated the first direct contract between an African farming cooperative and an American coffee roaster when they began purchasing coffee beans from the Abahuzamugambi Ba Kawa farming cooperative in Rwanda in 2002. Dr. Timothy Schilling, a coffee expert who has worked to revitalize Rwanda through agricultural development, was working for USAID when he approached Community Coffee to reestablish coffee agriculture in Rwanda. During the Rwandan genocide in 1994, farms and farmers were completely wiped out. Community Coffee and other coffee companies were brought in to financially support a new generation learning about coffee farming. The deal was facilitated through PEARL: Partnership for Enhancing Agriculture in Rwanda through Linkages, a United States–backed program that promotes agricultural initiatives in Rwanda. Community Coffee purchases about forty thousand pounds of coffee beans a year from the cooperative, and the coffee is used in several of the company's Private Reserve blends.

In 1995, in response to Starbucks' rapid expansion in the gourmet coffee realm, the Community Coffee brand expanded into the brick-and-mortar business by opening the first location of CC's Gourmet Coffee House at the corner of Jefferson Avenue and Magazine Street in New Orleans. Today, the business is known as CC's Coffee House, serves a variety of coffee drinks made with Community Coffee, and boasts over forty locations throughout Louisiana and Texas. The Saurage family owns the cafés, but it is a separate business from Community Coffee.

Matt Saurage, Dominick Blanda, and City Roots Coffee Bar

In 2019, Matt Saurage expanded his coffee footprint in Louisiana when he opened City Roots Coffee Bar in Mid City Baton Rouge with his business partner, Dominick Blanda. Blanda, a New Orleanian who grew up in an Italian family that shared a love of coffee, is a seasoned professional in the coffee industry. His journey began at various coffee shops in his teens, leading to a twelve-year tenure at Starbucks, where he worked his way through the ranks. He then served as a district manager at CC's Coffee House, gaining valuable insights into different coffee recipes, marketing and operational training.

Blanda's goal of running his own coffee business in Mid City Baton Rouge became a reality when he connected with Saurage, who wanted to take on a new venture apart from Community Coffee. The Electric Depot building on Government Street, where City Roots is located, is just a few blocks from where Saurage's great-grandfather first began roasting Community Coffee, creating a deep-rooted connection between Saurage and the space. Now the manager of the roaster and café, Blanda roasts all of City Roots' coffee weekly on a Loring S7 Nighthawk Roaster in small batches. The pair's goal for City Roots is to serve coffee in a family-friendly cafe with a menu that includes specialty coffee drinks and smooth espresso. They want to create a coffee experience that is unique and approachable to all coffee lovers, from the connoisseur to the casual drinker.

CoolBrew: An Easy Way to Cold Drip Coffee

If Phyllis Jordan introduced cold-brew coffee to New Orleanians, Phillip McCrory revolutionized it for home use with CoolBrew.

This coffee concentrate can be consumed hot or cold and comes in various flavors that can be enjoyed at home.

McCrory created CoolBrew in 1989 as the original cold-brewed, natural, fresh coffee concentrate made with arabica beans sourced from Central and South America. A pharmacist for the State Office of Public Health, McCrory got his first taste of cold-brewed coffee when he was given a Filtron cold-water coffee brewer. He enjoyed the coffee's low acidity so much that he set out to re-create the cold brew process on a much larger scale. Working from home, he converted stainless steel beer kegs into coffee extractors and equipped them with a solar-powered pump and filter. In CoolBrew's cold filtration process, the coffee is brewed slowly with cold water, removing the acidity usually found in hot coffee. The process leaves the acidity in the grounds and not the coffee.

Once McCrory had mastered the perfect cold brew coffee, his next move was to package it in an innovative bottle. Designed so that air can't infiltrate the coffee, CoolBrew's unusual bottle has a twin-neck design that allows for quickly measuring the coffee concentrate into one-ounce "shots." These shots make an eight- to ten-ounce drink that can be mixed with milk or water and enjoyed over ice or served hot. The bottle's design is so unique that the company includes instructions on the back of the bottle explaining how to use it.

Today, CoolBrew brews 150,000 gallons of coffee a year, and the company is run by Phillip's sons, Jeff and Greg McCrory. Although CoolBrew has inspired many imitators throughout the country seeking to create their own coffee concentrate, the McCrorys maintain that Phillip and his unique coffee-brewing style were the original. CoolBrew is available nationwide in Chocolate Almond, French Roast, Hazelnut, Mocha, and Vanilla; all the flavors except for French Roast contain chicory.

In "N.O. CoolBrew Celebrates 25 Years of Cold Drip Coffee," Cheramie Sonnier writes that CoolBrew goes through six to eight, 630-pound bags of arabica coffee beans a week. The McCrorys are dedicated to sustainability and donate CoolBrew's used coffee grounds to landscaping and soil companies for compost. According to the company's website, the New Orleans Coffee Company, which owns CoolBrew, was awarded the Sustainable Business Award from the City of New Orleans's Office of Environmental Affairs for the "Creative Reduction of Energy and Waste While Producing a Quality Product" in 2001. The New Orleans Coffee Company also donates its grounds to Laughing Buddha Nursery's Local Cooling Farms, which center on maximizing nutrient cycling and raising livestock with respect and integrity.

N.O. Brew: Cold Brew Coffee Easily Enjoyed at Home

In 2004, Fred Peer was working in advertising when he decided to enter the coffee industry. As cold brew coffee was gaining national popularity, Peer had the idea to bottle New Orleans–style cold brew coffee and sell it retail. Rather than create a coffee concentrate, Peer developed a cold brew coffee that combines well with water or milk but can also be enjoyed straight out of the bottle. He called his company N.O. Brew in honor of New Orleans, the company's hometown, because he considers the city one of the coffee capitals of the country and wanted to acknowledge New Orleans's unique relationship with the drink. Peer opened the first N.O. Brew facility with his business partner, Michael Stonebreaker, in a five-thousand-square-foot facility in the Faubourg Marigny neighborhood.

After Hurricane Katrina destroyed the Faubourg Marigny facility in 2005, Peer closed his advertising agency and entered the coffee industry full-time. He relocated N.O. Brew headquarters to its current facility in Gretna on the Westbank of the Mississippi River, just minutes away from the New Orleans city line. This move allowed N.O. Brew to expand its market presence to Dorignac's Food Center in Metairie. Furthermore, the company's partnership with

Whole Foods and United Natural Foods, Inc. (UNFI) further facilitated its expansion beyond the New Orleans market. Seven years after its launch, N.O. Brew increased its product line to include ground coffee, catering to customers who prefer to prepare their coffee at home.

N.O. Brew gets its 100 percent Arabica coffee blend from Nicaragua and Honduras and adds a touch of French chicory as a nod to traditional New Orleans chicory coffee. The company's coffee is roasted and ground at the Delicious Sips facility in New Orleans East and extracted at N.O. Brew's Gretna facility.

Since its inception over twenty years ago, N.O. Brew has built a strong following in Louisiana and expanded its reach to the Gulf Coast, the Florida Panhandle, Minnesota, and Wisconsin. The company's commitment to quality was recognized at the 2023 NOLA Coffee Festival, where N.O. Brew won in the "Best Cold Brew Coffee" and "Best Iced Coffee" categories.

MELLO JOY: A BELOVED CAJUN COFFEE

Mello Joy is a beloved Louisiana-based coffee brand and an integral part of the coffee culture of Lafayette, Louisiana. Brothers Louis and Will Begnaud had the idea for Mello Joy Coffee while working for Grimmer Coffee Company. In "You Can't Beat a Cup of Cajun Coffee," Jim Bradshaw explains that Grimmer Coffee Company was founded in 1921 by Charles Felix Grimmer, a grocery store, restaurant, and saloon owner, and produced Creole Belle coffee. With the motto "Cajun Belle in the Blue Package, the More You Drink, the More You Want," the brand is considered by many to be the first coffee packaged, roasted, and ground in Cajun country. In 1936, the Begnaud brothers used their savings to found Mello Joy, and the people of Acadiana quickly made the coffee brand their own. Soon Louis bought out his brother, and from the 1940s to the 1970s, Mello Joy became the number-one coffee brand in Louisiana. In

1976, Louis sold the company to a regional competitor, and the Mello Joy brand was phased out, much to the disappointment of Acadian Louisianians. In 2000, Mello Joy was resurrected in Lafayette under the guidance of owner Wayne Elmore and is available in grocery stores throughout Louisiana and parts of Texas.

8

Brew It Yourself

Grinding and Brewing Coffee at Home

Although coffee was frequently consumed at coffee exchanges, coffeehouses, and open-air markets throughout the nineteenth century in New Orleans, coffee was also prepared and enjoyed at home. Café noir and café au lait were consumed with breakfast, with the latter prepared traditionally with heated milk added to hot coffee.

The methods for preparing coffee at home have evolved over the years. When these processes started, they were more complex than today; as described in *Stir the Pot: The History of Cajun Cuisine,* green coffee beans were purchased at the local mercantile retailer, pan-roasted or *parched* at home, and ground by hand. The woman of the house ground and brewed the coffee in white, porcelain-coated drip pots called grègues. New Orleanians initially used a method called infusion brewing to brew their coffee. Begun in France around 1710, infusion brewing is a form of steeping thought to enhance coffee's flavor. However, in the nineteenth century, it was all done by hand with coffee grounds placed in a linen bag and steeped in hot water.

As time progressed, various products were invented to make the coffee grinding and brewing process more efficient. In the nineteenth and early to mid-twentieth centuries, myriad devices were developed to simplify the coffee making process, and multiple patents were filed for various gadgets to improve the quality of coffee made at home. However, the general theme remained unchanged: hot water is filtered through grounds to produce coffee. Over time, grinders have been perfected, and the list of all the various coffee brewing inventions throughout the years could go on and on. A few of the more well-known devices remain popular today.

COFFEE GRINDERS

Coffee grinding happens in a mortar and pestle in its most basic process: Beans are ground into a powder that is brewed to produce coffee. The first tool used for coffee grinding was invented in Turkey in the sixteenth century. The Turkish mill, used to grind coffee *and* spices, was improved in Damascus, Syria, and equipped with a folding handle and a receptacle for green coffee beans. Nicholas Book invented the first mill dedicated solely to grinding coffee in London in 1665. In Book's mill, coffee was placed in its top compartment and grounds deposited into its bottom compartment. William Ukers explains that by 1720, coffee grinders, made of iron, box-shaped, and often affixed to the wall, were so common in France they could be purchased for $1.20. These French coffee grinders were the early version of the modern burr grinder. The first coffee grinder with an electric motor, equipped with a belt-and-pulley system, was invented in 1898 in Troy, Ohio, by the Hobart Manufacturing Co., and the first American gear-driven electric coffee grinder was produced by the Enterprise Manufacturing Co. of Pennsylvania in 1900.

You can buy your coffee already ground, but coffee experts explain that when coffee is ground, it begins losing flavor. If you're serious about your coffee, consider taking the steps to grind your coffee yourself. When it comes to grinding, you have a few options. First, you can go to the grocery store and use one of their big industrial grinders to get the job done. Or, you can invest in a small grinder and grind your coffee fresh as a part of your morning routine. Before writing this book, I was someone who bought their coffee at a grocery store already ground. After investing in a small grinder and grinding my coffee beans at home, it was easy to taste the difference in coffee quality. When it comes to at-home coffee grinders, there are two choices, a blade grinder and a burr grinder.

Blade grinders are equipped with propellor-like blades that cut coffee beans apart, almost like a food processor for coffee. One of the pros of blade grinders is that they are relatively inexpensive and might be suitable for a coffee-grinding novice. However, coffee experts tell me that a big con of blade grinders is that they grind the coffee unevenly, leaving finer pieces mixed in with bigger pieces. If the secret to the perfect cup of coffee is the ideal grind, you will prefer more control over your final product.

A burr grinder is the coffee grinder that coffee experts recommend due to its ability to attain a precise, perfect grind. Burr grinders are typically made of carbon steel or ceramic and use two revolving abrasive elements, one spinning against the other, to crush coffee beans to the favored grind. There are two types of burr coffee grinders, the conical burr grinder, and the flat burr grinder. A conical burr grinder consists of two cone-shaped burrs with ridged edges, while a flat burr grinder consists of two plates with "teeth" that spin against each other. In both conical and flat burr grinders, the consistency of the coffee grounds will depend on how the abrasive plates are positioned. If they are further apart, they will create a coarser grind; if they are close together, they will make a finer grind.

Most commercial companies use roller grinders, which force coffee through a gap between two corrugated cylinders. When the cylinders rotate, the coffee is crushed into the desired grind. A roller grinder consists of two pairs of cylinders. Pre-breakers, the first pair of cylinders, crush the coffee beans, and the second pair of cylinders cut the crushed coffee into a desired size. *Barista Hustle* notes, in "Bench Top Roller Mill," that grind size is achieved by adjusting the speed and gap between the rollers. Other factors can also affect the grind, such as the rate of coffee fed into the grinder's hopper and the number of grinding stages.

Coffee Grinds

Any coffee connoisseur will tell you that the secret to the perfect cup of coffee starts with the correct grind, and the type of grind you want depends on what type of coffee you are brewing. For example, if you are making espresso, you want a fine grind; if you're making a pour-over, you will want a medium-fine grind. How you grind your coffee determines how the water will flow through the coffee and, ultimately, how the final product will taste. Like most things, there's a science to coffee grinding to ensure you are crafting the perfect cup of coffee.

In "Getting Your Grind Right," *Caffeine Brothers* explains that there are typically five types of coffee grinds. However, this varies a bit depending on how particular you are (some charts I came across had as many as seven different grinds!). Which grind is suitable depends on how you brew your coffee. A good rule of thumb is the longer you will be brewing your coffee, the coarser your grinds should be.

- **Coarse:** A grind with a large consistency. Slow brewing methods such as cold brewing and French press use a coarse grind because it takes a long time to brew.
- **Medium:** This is the most popular grind, and it's used in drip brewers.
- **Medium-Fine:** The coffee will have the texture of sand or sugar. This is the ideal grind for pour-over brewing.
- **Fine:** This grind works best for espresso. Because the coffee is so finely ground, it needs minimal contact with water to produce the desired result.

- **Ultra-Fine:** Also called extra-fine, this coffee is the consistency of powdered sugar or flour. The brewing time for ultra-fine ground coffee is very fast, and it is typically used for Turkish or Arabic coffee.

THE EVOLUTION OF BREWING COFFEE

Throughout history, people have tried various methods to brew their coffee, and the process has changed and evolved significantly over the years. Although there always seem to be new and exciting ways to add hot water to coffee grounds to produce coffee, many coffee enthusiasts prefer the classic methods that have been around for centuries. The type of brew method you choose could depend on how particular you are about how your coffee tastes, how fast (or slowly) you want to brew your coffee, or how much coffee you want to produce at a time.

In the late eighteenth century, the archbishop of Paris, Jean-Baptiste De Belloy, invented a percolation system, which would be known as the first coffee maker. According to Kathleen Rouser in "Drip, Percolate, and Brew: Coffee Makers Through History," De Belloy's coffeepot was a two-level pot design with a sock, or drip filter, in the top compartment. Hot water was poured through the coffee and filter in the top compartment, drained through holes, and then collected in the bottom compartment, typically made of metal or ceramic. Like today's coffee makers, the strength of the coffee depends on how fine the coffee grounds are and how much of the grounds are used.

BIGGIN POT

In 1780, around the same time that De Belloy was percolating his coffee, a device called a Biggin pot was invented, according to William Ukers, by someone named Mr. Biggin. He explains that by

1817, it had become England's favored method for brewing coffee. The Biggin pot has a long pour spot and comprises a filter cone lid, a second filter, and the coffeepot at the bottom. Much like the percolator, coffee is added to the filter, and hot water is poured through it into the coffeepot below. The hot water is to be poured slowly over the grounds until they are saturated and continually added until the desired coffee strength is achieved. The Biggin pot wasn't a perfect system—if the coffee was ground too finely, water had the habit of running out of the side of the lid, and if the grounds were too coarse, the coffee would be weak.

French Drip Coffeepot

The French drip coffeepot, which was the most common method in New Orleans coffee preparation in the late nineteenth and early twentieth centuries, was designed by Count Rumford, an inventor and physicist, in the early nineteenth century. Born Benjamin Thompson in Massachusetts, he began living abroad in the 1780s to protest the American Revolution. Rumford was mildly obsessed with coffee, outlining his love of coffee and his methods of brewing it in his 1813 essay "Of the Excellent Qualities of Coffee, and the Art of Making It in the Highest Perfection." In the essay, he details what would come to be known as the insulated French drip coffeepot, consisting of four pieces: the lid, the dripper, the basket, and the pot. Begin by bringing water to a boil in a kettle. Place the grounds into the filter of the coffeepot and pour the boiling water over the grounds in the filter basket until they are saturated. Once you have added the desired amount of water, replace the top of the coffeepot. Allow it to steep for five minutes and serve.

Vacuum Brewing and the French Press

The vacuum brewing machine was invented in Germany in the 1830s. This was similar to the percolator and the Biggin pot in that a two-chamber device used heat and cooling to force boiling water into the chamber above, which contained the coffee grounds. The device is then removed from the heat, and the change in temperature pulls the coffee into the lower chamber through vacuum pressure.

In 1852, the first design of the French press was patented by a Paris metalsmith and a merchant, Henri-Otto Mayer and Jacques-Victor Delforge. The device's design we are most familiar with today was patented by Italians Attilio Calimani and Giulio Moneta in 1929 and remains one of the most popular ways to prepare a cup of coffee. A French press works best with coffee that has a coarse grind with a 1:15 coffee to water ratio and forty grams of coffee. Start by boiling water and heating the French press. Experts suggest using warm water to heat the press until it is warm to the touch but not hot. Pour the water over the coffee on the top of the press and let the coffee sit for a minute and "bloom." As the coffee blooms, a crust will form on top of it—stir this mixture and add more water, if necessary, to ensure the grounds are evenly saturated. After the coffee is fully saturated, press the plunger to filter the brewed coffee from the grounds. Immediately pour into your preferred vessel and enjoy.

POUR-OVER AND CHEMEX

Melitta Bentz invented the pour-over brewing method in Germany in 1908 when she punched holes in the bottom of a tin cup and lined it with blotter paper. Although the pour-over method fell out of fashion with the invention of the French press, it has found new life among the more discriminating coffee fans as it is believed to create coffee with a more complex taste and less bitterness than other methods. Start with hot water in a slow-pouring kettle and freshly ground coffee. Some experts suggest wetting the filter before adding the grounds for the best results. Next, add a small amount of water and wait about forty-five seconds before adding more. As with the French press, letting your coffee bloom is essential. Continue adding water slowly until you reach the desired results with the amount of coffee brewed and color. Some more serious coffee drinkers involve a scale in the process for precise results. Like anything, it will take a bit of practice before you get the technique exactly right.

A German chemist, Peter Schlumbohm, invented the Chemex coffee maker in Massachusetts in 1941. This pour-over-style glass coffee maker is considered one of the best-designed coffee makers of modern times. The Chemex is an hourglass-shaped glass flask with a funneled neck, a heatproof wooden collar, and filters made of thick bonded paper. The thick filter is thought to filter out the coffee ground's oils, producing a cleaner and less bitter-tasting coffee. To brew coffee, the filter is folded into shape, placed in the neck of the flask, and then rinsed to remove any paper taste. Coarsely ground coffee is added to the filter, and hot water is slowly poured over the grounds and into the flask. The spout at the top of the coffee maker allows for airflow during the brewing process and easy pouring once the coffee is brewed.

Espresso Machines

According to Mark Pendergrast, the European coffee scene developed at the same rate as its American counterpart, with Europeans consuming high-quality coffee often roasted dark. Espresso, a brewing method that produces rich, thick, dark coffee, was first introduced in France by Edouard Loysel de Santais when he invented a coffee machine that could make two thousand cups of coffee in an hour. The word "espresso" comes from the Italian verb *esprimere,* which means to "press out" or "squeeze."

Italian inventor Angelo Moriondo patented an espresso machine in 1884 that used steam and boiling water to brew coffee. In 1901, another Italian inventor, Luigi Bezzera, improved Moriondo's machine by adding a boiler and four compartments holding the filters and coffee. This espresso machine produced coffee through rapid extraction with steam and hot water. The patent for Bezzera's machine was bought by Desiderio Pavoni in 1903, and espresso machines were mass-produced under his company, La Pavoni. In 1927, the first espresso machine in the United States was installed at Caffé Reggio in New York City, and by the 1930s, the machines were all over Europe.

In the years that followed, other variations of the espresso machine were developed, including a machine with a piston pump introduced in 1938. Like Bezzera's machine, this machine employed hot and not boiling water and produced coffee that had a more natural rather than burnt taste. Following World War II, Achilles Gaggia, an Italian, began commercially producing piston machines. Not only did these machines have faster and stronger filtration, but the piston caused the espresso to be topped with a layer of "crema," or foam, packed with intense aromas and flavors that add to the enjoyment of the drink. Today, espresso machines are commonplace in most coffee shops, and coffee enthusiasts don't hesitate to pay top dollar for a machine that will produce the perfect cup of espresso at home.

MOKA POT

The moka pot is a stovetop coffee maker invented by an Italian named Alfonso Bialetti in 1933. This gadget is named after the city of Mocha in Yemen, which is known for its coffee's quality. A moka pot consists of two pieces that screw together and a small metal filter that is packed with finely-ground coffee. Start by filling the bottom part of the moka pot with water up to its valve and filling the filter with grounds. It's important not to pack the grounds too tightly into the filter because you want the water to be able to flow through them. Screw the top of the moka pot onto the bottom half and place it on a stove with a low flame. The heat will force the wa-

Moka pot.
Wikimedia Commons.

ter through the filter into the top part of the moka pot. When this process is complete, the top part of the moka pot should be about three-quarters full and your coffee ready to pour.

Neapolitan Flip

Modeled after the coffeepot invented by De Belloy and partly inspired by the design of the moka pot is the Neapolitan flip coffeepot, also called *cuccumella, Napoletana,* or *cafetière Morize.* Believed to have been invented in Paris in 1819 by a tinsmith named Jean-Louis Morize, the Neapolitan flip was made of copper until 1886, when an aluminum design was introduced. Although the Neapolitan flip was invented in Paris, it was popular in Italy until the twentieth century. The design of the Neapolitan flip is very similar to the moka pot in that it consists of a lid, a filter with a filter cap, a water chamber, and a brewing/serving chamber. However, unlike the moka pot, the Neapolitan flip uses gravity rather than pressure to brew coffee.

Ever Meister, in "How to Brew Coffee in a Neapolitan Flip Pot," recommends using three level tablespoons of medium-coarse ground coffee per ten ounces of water. Fill the water chamber with water and the filter with coffee and secure the lid. Place the coffee filter into the base that holds the water chamber (the piece holding the coffee slips down into the base holding the water). Screw the brewing/serving chamber on top of the brewer, making sure that the spout of the serving chamber is covering the filter cap. Once the serving chamber is secure, put the pot on the stove and bring the water to a boil. The boiling process should take about ten minutes, and you will know the water is boiling when steam begins to escape from the vent. After the water boils, remove it from the stove and flip the pot so the water chamber is on top. The coffee will brew and deposit into the serving chamber below in about four minutes. When brewing is complete, remove the water chamber from the top of the pot and pour the coffee from the serving chamber.

Electric Drip Coffee Makers

The first variation of the electric drip coffee maker that we are familiar with came in 1954 with the invention of the Wigomat in Germany by Gottlob Widmann. This was the first coffee-making invention in which coffee didn't have to be brewed by hand, and it was considered revolutionary for its time. The coffee maker had a water reservoir, and water heated in the reservoir would rise through a tube and a coffee filter filled with coffee grounds. As the water filtered through the grounds, coffee would be collected in a glass coffeepot and heated by a hot plate.

In 1972, Vincent Marotta and Samuel Glazer invented the first automatic drip coffee maker for the home. Mr. Coffee took the same idea from the Wigomat and made it more compact with a hidden water reservoir in the back of the machine and the coffeepot and hot plate in the front. During brewing, gravity pulled water through a heating mechanism, filtered through the grounds, and dripped into the coffeepot below. Mr. Coffee, which was marketed as so easy a husband could master it, sold more than one million units by April 1974, and its invention changed the way people brewed their coffee at home.

When brewing coffee in a drip coffee maker, coffee experts suggest a ratio of one to two tablespoons of ground coffee per six ounces of water for coffee brewed into a twelve-ounce cup. Of course, you can add or subtract from that amount for more robust or lighter coffee. Food scientist and writer Alton Brown suggests adding a quarter teaspoon of salt to every six tablespoons of grounds to cut out coffee's bitterness and refresh the taste of stale tank water. I would suggest simply finding a coffee that best suits your palate and changing the water in your automatic coffee maker daily to avoid these issues.

Single-Serve Coffee Brewing

No breakdown of the various ways to brew coffee is complete without the trend that has made brewing coffee as simple as loading a pod into a machine and pressing a button. While Keurig might have made single-serve coffee brewers famous, the company wasn't the first with the concept of one-cup coffee making. According to its company website, in 1958, Rombouts Coffee debuted a prefilled One Cup Coffee Filter, consisting of a single-use drip coffee filter placed over a cup, for the Brussels World Exhibition. The company began marketing the filter in 1964 and continues to sell the filters today.

Keurig launched its first brewers and K-Cup pods, single-use pods filled with one serving of coffee, in 1998. The pod consists of a coffee-filled plastic cup lined with a paper filter and topped with an aluminum foil lid. The machine brews the coffee by piercing the foil lid with a spray nozzle and piercing the bottom of the pod with a discharge nozzle. Hot water is pushed through the spray nozzle, over the grounds and filter, and brewed coffee is forced out of the bottom of the pod. As the Keurig brewer has gained in popularity, other variations of the machine have been introduced that brew cold coffee, tea, cocoa, and other drinks. In 2005, the company introduced reusable K-Cup pods that could be filled with a coffee of the user's choice.

Keurig's next step in sustainability is the introduction of K-Rounds, which the company describes as plastic and aluminum-free pods of roasted premium coffee wrapped in a plant-based coating that protects the coffee's integrity. K-Rounds are currently being tested and will be available in various sizes, ideal for brewing espresso, traditional coffee, and cold brews. Keurig hopes that the K-Rounds, which can be disposed of like traditional coffee grounds, will reduce the amount of waste that ends up in landfills.

AEROPRESS

One of the more modern coffee brewing inventions is the AeroPress. Avid inventor Alan Adler developed this coffee maker in 2005 to reduce coffee's acidity and bitterness. Many coffee lovers use the AeroPress, especially when traveling, because it's compact, easy to use, and brews a cup of coffee in about two minutes. An AeroPress consists of a cylindrical chamber and a plunger with an airtight silicone seal.

In "How to Brew Perfect Coffee with AeroPress," Stumptown Coffee Roasters outlines the steps, starting with two and a half tablespoons of finely ground coffee. Place a paper filter in the AeroPress basket and rinse the filter with hot water to eliminate a paper taste. Discard that water and place the AeroPress on top of the vessel you will be "pressing" the coffee into, ensuring it's big enough to hold all the coffee you'll be brewing. Fill the AeroPress with coffee and the desired amount of hot water. Stumptown recommends 220 grams (7.76 ounces) for two and a half tablespoons of coffee.

Stir the coffee and water so that the grounds are completely saturated. Place the plunger on the brew chamber and pull up to create a pressure seal. Remove the plunger and stir the coffee and water mix again to ensure complete extraction. Replace the plunger and let it sit for a minute before pressing. Slowly press down until the coffee fills the vessel. Your coffee is now done and ready to enjoy!

For further reading on coffee history, brewing, grinding, and roasting, I recommend William Ukers's essential work *All About Coffee.* His book, published in 1922, is available to read for free online and outlines, in exquisite detail and illustration, coffee preparation methods from the eighteenth century through the early twentieth century.

CONCLUSION

Still Brewing After All These Years

No city in the United States has been as diverse in history, culture, and population since its inception as New Orleans. In the nation's early years, the Port of New Orleans was the gateway through which goods were imported into the country, and New Orleans was the destination for those who wanted to do business or start a new life. The importation of coffee made the city a prime commerce capital in the eighteenth and nineteenth centuries. Technology moved forward, allowing the Port of New Orleans to expand into a hub of imports and exports, and the city became a welcome home to traders, vendors, and brokers.

Over time, the coffee that New Orleans imported and exported transcended its status as a commodity, becoming an integral part of New Orleans's vibrant culture. It was a staple at the city's open-air markets, and the enslaved used it to secure their freedom. Coffee rituals became a tradition at home and during social gatherings, and New Orleanians incorporated coffee practices from other cultures into their own. Many would argue that no holiday season is complete without the sweet smell and warmth of a café brûlot. Kicking off my Mardi Gras with a frozen Irish coffee and watching the Zulu parade with an icy cup in my hand has become a highlight of my parade season.

The coffee exchanges of the past, where ideas were shared among citizens, coffee stands like Café du Monde and Morning Call Coffee Stand, and the second-wave coffee shops of the 1990s have given way to the diverse array of shops and roasteries we enjoy today. The influence of New Orleans coffee has even extended to the rest of the country. Folgers is a famous national brand that calls the city home, and other locally born brands like Community Coffee, French Market Coffee, and PJ's Coffee, are enjoyed by those outside of the local area code who crave a taste of New Orleans coffee even when they don't have the pleasure of being in the city. Café du Monde coffee is the brand most frequently used in Vietnamese cà phê sữa đá, iced coffee served with sweetened condensed milk, adding a piece of New Orleans history to a crucial cultural coffee practice.

New Orleans is currently experiencing a coffee renaissance, with a rich specialty coffee scene that continues to grow and evolve. This is most evident in the passionate roasters who have dedicated their lives to coffee, fueling the city's coffee culture. The inception of the NOLA Coffee Festival, a celebration of coffee and those who love it, is a testament to the city's growing influence in the coffee world. Coffee is as much of a part of the culture of New Orleans as the music on Frenchmen Street or the streetcars that rattle down St. Charles Avenue. It has tied the city's different societies together since Bienville put down roots. The future of New Orleans's coffee industry is promising, and the city is poised to become a destination for coffee lovers, rivaling the likes of Portland and Seattle.

ACKNOWLEDGMENTS

So much love went into writing *Coffee Culture New Orleans.* When I began my work on this book, I had no idea where the path would lead. I knew that I wanted to cover the roots of the New Orleans coffee industry throughout the city's history and so many of the incredible people who spend their days making the local and national coffee system work. I am grateful to everyone I spoke with while researching this book and piecing it all together. Myriad coffee professionals, roasters, and baristas gave me tidbits of what I should include and suggested whom I should speak with. I am immensely grateful for all of them. Without these people taking time out of their busy schedules to explain the coffee business, *Coffee Culture New Orleans* wouldn't be what it is.

Jenny Keegan, the acquisitions editor at LSU Press, once again trusted me with an incredible project. When I approached Jenny with the idea for this book, she was supportive and did everything in her magical publishing power to make it happen. *Coffee Culture New Orleans* wouldn't exist without Jenny's expertise and encouragement.

Alisa Plant, the director of LSU Press, was another person in my corner when I was considering penning this book. Alisa is an incredible director, and I am always astounded by the great work that LSU Press produces. I am honored to add another of my books to that list, and I'm immensely proud to be a part of the LSU Press family.

Thanks to everyone at LSU Press who touches these books before the world does. I am appreciative of their hard work and the work of the incredible peer reviewers and editors who lovingly shape manuscripts into their final forms.

David Rodrigue took some of the photographs in *Coffee Culture New Orleans*. It's always fun to bring your friends in on your special projects, and Dave was more than happy to join me as I sipped and tasted coffee. Dave is an expert at capturing the magic of these moments, and I am so delighted that he lent his skills to this book.

David W. Brown, a brilliant author and friend, was the first to read *Coffee Culture New Orleans* and kindly bestowed his feedback and suggestions. Being friends with a skilled writer like David improves my writing, and this book is better because of his expertise, support, insight, and encouragement.

Bob Arceneaux, who showed me around Orleans Coffee, explained the process of working with importers and how coffee gets from the roaster to grocery store shelves and customers. Bob is one of New Orleans's foremost coffee experts, and it was so kind of him to take the time to talk coffee with me and answer my questions about the industry.

Paola Barona, the roaster and founder of Del Alto Valle Coffee, uses her coffee to help farmers and the children of Colombia. Matt Cronin, the roastmaster at Mojo Coffee Roasters, was generous with his time and explained the magic of Mojo's roasting process, namely Mojo's countries of origin for its coffee beans. Andrew Madary of Delicious Sips is a descendant of a coffee legend and explained his family's coffee roots and his wonderful coffee-roasting business.

Drew Cambre from the International Coffee Corporation explained what coffee brokers do and reviewed the history of ICC. Drew, a certified Q Grader, has a long history in the coffee industry and was kind enough to answer all my questions about coffee brokering and the different types of coffee buying.

Lauren Fink of Cherry Coffee, Mia Patterson of Cora's Girls Coffee, Angela Jackson of Mojo Coffee Roasters, and Alyssa Johnson of Undergrowth Coffee are incredible women in the New Orleans coffee industry who explained the ins and outs of the coffee business, how coffee gets from seed to cup, and gave me networking suggestions that made this book what it is. These incredible women are doing amazing things in the New Orleans coffee industry.

Peter Giuliano of the Specialty Coffee Association did an excellent job of describing the different coffee waves, especially to a complete novice like myself who was unfamiliar with the "coffee scene" and needed a quick education so that I could add some depth to my book. Peter is an incredible source of information, and it's evident that he chose the right profession!

David Hennessey gave me information on Morning Call's background and what makes the restaurant's coffee stand out. Bruna Iljazi and Alfred La Nasa filled in some blanks regarding the history of some Reily Foods coffee brands. Mark Ricard and Brenda Toepfer shared some insights about their time at Folgers during Katrina.

Ted Hood, who shared the inside scoop on Kaldi's Coffee House, a shop long gone before good coffee was a part of my consciousness. Thank you for painting the picture of what an incredible place Kaldi's was.

Felton Jones Jr., the chief roastmaster and brand ambassador of PJ's Coffee, taught me much about sourcing coffee and ethical farming practices. Felton is an asset to not only PJ's Coffee but the New Orleans coffee industry as a whole. Ashless Voss, the director of roaster operations for PJ's Coffee, explained the company's coffee buying and packaging process.

Sarah K. Lambeth, founder of Pretty Coffee, shared the incredible story of starting her coffee business after working in other facets of the industry. Speaking with Sarah was especially remarkable because she's a certified Q Grader with insight into the specialty coffee industry throughout the country.

Bob Lutz, Abby King, Lauren McCabe, and Jerico Cyres shared the story of Try-Me Coffee from the past to the present. Seeing the antique coffee roasters and learning about this one-hundred-year-old company was a highlight of writing this book.

Kellan Lyman is introducing specialty coffee from the Philippines to New Orleans and beyond through her company, New Orleans Coffee Import Co. Kellan is doing incredible work to support small farmers in the Philippines and El Salvador.

Catherine Mansell is a certified Q Grader and coffee expert doing impressive work at Current Crop Roasting Shop. Current Crop is a "must visit" for any coffee lover in New Orleans. Her coffee education classes are creating a new generation of coffee enthusiasts who are developing an understanding and appreciation for specialty coffee. Attending a cupping and roasting class was one of the highlights of my book research!

Michael Matthews was an incredible source of information and detailed the relationship between a coffee roaster and coffee farmers. His in-depth knowledge of coffee is extensive, and if you have any questions about the coffee industry, Michael is the person to speak to.

Trey Monaghan told me the story of his grandfather's delicious Frozen Irish Coffee, a truly iconic New Orleans cocktail. Frozen Irish Coffee is such a pivotal part of the New Orleans coffee story that I almost can't imagine a St. Patrick's Day without one. I was delighted to learn the origin of the drink.

Janet Colley Morse and Shelby Westfeldt Mills shared the history of their family-owned coffee storage and import companies with me. These companies are essential to the New Orleans coffee industry and its history, and I was honored that these ladies took the time to speak with me.

Geoffrey Meeker, the founder of French Truck Coffee, is building a specialty coffee empire in New Orleans and beyond. Thank you for introducing me to the Loring Roaster and explaining its incredible benefits in coffee roasting.

Tom Oliver and Scott Perry are the coffee geniuses at Coffee Science. Tom is one of the O.G. coffee professionals in the city and was an incredible source of information. He told me about his early days in the New Orleans coffee business and what inspired him to open Coffee Science. Scott explained every detail of how the Bellwether Coffee Roaster works and walked me through the process step-by-step so I could explain it in this book.

Kevin Pedeaux is one of the city's most knowledgeable coffee experts. He generously shared his knowledge with me, and I was thrilled to hear the story of CR Coffee Shop and his thoughts on the future of New Orleans coffee.

Fred Peer is the founder of N.O. Brew, an innovative coffee company that bottles New Orleans–style cold brew. He explained his company history and gave insight into the local coffee industry. David Privat-Gilman gave me wonderful insight into his roaster, Junk Drawer Coffee, and his efforts to be an ethical coffee roaster.

Jim Curie and Kevin Richards are the founders of the NOLA Coffee Festival. When I began researching this book, I knew that I had to attend the festival, and I learned so much in just one day! Sitting in on the festival's lectures and tasting coffee from roasters worldwide lit a fire under me to dive deep into coffee, devour industry knowledge, and write *Coffee Culture New Orleans.*

Baruch Rabasa and Melissa Stewart of Applied Arts Coffee are New Orleanians who spent time in Portland perfecting their coffee skills so they could share their expertise and delicious coffee with New Orleans coffee lovers.

Jonathan Riethmaier at Mammoth Coffee Company is doing incredible things with specialty coffee in New Orleans by working with companies that help him ethically source his coffee. I appreciate his insight and education on the practices that will ensure a sustainable living for coffee farmers.

Greg Rodrigue at HEY Coffee Co. explained how coffee roasting works in incredible detail. I knew I wanted to explain it for this book, and he patiently went over all the steps with me and suggested reading material I could use to expand my understanding of the roasting process.

Brice Sanderford at Riverboat Coffee Company is revolutionizing the future of cold brew coffee with sustainable practices, cold brew kegs, and coffee delivery.

Matt Saurage, the chairman of Community Coffee, provided background on his family's company and shared how Community Coffee gets its coffee from seed to cup. Matt was also kind enough to send me a book about Community Coffee's history, which was a great help in my research. Dominick Blanda, Matt's business partner at City Roots Coffee Bar, explained how their café brings delicious coffee to the people of Baton Rouge.

Craig Seaman is a cocktail expert who detailed the classes he teaches at Current Crop Roasting Shop. His coffee cocktails are innovative and interesting!

Zoe Underhill, Grace Murphy, and Patrick Brennan welcomed me into Congregation Coffee's roastery, told me about their business, gave me a tour of the facility, and shared their thoughts on the local coffee scene. With this incredible team, the next chapter of Congregation Coffee's story is sure to be a good one.

Elizabeth Williams, author, historian, and founder of the Southern Food and Beverage Museum, is always a vast source of knowledge and has exciting stories to tell. I can go to Elizabeth with any food query, and she'll give an interesting answer. This knowledge extends to coffee as well!

Turgay and Amy Yildizli, Turkish coffee experts and owners of Specialty Turkish Coffee, explained Turkish coffee, the world of coffee competition, and its importance to the coffee industry.

Jeffery Chauvin, my partner in love and life, is endlessly supportive of everything I do. Jeffery is always first in line to cheer me on and encourage me, even when I'm not as confident as I would like.

My father, Robert, has always been my number-one fan and has done everything he can to support me and ensure I reach my personal and professional goals. This book and my previous book, *The Absinthe Frappé,* wouldn't have happened without his support.

Sources

Online Sources

"Abol, Tona, Baraka: Behind the Coffee Ceremony." *Coffee Behind the Scenes* blog. www.coffeebehindthescenes.com/en/2019/01/08/abol-tona-baraka-behind-the-coffee-ceremony.

Andermann, Robyn Rene. "Brewed Awakening: Re-imagining Education in Three Nineteenth-Century New Orleans Coffee Houses." Ph.D. Diss., Louisiana State University, 2018. https://repository.lsu.edu/gradschool_dissertations/4572/.

Avey, Tori. "The Caffeinated History of Coffee." PBS Food: The History Kitchen, April 8, 2013. www.pbs.org/food/the-history-kitchen/history-coffee.

Babür-Winter, Oset. "10 Best Coffee Brands from All Over the Country." *Food & Wine,* February 27, 2023. www.foodandwine.com/best-coffee-brands-7152027.

Bankston, Carl L., III. "Vietnamese in Louisiana." *64 Parishes,* March 10, 2022. https://64parishes.org/entry/vietnamese-in-louisiana.

"Becoming a Leader in Coffee Imports: A Marvelous Development in the Port's Trade." *Times-Picayune,* September 1, 1903, 43.

"Beginners Guide to Coffee Grinders." *Whole Latte Love* blog, September 15, 2022. www.wholelattelove.com/blogs/quick-tips/a-beginners-guide-to-coffee-grinders.

"Bench Top Roller Mill?" *Barista Hustle* blog, May 30, 2020. www.baristahustle.com/blog/bench-top-roller-mill.

"Bigger Than Coffee." *Times-Picayune,* January 21, 1994.

Bolton, Dan. "Coffee Gateway to the USA." *STiR Coffee and Tea Magazine,* August 15, 2018. https://stir-tea-coffee.com/features/coffee-gateway-to-the-usa.

Bradshaw, Jim. "Saint-Domingue Revolution." *64 Parishes,* April 21, 2023. https://64parishes.org/entry/saint-domingue-revolution.

———. "You Can't Beat a Cup of Cajun Coffee." *Abbeville Meridional,* January 3, 2010. www.newspapers.com/article/abbeville-meridional-abbeville-meridiona/139540893.

Brasted, Chelsea. "Skip the Hurricane—Frozen Irish Coffee is a New Orleans Staple Worth Sipping." Food52, August 8, 2022. https://food52.com/drinks/cocktails/27563-the-inimitable-experience-of-ordering-a-frozen-irish-coffee-in-new-orleans.

Brunn, E. M. "The New York Coffee and Sugar Exchange." *Annals of the American Academy of Political and Social Science* 155 (1931): 110–18. JSTOR, www.jstor.org/stable/1018010.

Burkhardt, Kai. "How to Make the Perfect Cup of Pour-over Coffee, According to Experts." CNN Underscored, January 26, 2023. www.cnn.com/cnn-underscored/health-fitness/how-to-make-pour-over-coffee.

"Burned Docks Will be Replaced by Concrete Wharves." *Times-Picayune,* November 19, 1925, 1–2.

Campanella, Richard. "From Poydras Market to South Market District: Food Retail in New Orleans' Central Business District." Tulane School of Architecture, December 2016. https://richcampanella.com/wp-content/uploads/2020/02/article_Campanella_Preservation-in-Print_2016_Dec_Poydras-Market.pdf.

———. "Gallier and Dakin's Merchants' Exchange." Preservation Resource Center of New Orleans, September 1, 2016. https://prcno.org/gallier-dakins-merchants-exchange.

Chamberlain, Orville W. Automatic drip-coffee pot. US1174683A, United States Patent and Trademark Office, March 7, 1916. https://patents.google.com/patent/US1174683A.

Cleaver, Molly. "What's the Difference Between Cajun and Creole—or Is There One?" The Historic New Orleans Collection, October 16, 2020. www.hnoc.org/publications/first-draft/whats-difference-between-cajun-and-creole-or-there-one.

"Coffee Control May Be Benefit to New Orleans: Board of Trade Believes Recent Action Will Help Port." *Times-Picayune,* October 24, 1918, 6.

"Coffee Cupping: A Step-by-Step Guide." *Methodical Coffee* blog, March 21, 2022. https://methodicalcoffee.com/blogs/coffee-culture/coffee-cupping-a-step-by-step-guide.

"Coffee Grades: Understand the Basics." Trabocca, October 6, 2020. www.trabocca.com/coffee-knowledge/quality/coffee-grades-understanding-the-basics.

"Coffee Importation Restrictions Named." *Times-Picayune,* April 29, 1918, 6.

Coffee Trade and Port of New Orleans. Exhibition. Louisiana State Museum. www.crt.state.la.us/louisiana-state-museum/online-exhibits/coffee-trade-and-port-of-new-orleans/j-aron-and-company-the-role-of-the-coffee-importer.

"Coffee Trade Perks up in N.O. as Beans Fill Silos." *Times-Picayune,* August 22, 1993, F-1, F-3.

"Community Coffee Firmly in Family Hands at 100." *Times-Picayune,* February 22, 2019. Last updated July 22, 2019. www.nola.com/entertainment_life/community-coffee-firmly-in-family-hands-at-100/article_d7f7fdcc-831e-533f-94b7-58ba918e476e.html.

Dekker, Nicholas. "Coffee: What Is Kyoto-Style Cold Brew?" *Breakfast with Nick* blog, May 20, 2014. https://breakfastwithnick.com/2014/05/20/coffee-what-is-kyoto-style-cold-brew.

"Designed to Lower Impact." Loring. https://loring.com/efficiency.

"The Differences Between 1st, 2nd, and 3rd Wave Coffee." *Driven Coffee Roasters* blog, May 17, 2019. www.drivencoffee.com/blog/coffee-waves-explained.

"Dock's New $2,000,000 Coffee Shed Dedicated. *Times-Picayune,* October 4, 1928, 2.

"Fashionable Rebellion." Women and the American Story. https://wams.nyhistory.org/settler-colonialism-and-revolution/settler-colonialism/fashionable-rebellion.

"Flames Sweep Coffee Docks." *Times-Picayune,* November 18, 1925, 1–2.

"Folgers Continues to Grow New Orleans East's Economy." *Biz New Orleans,* January 25, 2018. www.bizneworleans.com/folgers-continues-to-grow-new-orleans-easts-economy.

Frania, Lisa. "History of the Coffee Break." *Death Wish Coffee* blog, January 17, 2023. www.deathwishcoffee.com/blogs/lifestyle/history-of-the-coffee-break.

Gershon, Marshall. "Steamboats: The Engine That Drove Economic Development in New Orleans." ViaNolaVie, December 9, 2021. www.vianolavie.org/2021/12/09/steamboats-the-engine-that-drove-economic-development-in-new-orleans.

"Getting Your Grind Right: The Most Common Grind Types for Your Coffee Equipment." Caffeine Brothers, April 13, 2021. https://caffeinebrothers.co/common-grind-types.

Green, Steve. "Green Coffee Buying Basics." *Mill City Roasters* blog, October 26, 2023. https://millcityroasters.com/blogs/coffee-articles/green-coffee-buying-basics.

Haines, Dena. "What Is Arabica Coffee?" Enjoy Java, January 5, 2023. Updated on September 18, 2025. https://enjoyjava.com/arabica-coffee.

———. "What Is Robusta Coffee?" Enjoy Java, January 5, 2023. https://enjoyjava.com/robusta-coffee.

Hansrod, Zeenat. "18th Century Manuscripts Reveal Life in Louisiana Under French Rule." Radio France Internationale, October 1, 2019. www.rfi.fr/en/americas/20190109-louisiana-colonial-documents.

"The Historic French Market Celebrates 200 Years of Commerce, Community & Culture." French Market District. www.frenchmarket.org/history.

"The History of Coffee Part 4: 1900–Present." The Coffee Pot. www.thecoffeepot.com/coffee-history-1900-now.

"The History of Using Chicory." *New Orleans Roast.* www.neworleansroast.com/history-of-using-chicory.

"History of Vietnamese Immigration to New Orleans." *Clarion Herald,* July 1, 2014. https://clarionherald.org/news/history-of-vietnamese-immigration-to-new-orleans.

"How a Coffee Dry Mill Works: 7 Step Breakdown." Trabocca. www.trabocca.com/coffee-knowledge/coffee-supply-chains/how-a-coffee-dry-mill-works-7-step-breakdown.

"How Is Coffee Decaffeinated?" *Stokes Tea and Coffee* blog. https://stokescoffee.com/blogs/journal/how-is-coffee-decaffeinated.

"How Many People Drink Coffee? 11 Coffee Drinking Statistics." *Joe's Garage Coffee* blog. https://joesgaragecoffee.com/blog/coffee-drinking-statistics.

"How to Brew Perfect Coffee with AeroPress." Stumptown Coffee Roasters. www.stumptowncoffee.com/pages/brew-guide-aeropress.

Kolb, Carolyn. "The Orleanian at the Automat." *New Orleans Magazine,* May 31, 2019. www.myneworleans.com/the-orleanianan-at-the-automat.

Kristoff, Paul. "Bánh Mì Hòa Mã, District 3." The City Lane. https://thecitylane.com/banh-mi-hoa-ma-district-3.

Lamour, Joseph. "Alton Brown's Coffee-Brewing Trick Is Strange, but It Works." The Kitchn, April 30, 2019. www.thekitchn.com/alton-brown-coffee-tip-salt-267757.

Landsel, David. "The Best Coffee Shops in Every State." *Food & Wine,* March 11, 2022. www.foodandwine.com/coffee/best-coffee-shops-in-america.

Larino, Jennifer. "The Untold Story Behind How Café Du Monde Stands Ended up in Japan." *Times-Picayune,* May 8, 2019. Last updated July 25, 2019. www.nola.com/news/business/the-untold-story-behind-how-cafe-du-monde-stands-ended-up-in-japan/article_e1517fc7-d618-5430-8064-e85100b8ffcb.html.

Latvakangas, Sampo. "Coffee Roasting Basics: Developing Flavour by Roasting." *Barista Institute* blog, April 4, 2022. www.baristainstitute.com/blog/sampo-latvakangas/april-2022/coffee-roasting-basics-developing-flavour-roasting.

"Light Roast vs. Dark Roast: Comparing Coffees." *Breville Coffee Journey* blog. www.breville.com/us/en/blog/coffee-and-espresso/light-roast-vs-dark-roast.html.

"Little Story Behind Chicory Root." Gourmetpedia. http://gourmetpedia.net/products/articles/chicory-root-story.

Llewellyn, Jennifer, and Steve Thompson. "French Colonialism in Vietnam." *Alpha History,* August 2, 2019. https://alphahistory.com/vietnamwar/french-colonialism-in-vietnam.

Loyacano, Shelby. "Coffee in New Orleans." New Orleans Historical. https://neworleanshistorical.org/items/show/1393.

Massicot, Kelly. "Felton Jones, Jr." *New Orleans Magazine,* October 1, 2021. www.myneworleans.com/felton-jones-iii.

Meister, Ever. "How to Brew Coffee in a Neapolitan Flip Pot." *Serious Eats* blog, August 9, 2018. www.seriouseats.com/how-to-brew-coffee-in-a-neapolitan-flip-pot-hack-instructions.

"Mello Joy Cajun Coffee." Louisiana Tastebuds. www.louisiana-tastebuds.com/mellojoy.html.

Mingo, Cirilo. Method of Aging Coffee. US505883A, United States Patent and Trademark Office, October 3, 1893. https://patents.google.com/patent/US505883A.

"Miscellaneous. The New York Coffee Exchange." *Daily Picayune,* March 8, 1882, 6.

Mizell-Nelson, Michael. "No Such Thing as a Free Lunch Anymore." *64*

Parishes, fall 2013. https://64parishes.org/no-such-thing-as-a-free-lunch-anymore.

Monaco, Emily. "The French Influence of Vietnamese Cuisine." *Epicure & Culture,* September 19, 2025. https://epicureandculture.com/vietnamese-cuisine-french-influence/.

Moss, Tyler, "The 19th-Century Swill Milk Scandal That Poisoned Infants with Whiskey Runoff." Atlas Obscura, November 27, 2017. www.atlasobscura.com/articles/swill-milk-scandal-new-york-city.

"Multiple Storied Coffee Wharf May Rise Out of Ruins." *Times-Picayune,* November 20, 1925, 1–2.

"National Coffee Day." Calendarr. www.calendarr.com/united-states/national-coffee-day.

"The NCA U.S. Coffee Impact Report." National Coffee Association. www.ncausa.org/Research-Trends/Economic-Impact.

"New Orleans." History, October 17, 2022. www.history.com/topics/us-states/new-orleans.

"New Orleans and Coffee." Louisiana State Museum. www.crt.state.la.us/louisiana-state-museum/online-exhibits/coffee-trade-and-port-of-new-orleans/new-orleans-and-coffee.

"New Orleans Board Asks for Removal of Certain Restrictions." *New York Times,* November 17, 1918, 30. https://nyti.ms/43MYLsG.

Nguyen, Sahra. "How Café du Monde Became a Vietnamese American Staple." Nguyen Coffee Supply. https://nguyencoffeesupply.com/blogs/news/how-cafe-du-monde-became-a-vietnamese-american-staple.

Pontchartrain, Blake. "How a New Orleans Social Worker Started a National Coffee Chain." *The Gambit,* July 16, 2023. www.nola.com/gambit/news/blake_pontchartrain/blake-pontchartrain-how-a-new-orleans-social-worker-started-a-national-coffee-chain/article_4347f38c-1f54-11ee-9876-db8ae256fd46.html.

"Port of New Orleans." World Port Source. www.worldportsource.com/ports/review/USA_LA_Port_of_New_Orleans_254.php.

"Poydras Street Dock to Double Cargo Capacity." *Times-Picayune,* June 11, 1926, 1, 11.

Price, Chris. "Brew Orleans." *Biz New Orleans,* March 3, 2017. www.biznew orleans.com/brew-orleans.

Redard, Thomas, E. "The Port of New Orleans: An Economic History, 1821–1860." PhD. diss., Louisiana State University, 1985. https://digitalcom

mons.lsu.edu/cgi/viewcontent.cgi?article=5150&contex=gradschool_disstheses.

Rhodes, Kalie. "The Native Roots of the French Market." New Orleans Historical, April 19, 2021. https://neworleanshistorical.org/items/show/1641.

"A Rich Heritage and an Even Brighter Future." Sazerac Co. Inc. www.sazerac.com/our-company/our-story.html.

"The Rich History of Turkish Coffee." Bodrum NYC. www.bodrumnyc.com/blog/turkish-coffee.

Rosa, Deborah Belintani, et al. "The Transition of Vietnamese Refugees in America." Kent State University. www-s3-live.kent.edu/s3fs-root/s3fs-public/file/The-Transition-of-Vietnamese-Refugees-in%20America.pdf.

Rouser, Kathleen. "Drip, Percolate, and Brew: Coffee Makers Through History." *Heroes, Heroines, and History* blog, July 21, 2018. www.hhhistory.com/2018/07/drip-percolate-and-brew-coffee-makers.html.

Rumford, Count Benjamin. "Of the Excellent Qualities of Coffee, and the Art of Making It in the Highest Perfection." 1813. https://archive.org/details/b29307156.

Ryu, Airi. "Visualizing the Global Coffee Trade by Country." *Visual Capitalist,* November 24, 2023. www.visualcapitalist.com/cp/global-coffee-trade.

Sanchez, Elise. "Interview Series: Westfeldt Brothers Inc. Coffee Importers." Flavor Wave, July 8, 2022. www.flavorwaves.com/post/interview-series-westfeldt-brothers.

Sanford, Aysegul. "How to Make Turkish Coffee." Foolproof Living, September 19, 2023. https://foolproofliving.com/how-to-make-turkish-coffee.

Scherck, Lewis A. Multiple drip coffee urn. US2491336A, United States Patent and Trademark Office, November 15, 1947. https://patents.google.com/patent/US2491336A/en.

Shen, Kona. *The Haitian Revolution Timeline.* https://thehaitianrevolution.com.

Smith, K. Annabelle. "The History of the Chicory Coffee Mix That New Orleans Made Its Own." *Smithsonian Magazine,* March 5, 2014. www.smithsonianmag.com/arts-culture/chicory-coffee-mix-new-orleans-made-own-comes-180949950.

Solano, Fabiola. "French Press—The History & Brewing Guide." *Perfect Daily Grind,* May 10, 2015. https://perfectdailygrind.com/2015/05/french-press-the-history-brewing-guide.

Sonnier, Cheramie. "N.O. CoolBrew Celebrates 25 Years of Cold Drip Coffee."

The Advocate, August 11, 2014. www.theadvocate.com/baton_rouge/entertainment_life/n-o-coolbrew-celebrates-25-years-of-cold-drip-coffee/article_7c8685f0-07cc-5ed2-afbf-63afbd65814b.html.

"SP History." Southern Pacific Historical & Technical Society. https://sphts.org/sp-history.

"St. Charles Avenue Streetcar Line, 1835." American Society of Mechanical Engineers Regional Transit Authority, December 9, 1984. www.asme.org/wwwasmeorg/media/resourcefiles/aboutasme/who%20we%20are/engineering%20history/landmarks/101-st-charles-avenue-streetcar-line-1835.pdf.

Starbucks Everywhere blog. New Orleans. www.starbuckseverywhere.net/index.htm.

Stevens, Ryen. "Caffeinating the Port of New Orleans." Digital Humanities Studio, December 19, 2019. https://docstudio.org/2019/12/19/caffeinating-the-port-of-new-orleans.

Stilwell, Blake. "A Brief History of Trying (In Vain) to Replace Coffee with Chicory." *Coffee or Die Magazine,* August 8, 2021. https://coffeeordie.com/coffee-chicory.

Thompson, Charles L. *Chronological History of The Old French Market.* Tulane University Digital Library. New Orleans, 1950. https://digitallibrary.tulane.edu/islandora/object/tulane%3A55023.

Tooker, Poppy. "The Mother of All Iced Coffee." *Biz New Orleans,* June 29, 2018. www.bizneworleans.com/the-mother-of-all-iced-coffee.

"Understanding the Weird History of Decaffeinated Coffee and How It's Made." *Compass Coffee* blog. www.compasscoffee.com/blogs/the-daily-grind/understanding-the-weird-history-of-decaffeinated-coffee.

Vargas, Paul. "French Market Coffee, New Orleans." New Orleans 1920. https://paulvargas1.wordpress.com/french-market-coffee-new-orleans

———. "The French Market at New Orleans." New Orleans 1920. https://paulvargas1.wordpress.com/the-french-market-at-new-orleans.

"What Is Chicory Coffee? Some History and Brewing Experiments." Manual Coffee Brewing. https://manualcoffeebrewing.com/chicory-history-blending-and-new-orleans-style-coffee.

"What Is Excelsa Coffee?" Perfect Daily Grind, May 12, 2021. https://perfectdailygrind.com/2021/05/what-is-excelsa-coffee.

Printed Sources

Arthur, Stanley Clisby. *Old New Orleans: A History of the Vieux Carré, Its Ancient and Historical Buildings.* Harmanson, 1936.

Bienvenu, Marcelle, et al. *Stir the Pot: The History of Cajun Cuisine.* Hippocrene Books, 2005.

Brault, Len. *Coffee Roaster's Handbook: A How-To Guide for Home and Professional Roasters.* Rockridge, 2020.

Campanella, Richard. *Bienville's Dilemma: A Historical Geography of New Orleans.* University of Louisiana Press, 2018.

Clark, Emily. *The Strange History of the American Quadroon: Free Women of Color in the Revolutionary Atlantic World.* University of North Carolina Press, 2013.

Cole, Catherine. *The Story of the Old French Market, New Orleans.* New Orleans Coffee Company, 1916.

Dessens, Nathalie. *From Saint-Domingue to New Orleans: Migration and Influences.* University Press of Florida, 2007.

Haggerty, Richard A. *Haiti: A Country Study.* U.S. Government Printing Office, 1989.

Hall, Basil. *Travels in North America in the Years 1827 and 1828.* Vol. 3. Edinburgh, 1830. Copy located at University of Pittsburgh, Darlington Memorial Library.

Hayton, Bill. *A Brief History of Vietnam.* Tuttle, 2022.

Jacob, H. E. *Coffee: The Epic of a Commodity.* Skyhorse, 2015.

James, C. L. R. *The Black Jacobins: Toussaint l'Ouverture and the San Domingo Revolution.* Penguin Books, 1938.

Landweber, Julia. "Domesticating the 'Queen of Beans': How Old Regime France Learned to Love Coffee." *World History Bulletin.* Montclair State University.

Pendergrast, Mark. *Uncommon Grounds: The History of Coffee and How It Transformed Our World.* Basic Books, 1999.

The Picayune's Creole Cook Book. Times-Picayune Publishing, 1987.

The Picayune's Guide to New Orleans. 5th ed. The Picayune, 1903.

Saurage, H. Norman, III, and Matthew C. Saurage. *The Community Coffee Story.* Community Coffee Company, 2019.

Saxon, Lyle. *Fabulous New Orleans.* 1928. D. Appleton, 1939.

———. *Old Louisiana.* Century, 1929.

Simmonds, P. L. *Coffee and Chicory: Their Culture, Chemical Composition, Preparation for Market, and Consumption, with Simple Tests for Detecting Adulteration, and Practical Hints for the Producer and Consumer.* London, 1864.

Spary, Emma C. *Eating the Enlightenment: Food and the Sciences in Paris, 1670–1760.* University of Chicago Press, 2013.

Stall, Gaspar J. "Buddy." *Proud, Peculiar New Orleans: The Inside Story.* Claitor's Publishing Division, 1984.

Stone, Suzanne, and David Feldman. *New Orleans Coffee: A Rich History.* History Press, 2019.

Strachan, Sue. *The Café Brûlot.* Louisiana State University Press, 2021.

Thurston, Robert W. *Coffee: From Bean to Barista.* Rowman & Littlefield, 2018.

Ukers, William H. *All About Coffee.* 2nd ed. Martino Fine Books, 2011.

INTERVIEWS BY THE AUTHOR

Arceneaux, Bob. January 17, 2024. In-person interview.

Barona, Paola. April 5, 2024. Phone interview.

Blanda, Dominick. August 6, 2024. Phone interview.

Brennan, Patrick. February 19, 2024. In-person interview.

Cambre, Drew. February 2, 2024; December 3, 2024. Phone interviews.

Colley Morse, Janet. January 19, 2024. Phone interview.

Cronin, Matt. March 19, 2024. Phone interview.

Currie, Jim. January 16, 2024. Phone interview.

Cyres, Jerico. August 23, 2024. In-person interview.

Fink, Lauren. January 8, 2024. In-person interview.

Giuliano, Peter. February 22, 2024. Phone interview.

Hennessey, David. January 31, 2024. Phone interview.

Hood, Ted. February 16, 2024. In-person interview.

Iljazi, Bruna. February 19, 2024. Phone interview.

Jackson, Angela. January 23, 2024. In-person interview.

Johnson, Alyssa. December 15, 2023. In-person interview.

Jones, Felton, Jr. March 7, 2024. Phone interview.

King, Abby. August 23, 2024. Phone interview.

La Nasa, Alfred. November 22, 2023. Phone interview.

Lambeth, Sarah K. March 4, 2024. Phone interview.

Lutz, Bob. August 23, 2024. In-person interview.

Lyman, Kellan. February 5, 2024. Phone interview.
Madary, Andrew. April 3, 2024. Phone interview.
Mansell, Catherine. February 7, 2024. Phone interview.
Matthews, Michael. January 30, 2024. Phone interview.
McCabe, Lauren "Mermaid." August 23, 2024. In-person interview.
Meeker, Geoffrey. February 7, 2024. In-person interview.
Monaghan, Trey. October 4, 2023. Phone interview.
Murphy, Grace. February 19, 2024. In-person interview.
Oliver, Tom. January 23, 2024. In-person interview.
Patterson, Mia. April 15, 2024. Phone interview.
Pedeaux, Kevin. February 26, 2024. In-person interview.
Peer, Fred. August 8, 2024. Phone interview.
Perry, Scott. January 23, 2024. In-person interview.
Privat-Gilman, David. December 3, 2024. Phone interview.
Rabasa, Baruch. March 20, 2024. In-person interview.
Ricard, Mark. July 11, 2024. Phone interview.
Richards, Kevin. January 16, 2024. Phone interview.
Riethmaier, Jonathan. February 27, 2024. In-person interview.
Rodrigue, Greg. January 8, 2024. In-person interview.
Sanderford, Brice. April 19, 2024. Phone interview.
Saurage, Matt. May 9, 2024. Phone interview.
Seaman, Craig. November 5, 2024. Phone interview.
Stewart, Melissa. March 20, 2024. In-person interview.
Toepfer, Brenda. July 2, 2024. Phone interview.
Underhill, Zoe. February 19, 2024. In-person interview.
Voss, Ashlee. August 7, 2024. Phone interview.
Westfeldt Mills, Shelby. January 23, 2024. Phone interview.
Williams, Elizabeth. March 29, 2024. Phone interview.
Yildizli, Amy. March 27, 2024. In-person interview.
Yildizli, Turgay. March 27, 2024. In-person interview.

Lectures and Correspondence

Bienvenu, Marcelle. Email correspondence. June 27, 2024.
Cambre, Drew. Lecture at NOLA Coffee Festival. September 28, 2024.
Coates, Amanda. Provided Port of New Orleans coffee import statistics via email. January 13, 2024.

Lelko, Moss. Instructor, Cherry Coffee Roasters. Coffee cupping demonstration and specialty coffee talk. April 28, 2024.
Lobo, Prince. Lecture at NOLA Coffee Festival. September 16, 2023.
Mansell, Catherine. Instructor, Current Crop Roasting Shop, "Discover the Art of Coffee: Roast, Cup, and Savor." April 4, 2024.
Williams, Elizabeth. Lecture at NOLA Coffee Festival. September 16, 2023.
Winter. Email correspondence. December 4, 2024.

INDEX

Abahuzamugambi Ba Kawa farming cooperative, Rwanda, 175
Abstract Bookshop and Café, 96
Acadians, 90
Addis NOLA, 18, 141–42
Adler, Alan, 193–94
AeroPress, 193–94
Africa/African coffee, 7–8, 21, 30, 54, 101, 106, 147, 175. *See also* Ethiopia; Rwanda
Age of Enlightenment, 58
Agua Fresca Coffee, 145–46
Alciatore, Antoine, 66–67
Alciatore, Jules, 66
alcohol, 23, 58, 66–68
Alemayehu, Biruk, 141
Alinea Coffee Roasters, 132–35
All About Coffee (Ukers), 10, 33, 194
American Coffee Company, 172
American colonies, 24–25
Americanization of Creole culture, 62
American work culture, 86–87
Andermann, Robyn, 58, 61
Angelo Broacto's, 102
Annex Warehouse, 146
Antoine's Restaurant, 66–67, 82
Applied Arts Coffee, 126–27
Arabia, 21
arabica beans/coffee, 7–8, 155–57, 167, 170, 177, 179
Arabs, 19
Arceneaux, Bob, 111–13, 114, 125, 146–47
Arnold, Benjamin G., 36
Aron, Jacob, 32–33, 169–70
Arthur, Stanley Clisby, 59, 61
Atha, Frank P., 161
auctions, 59, 62
Austin, Denise, 97
Australia, 51
automats, 85–86
Avey, Tori, 21

Baba Budan, 21
baguettes, 154
Bakery Bar, 119
Ballard, Paul, Steven, and Scott, 166
Ballard Brands, 166
bánh mì, 154
Bankston, Carl L. III, 151–52
Barbason de Pailloux, Jean, 70
Barbé-Marbois, François, 56
Barcolo Manufacturing, 87
Barista Guild of America, 130
Barista Hustle, 183
Barona, Paola, 124
Barrilleaux, Ian, 117
Bartlett family, 171
Battle of Điện Biên Phủ, 153
Battle of Vertières, 55
Bearcat Café, 133
Beck, Brian, 169
Begnaud, Louis and Will, 179–80
beignets, 79–84
Bell, Henry, 29
Bellwether Coffee Roaster, 115–17, 139
"Bench Top Roller Mill" (*Barista Hustle*), 183
Bentz, Melitta, 187–88
Berlin Decree, 88

"best by" dates, 173
Bezzera, Luigi, 188–89
Bialetti, Alfonso, 189–90
Bienvenu, Marcelle, 65, 181
Bienville's Dilemma (Campanella), 57
Biggin pot, 185–86
Big Shoulders Coffee Chicago Roaster Workshop Competition, 132
Bird, Aaron, 60
Biz New Orleans, 162
Black Code of 1806, 76
The Black Jacobins (James), 55
blade grinders, 183
Blanda, Dominick, 176
Blanque, Jean, 59
Bolton, Dan, 52
Book, Nicholas, 182
Boston Tea Party, 24–25
Bovee, William H., 161
Bradshaw, Jim, 53–56, 179
Brazil, 25, 33–34, 35, 41, 46, 51
Brennan, Patrick, 117–18
Brennan's Restaurant, 118
"Brewed Awakening" (Andermann), 58
brewing coffee at home, 181–94; with AeroPress, 193–94; and Chemex, 188; coffee grinds, 184–85; with electric drip coffee makers, 191–92; with espresso machines, 188–89; with French press, 187; infusion brewing, 181; with moka pot, 189–90; with Neapolitan flip coffeepot, 190–91; pour-over brewing method, 187–88; single-serve coffee brewing, 192–93; vacuum brewing, 186–87
A Brief History of Vietnam (Hayton), 152
Britain, 30
British East India Company, 24
Brocato's gelato, 96
brokers, 49–51
Brown, Alton, 192
Brunn, E. M., 35–36
Brussels World Exhibition, 192
bubonic plague, 73
Buckley, Mike, 164
Burkenroad, William B., 32–33
Burns Jubilee Coffee Roaster, 121
burr grinders, 183
Butcher's Hall, 80
Butler, Edward S., 43–44
Butler, Willie, 103

café au lait, 64–66, 69, 78, 79, 81–82, 84, 92, 96, 134, 181
Café Beignet, 113
The Café Brûlot (Strachan), 66
café brûlot diabolique, 66–68
Café de la Bourse, 59
Café des Améliorations, 62
Café des Réfugiés, 61
Café du Monde, 3, 79–82, 196; Café du Monde coffee, 4, 80, 156–57, 170, 196; CDM Coffee, 156–57, 170–71; and chicory, 87; City Park spot, 84; in Japan, 81–82; in second-wave coffee movement, 95–96; and Vietnamese coffee, 4, 155–57; and Vietnamese refugees, 151
Café du Procope, 22–23
café noir, 64–66, 181
"Café-NOLA (Brulo)," 67
"The Caffeinated History of Coffee" (Avey), 21
"Caffeinating the Port of New Orleans" (Stevens), 41
caffeine, 16–18
Caffeine Brothers, 184
Caffé Reggio, New York City, 189
Cage and Drew, 33
Cairo, Egypt, 10
Cajuns, 64–66, 90
Calimani, Attilio, 187
Cambodia, 153
Cambrai, France, 89
Cambre, Drew, 50–51, 98–99, 147
Campanella, Richard, 57, 59–60, 74
Campos (steam merchant ship), 41
cà phê đá (black iced coffee), 155–57

cà phê sữa đá (Vietnamese iced coffee), 155–58, 196
carbon dioxide extraction method, 17–18
Caribbean Islands, 28, 30, 90
Carrollton Railroad Company, 74
Casino Building, 84
Catholic Charities, 150–51
CC's Coffee House, 98–100, 114, 147, 175–76
CC's Gourmet Coffee House, 175
Ceylon, 21
Cezve/Ibrik Championship, 140
Chalmette Slip, 44
Chamberlain, Orville Walter, 63–64
charity projects, 162–63, 174
Charles II (King), 23–24
Charlotte Dundas (boat), 29
Chemex, 188
Cherry Coffee Roasters, 104–7, 145
chicory, 3, 69, 87–88; in café brûlot, 67; and Café du Monde coffee, 156, 170; and CDM coffee, 170; and coffee in modern-day New Orleans, 92–93; and Community Coffee, 172; and Congregation Coffee, 118; consumption history of, 88–89; and Cora's Girls Coffee, 120; and Delicious Sips, 121; and Junk Drawer Coffee, 139; making its way to New Orleans, 90–91; and Mojo Coffee, 110; and Morning Call Coffee Stand, 82; and N.O. Brew, 179; and swill milk scandal, 91–92
chicory plantations, 89
China, 153–54
Christophe, Henri, 55
Chronological History of the Old French Market (Thompson), 70
Church Alley Coffee Bar, 119
City Roots Coffee Bar, 176
Civil War, 33–35, 79, 90–91
Clarion Herald (newspaper), 150
Clark, Emily, 54, 57, 76
Clark and Company, 33
Clay, Henry, 171
Cleaver, Molly, 56–57
Coast Roast Coffee and Tea, 128
cocktails, 66–68
Code Noir (Black Code), 75–76, 79
Coffee, Sugar, and Cocoa Exchange, Inc., 36
Coffee and Chicory (Simmonds), 89
Coffee Bean Corral, 100–101
coffee beans: arabica, 7–8, 155–57, 167, 170, 177, 179; beginning of, 5–7; and chicory, 88–89; and coffee grinders, 182–83; coffee imports, 47; Creole coffee, 65; decaffeinated coffee, 17; defects in, 94–95; Dupuy Storage and Forwarding, 47; and fluid bed coffee roasting, 115; Folger's, 161–62; robusta, 7–8, 157, 170; types of, 7–8. *See also* green coffee beans/coffee; coffee-roasting process
coffee brands, 160–80; CDM Coffee, 170–71; City Roots Coffee Bar, 176; Community Coffee, 172–76; CoolBrew, 176–78; Folgers, 160–63; French Market Coffee, 171–72; Luzianne Coffee, 169–70; Mello Joy, 179–80; N.O. Brew, 178–79; PJ's Coffee, 163–69
coffee business and customs: automats, 85–86; Café du Monde, 79–82; Code Noir (Black Code), 75–76; coffee break, 86–87; coffee with chicory, 87–93; French Market, 69–75; Morning Call Coffee Stand, 82–84; and Nicaud, 77–79; and swill milk scandal, 91–92. *See also* specialty coffee
Coffee Chateau, 114
coffee cherries, 5–6
"Coffee Cocktail Creation" class, 102
coffee contracts, 35–36
"Coffee Cupping: A Step-by-Step Guide," 14
coffee cupping or coffee tasting, 12–14
coffee dock, 46
coffee dock fire of 1925, 27, 42–43

coffee exchanges, 2, 35–39, 58–62, 196
coffee farmers, 26, 48–49, 109–10, 122, 131, 135, 145–46, 167–68, 174–75. *See also* coffee plantations
coffee farms, 145–46
Coffee Federation of Colombia, 146
coffee flavor wheel, 13
"Coffee Gateway to the USA" (Bolton), 52
"Coffee Grades," 94–95
coffee grinding, 181–85; blade grinders, 183; burr grinders, 183; coffee grinders, 182–84; coffee grinds, 184–85; roller grinders, 183–84; Turkish mill, 182
coffeehouses, 2–3, 19, 20, 22–23, 24–25, 35–36, 58–59, 67, 79, 96
coffee imports, 27–52; during the Civil War, 33–35; and coffee brokering, 49–51; and coffee exchange, 35–36; and coffee shed, 46; and Dupuy Storage and Forwarding, 46–48; growth of, 30–31; and J. Aron and Company, 32–33; in modern-day New Orleans, 51–52; and Napoleon's Continental System, 88–89; in New Orleans in the nineteenth century, 27–29; from the Philippines, 48–49; and the Port of New Orleans, 51–52; and Poydras Wharf, 45; and railroads, 37–39; rebuilding the docks for, 43–44; Silocaf, 162; trade restrictions during World War I, 39–40; Westfeldt Brothers, Inc., 31–33
Coffee in Good Spirits, 140
coffee origins, 5–26; beginning of a coffee bean, 4–7; coffee beans, types of, 7–8; and coffee cupping or tasting, 12–14; and coffee roasts, 12; decaffeinated coffee, 16–18; Ethiopian legend, 18–19; in Europe, 21–24; introduction of coffee into the United States, 24–26; three waves of coffee, 14–16; Turkish coffee, 19–21
coffee plantations, 19, 22, 55, 57, 90
coffee prices, 32, 33–34, 35–36, 43, 50, 140
Coffee Quest, 107
Coffee Rani, 128
Coffee Roasters Guild Retreat, 133–34
Coffee Roasters of New Orleans, 111
coffee-roasting process, 8–12
coffee roast types, 12
Coffee Science, 112, 113–17
coffee shed, 46
coffee shipping, 145–48
coffee shops, 98–99, 110, 111, 114, 145
coffee sniffers, 89
coffee terminal, 44–45
Coffee Trade and Port of New Orleans (online exhibit), 32
coffee upgrading, 47
cold brew coffee: coffee kegs, 137–38; CoolBrew, 176–78; Japanese cold brew method, 164–66; nitro cold brew coffee, 138; and N.O. Brew, 178–79; and PJ's Coffee, 164–66; and Riverboat Coffee Company, 137–38
Cole, Catherine, 71, 77–78, 80
Colley, Allan, 46–48
Colley Morse, Janet, 46–48, 147
Colombia, 51
Colombian coffee, 108, 120, 124–26, 146, 175
Comédie-Française, 22
Committee of Public Safety, 59
commodity coffee, 15, 134, 147–48
Community Coffee, 4, 102, 134, 147, 172–76, 196
Compass Coffee blog, 17
competitions, 16, 132–34, 140
Compilation of the Laws of the Kingdoms of the Indies, 70
Confederacy, 79
Congregation Coffee, 117–18
Continental System, 3, 88–89, 90
Continental Terminals, 146
CoolBrew, 176–78
Cora's Girls Coffee, 120
Cottraux, E. P., 33
Court of Two Sisters, 102
Covington Farmer's Market, 128

CR Coffee Shop, 127–29
Creole Belle coffee, 179
Creole coffee (café à la Creole), 64–66
Creole Creamery, 113
Creoles, 56–57, 62, 64–66
Cronin, Matt, 109
Cuba, 28, 30, 57
Current Crop Roasting Shop, 100–102
Currie, Jim, 142–46
Curtis D500 Brewer, 115
Cutner, Sandy, 111
Cyres, Jerico, 103

Daily Picayune (newspaper), 74
Darby, William, 57
dark-roast coffee, 139. *See also* chicory
Davis, Aaron P., 8
De Belloy, Jean-Baptiste, 185
decaffeinated coffee, 16–18
Declaration of the Rights of Man and of the Citizen, 55
Dee's Coffee, 99–100
defects, 94–95
de France, W. H., 44
de Genouilly, Charles Rigault, 152
Del Alto Valle Coffee, 124–26
Delforge, Jacques-Victor, 187
Delicious Sips, 120–21, 179
demitasse cups, 66
Department of Public Property, 73
Dessalines, Jean-Jacques, 55
Dessens, Nathalie, 57
Diedrich Coffee Roaster, 10
Diedrich Roaster, 107
Dittmann, Charles S., 41
Division of Public Markets, 73
Dock Board, 43–46
Dock Commission, 41
Dodge family, 171
"Domesticating the 'Queen of Beans'" (Landweber), 22
Dorignac's Food Center, 125, 178
"Drip, Percolate, and Brew: Coffee Makers Through History" (Rouser), 185
dry milling, 6
Dunn, Debra, 96
Dupuy, John, 46–48
Dupuy Storage and Forwarding, 46–48, 136, 147
Duskin Co. Ltd., 81
Dussau de la Croix, 59
Dutch-style coffee, 166

Eating the Enlightenment (Spary), 58
ECOM Foundation, 174
E. Johnston and Company, 41
electric drip coffee makers, 191–92
Elford's white iron roaster, 10
Elkin's Exchange, 59
Elmore, Wayne, 180
El Salvador, 147–48
England, 10, 23, 186
enslaved people, 2–3, 53–55, 59, 75–79, 195
Enterprise Manufacturing Co., 182
epidemics, 32, 34–35, 73
Erie Canal, 37
Erin Rose, 68
espresso machines, 188–89
Estrehan, Jean Noël d', 59
ethically sourced coffee, 126–27, 131, 168, 174–75
Ethiopia/Ethiopian coffee: arabica beans/coffee, 7; coffee ceremony, 141–42; and HEY Coffee Co., 107–8; and origins of coffee, 18–19; and Turkish coffee, 140
Europe, coffee in, 21–24, 188–89
excelsa coffee, 7–8
Exchange Coffee House, 59

Fabulous New Orleans (Saxon), 86
Fair Grinds, 114
Farm Gate price, 131
Farragut, David, 33
"Fashionable Rebellion," 76
Fatma's Cozy Corner, 141
Feldman, David, 30–31
female street vendors of color (*les vendeuses*), 76

Fernandez, Hubert, 80–81
Fernandez, June, 80–81
Fernandez Wine Cellar, 80
Fink, Lauren, 104–7
First Indochina War, 153
Fitzpatrick, Harry W., 44
flatboats, 28–29
fluid bed coffee roasting, 115–17
Folger, James, Henry, and Edward, 160–61
Folger, James II, 161
Folgers, 3, 134, 146, 160–63, 164, 174, 196
"Folgers Continues to Grow New Orleans East's Economy" (*Biz New Orleans*), 162
Food Administration, 39–40
food regulations, 91–92
Food & Wine (magazine), 117, 130
Ford, Gerald, 149–50
Foreign Trade Bureau of the Association of Commerce, 46
forward buying, 50–51
Foucher, Pierre, 59
France, 3, 22–23, 30, 89, 90
Frania, Lisa, 87
Frederick the Great (King), 23, 89
free lunch, 62–63
free people of color, 54–55, 61, 69, 78–79
French colonialism in Vietnam, 152–54, 155
"French Colonialism in Vietnam" (Llewellyn and Thompson), 153
French Creoles, 62
French drip coffeepot, 186
French Indochina, 153
"The French Influence on Vietnamese Cuisine" (Monaco), 153–54
French Market, 69–75, 77–78, 79–81, 84, 102
"The French Market at New Orleans" (Vargas), 72
French Market Business Men's Association, 73
French Market Coffee, 80, 171–72, 196
"French Market Coffee, New Orleans" (Vargas), 80
French Market Corporation, 73–75
French Market Mills, 171
French National Assembly, 55
French Opera House, 83
French press, 187
French Quarter, 68, 84, 98, 111, 151
French Truck Coffee, 121–24
French West Indies Company, 54
"From Poydras Market to South Market District" (Campanella), 74
From Saint-Domingue to New Orleans (Dessens), 57
frozen coffee cocktail, 68
Frozen Irish Coffee, 68
Full Weight Grocery, 172
Fulton, Robert, 29

Gaggia, Achilles, 189
"Gallier and Dakin's Merchants' Exchange" (Campanella), 59
Geisha coffee, 126
Geneva Accord of 1954, 153
George (King), 24
Germany, 22–23, 25, 30, 47, 51, 85, 186, 187, 191
Gershon, Michael, 29
Gervais Favrot and Co. Construction, 73
"Getting Your Grind Right" (Caffeine Brothers), 184
Giraud, Charles, 89
Girod Street Wharf, 42–43
Giuliano, Peter, 95–96, 100
Glass Half Full, 137–38
Glazer, Samuel, 191–92
Golden, Evan, 137–38
Golden Cup Standard, 115
Gonzalez, Mark, 97
Gothot Coffee Roaster, 98
Government Wharf, 45
Great Britain, 56, 88
Great New Orleans Fire of 1794, 61
Green Coffee Association, 44
green coffee beans/coffee: beginning of, 6; and coffee brokers, 50; and coffee grinders, 182; in coffee imports, 52; and

coffee innovators, 63; and Coffee Science, 116–17; coffee trade restrictions of, during World War I, 39–40; and Current Crop Roasting Shop, 100–101; decaffeination process, 17–18; and Dupuy Storage and Forwarding, 47; and Ethiopian coffee ceremony, 141–42; and Folgers, 161–63; and French Truck, 122; and J. Aron and Company, 32–33; and Junk Drawer Coffee, 139; and New Orleans Coffee Import Co., 48–49; and Orleans Coffee, 112; and PJ's Coffee, 167–69; and Poydras Wharf, 41; preparing coffee at home with, 181; and Try-Me Coffee Roasters, 103; and Westfeldt Brothers, Inc., 31–32. *See also* coffee-roasting process
grègues, 181
Grimmer, Charles Felix, 179
Grimmer Coffee Company, 179
grinding coffee. *See* coffee grinding
Ground Control Coffee Brewer, 127
Guatemala, 51
Guthrie, Eliot, 117
Gwathmey, John, 61
Gwathmey's Coffee House, 61

Haggerty, Richard A., 54–55
Haiti, 55
Haiti (Haggerty), 54–55
Hannan, Philip M., 150
Hard, Anson Wales, 39
Hardart, Joseph Horn and Frank (né Franz Hardardt), 85
Hawaii, 7
Hayton, Bill, 152–53
Hennessey, David Michael, 82
Hennessey, Robert "Bob" F., 82
Hewlett, John, 59
Hewlett's Exchange, 59–60
HEY Coffee Co., 10–11, 107–8, 145
HEY Coffee Roasters, 134
high coffee, 65
Hill, Greg, 112
Hipp, Juan, 107
Historic New Orleans Collection, 78
"The History of the Chicory Coffee Mix That New Orleans Made Its Own" (Smith), 90
Hồ, Chí Minh, 153
Hòa Mã, 154
Hobart Manufacturing Co., 182
Hoffman, Daniel H., 33
Hoffman, D. H., 80
Holland, 88
Honduras, 147–48
honey-processed coffee, 126
Hood, Ted, 97–98
Horn, Brady, 137–38
Horn and Hardart Automat, 85–86
Hotel Grunwald Caterers, 67
"How Café du Monde Became a Vietnamese American Staple" (Nguyen), 156
Howell, Mark, 174
"How to Brew Coffee in a Neapolitan Flip Pot" (Meister), 191
"How to Brew Perfect Coffee with AeroPress" (Stumptown Coffee Roasters), 193–94
Hurricane Katrina, 98–99, 103–4, 108–9, 111–12, 117, 127–28, 162

Iljazi, Bruna, 171–72
Illinois Central, 37
Indigenous groups, 70
Indochina Migration and Refugee Assistance Act, 150
Indonesia, 51
Industrial Revolution, 25
infusion brewing, 181
InterAmerican, 147
International Coffee Corporation (ICC), 49–51, 121, 147
International Coffee Day, 26
International Coffee Organization (ICO), 26
Israel, Leon, 32
Israel, Samuel, 46

Jabez Burns & Sons Roaster, 103
Jackson, Andrew, 59, 171–72
Jackson, Angela, 108–10
Jackson, MS, 100–101
J. A. Folger & Co, 161
James, C. L. R., 55
Jamila's Café, 141
Japan, 81–82, 153
Japanese cold brew method, 164–66
J. Aron and Company, 32–33, 49–50, 120–21
Jefferson, Thomas, 56
J. M. Smucker Company, 163
Johnson, Alyssa, 135–37
Jones, Felton Jr., 166–69
Jones, W. T., 33
Jordan, Phyllis, 3–4, 96, 114, 163–66, 167
Junction Bar & Grill, 68
Junk Drawer Coffee, 138–39
Jurisich, Alvin "Al" P., 82
Jurisich, Carol, 82
Jurisich, Joseph, 82

Kaffee HAG, 17
Kahveci Usta, 20
Kailua-Kona, Hawaii, 7
Kaldi (Khalid), 18–19
Kaldi's Coffee House, 97–98, 114
kaveh kanes, 19
K-Cup pods, 192–93
keelboats, 28–29
Kepler, Henry, 102–3
Keurig, 192–93
King, Abby, 104
Knipmeyer, John, 99
Koehlar, Troy and Angie, 68
Koeniger, Fred, 80
Kolb, Carolyn, 85–86
Kona coffee, 7
Krewe of the Rolling Elvi, 104
Kristoff, Paul, 154
K-Rounds, 193
Kuntz, F. W., 43
Kyoto-style coffee, 166

La Bourse de Maspero, 59
Lafitte, Jean, 59
La Harpe, Bernard de, 70
Lake Pontchartrain, 28, 37, 81
Lambeth, Sarah K., 118–19
La Nassa, Alfred, 157, 170–71
Landweber, Julia, 22
Laos, 153
La Pavoni, 189
Larino, Jennifer, 81
La Roque, Jean de, 22
Laughing Buddha Nursery's Local Cooling Farms, 178
Lê, Minh Ngọc, 154
Leach, Neal M., 44
LeClerc, Charles Victoire Emmanuel, 56
Le Moyne, Jean-Baptiste, Sieur de Bienville, 27–28
Le Moyne de Bienville, Jean-Baptiste, 70
Le Moyne d'Iberville, Pierre, 70
Leon Israel and Brothers, Inc., 46
liberica coffee, 7–8
licenses, 40
LIFT program, 136
Living Room Coffeehouse, 96
Livingston, Edward, 59
Livingston, Robert, 56
Llewellyn, Jennifer, 153
Lobo, Prince, 18, 141–42
London, England, 23, 58, 182
Longevity Brand, 155
Lonsdale, Henry T., 31, 34
Loring Coffee Roaster, 122–24, 126
Loring S7 Nighthawk Roaster, 176
Los Wigwam Weavers, 87
Louis XIV (King), 22, 75
Louisiana's sale to the United States, 55–56
Louisiana World Exposition, 81
L'Ouverture, Toussaint, 55
Loysel de Santais, Edouard, 188
Lutz, Bob, 102–4
Lutz, Carolyn, 103
Lutz, John Patrick "J. P." Jr., 103

Luzianne Café, 157
Luzianne Coffee, 169–70
Luzianne Iced Tea, 170
Lyman, Kellan, 48–49

Macarty, Augustin de, 59
Madary, Andrew, 120–21
Madary, William G. II, 50, 120–21
Mae's Bakeshop, 120
Maher, Sylvia, 81
Maiorica, Girolamo, 152
Mammoth Coffee Company, 129–31
Mammoth Espresso, 130
Manila Marn (coffee ship), 42
Mansell, Catherine, 101–2
Marotta, Vincent, 191–92
Mary Queen of Vietnam Church, 151, 159
Maspero, Pierre, 59
Maspero's Exchange, 59
Matthews, Michael, 132–35
Mayer, Henri-Otto, 187
McCabe, Lauren "Mermaid," 104
McCrory, Jeff and Greg, 177–78
McCrory, Phillip, 176–78
medicinal properties of coffee, 19, 22, 64
Meeker, Geoffrey, 122–23
Meigō Sakusen (Operation Bright Moon), 153
Meister, Ever, 191
Mello Joy, 179–80
Merchants Coffee Co. of New Orleans, Inc., 172
Merchants' Coffee House, 61
Merchants' Exchange, 60–61
Mercon Specialty, 136
Methodical blog, 14
Mexico, 51
Meyer, Karen, 82
Miller, Lloyd, 68
Milneburg, 37
Mingo, Cirilo, 63
Miró, Esteban Rodríguez, 76
Mississippi River, 28, 45, 56
Mister Donut, 81
Mizell-Nelson, Michael, 62–63
Mojo Coffee, 108–10
Mojo Coffee House, 100
moka pot, 189–90
Molly's at the Market, 68
Monaco, Emily, 153–54
Monaghan, Jim Sr., 68
Monaghan, Jim "Trey" III, 68
Moneta, Giulio, 187
Monroe, James, 56
Montella, Shawn, 128
Monte Vista Coffee, 107, 145–46
Morgan, Benjamin B., 59
Moriondo, Angelo, 188–89
Morize, Jean-Louis, 190–91
Morning Call Coffee Stand, 82–84, 87, 196
"The Mother of All Iced Coffee" (Tooker), 166
Mr. Coffee, 191–92
multiple-drip coffee urn, 64
Murad IV (Sultan), 20
Murphy, Grace, 117–18

Napier and Company, 41
Napoleon Bonaparte, 3, 55–56, 88–89, 90
National Coffee Association, 25–26, 166
National Coffee Day, 26
"The Native Roots of the French Market" (Rhodes), 70
Naylor, James, 96
Neapolitan flip coffeepot, 190–91
Neutral Ground Coffee House, 96
New Orleans (steamboat), 29
New Orleans and Carrollton Railroad, 37
New Orleans Board of Trade, 40
New Orleans City Council, 168
New Orleans City Park, 84
New Orleans Coffee (Stone and Feldman), 30–31
New Orleans Coffee Company, 33, 80, 171, 178
New Orleans Coffee Import Co., 48–49
New Orleans Coffee Works, 111

New Orleans Roast, 89
New Orleans Roast, LLC, 166
New Orleans social life, 53–68; and café brûlot diabolique, 66–68; and coffee exchanges, 58–62; and coffee innovators, 63–64; and Creole and Cajun coffee, 64–66; and free lunch, 62–63
New York, 40, 45
New York Board of Trade, 36
New York Cocoa Exchange, 36
New York Coffee and Sugar Exchange, 36
"The New York Coffee and Sugar Exchange" (Brunn), 35
New York Coffee Exchange, 35–36, 40
New York Cotton Exchange, 36
Nguyen, Sahra, 156
Nguyễn, Thị Tịnh, 154
Nguyễn dynasty, 152
Nica Nola Coffee, 145–46
Nicaragua, 51, 147–48
Nicaud, Rose, 2–3, 69, 77–79
nitro cold brew coffee, 138
N.O. Brew, 178–79
"N.O. CoolBrew Celebrates 25 Years of Cold Drip Coffee" (Sonnier), 177–78
NOLA Coffee Festival, 126, 142–44, 179, 196
"No Such Thing as a Free Lunch Anymore" (Mizell-Nelson), 62

Oak Street Po-Boy Festival, 154
office coffee culture, 138
"Of the Excellent Qualities of Coffee, and the Art of Making It in the Highest Perfection" (Rumford), 186
Ogden, George, 59
Oji Tower, or Yama Tower, 164–66
Old Louisiana (Saxon), 61
Old New Orleans (Arthur), 59
Old Road Coffee Shop, 120
Oliver, Tom, 112, 113–17
One Cup Coffee Filter, 192
open markets and coffee stands, 3, 69, 74, 75, 78, 79, 170, 195–96. *See also* Café du Monde; French Market; Morning Call Coffee Stand
Operation New Life, 150
O'Reilly, Alexander, 70
"The Orleanian at the Automat" (Kolb), 85–86
Orléans, Philip II, Duke of, 28
Orleans Coffee, 111–13
Orleans Coffee Exchange, 111–12, 114
Orleans Levee Board, 73
Oumas Indians, 70
Ozdemir Pasha, 19–20

Pác Bó, Vietnam, 153
Panama, 148
Pan-American Coffee Bureau, 87, 164
Panic of 1837, 31
Parish Coffee, 113
Parker, John M., 40
Parnahyba (boat), 42
patents, 63–64
Patterson, Mia, 120
Pavoni, Desiderio, 189
PEARL: Partnership for Enhancing Agriculture in Rwanda through Linkages, 175
Pebdani, Artemis, 115
Pedeaux, Kevin, 127–29
Peer, Fred, 178–79
Peet, Alfred, 95
Pendergrast, Mark, 19, 21, 22–23, 24–25, 33, 36, 188
penny universities, 23
Perfect Daily Grind, 8
Perry, Scott, 115–16
Peters, Samuel Jarvis, 60
petit blancs, 54
Peychaud, Antoine Amedie, 61
Peychaud's Bitters, 61
Philippines, 48–49
phin filter, 157–58
Phoenix Oyster and Beefsteak House, 61
The Picayune's Creole Cook Book, 64, 65
The Picayune's Guide to New Orleans, 62

Pilie Market, 74
Pioneer Steam Coffee and Spice Mills, 161
PJ's Coffee, 3–4, 96, 99–100, 114, 127, 134, 147, 163–69, 196
Place de Armes, 71
Plantation Coffee House, 96
Pond Coffee, 119
Pontchartrain Railroad Company, 37
Portage Road, 70
Port Authority of New York, 40
Port of New Orleans, 2, 195; and Civil War, 33–34, 90; and coffee imports, 51–52; in Louisiana's sale to the United States, 56; and NOLA Coffee Festival, 143; and specialty coffee, 145–47; and steamboats, 29–30; in the twentieth century, 41–42
"The Port of New Orleans" (Redard), 30
pour-over brewing method, 187–88
Poydras Market, 74
Poydras Wharf, 41–42, 45, 46
preparing coffee at home. *See* brewing coffee at home
preshipment samples, 51
Pretty Coffee, 118–20
Privat-Gilman, David, 138–39
"A Proclamation for the Suppression of Coffee Houses," 23–24
Procope, Francois, 22–23
Procter & Gamble, 162–63
Proud, Peculiar New Orleans (Stall), 86
Prussian Empire, 3, 89
Public Works Administration, 73
Puckett, John, 101

Q Graders, 13

Rabasa, Baruch, 126–27
railroads, 37–39
Ralph Brennan Restaurant Group, 118
Rand, George C., 39
Randazzo's Bakery, 127
Raving Brands, 166
Rebirth Coffee, 146
Redard, Thomas E., 30
Red Fox Coffee Merchants, 105, 107
Reed, Scott, 167
Reily, William B., 169–70
Reily, William B. Jr., 170
Reily Foods Company, 147, 157, 169–70, 171–72
Rescoe, Zack, 135–37
Rhodes, Alexandre de, 152
Rhodes, Kalie, 70
Rhythm and Blues, 96
Ricard, Mark, 162–63
Richards, Kevin, 142–44, 146
Riethmaier, Darlene, 129–31
Riethmaier, Jonathan, 129–31
Riverboat Coffee Company, 137–38
Riverwalk Marketplace, 42
robusta beans/coffee, 7–8, 157, 170
Rodrigue, Greg, 10–11, 107–8
roller grinders, 183–84
Roman, Cynthia, 81
Roman, Jay, 151
Rombouts Coffee, 192
Roosevelt, Nicholas, 29
Roppolo, Jerry, 96
Rose, Erin, 68
Roselius, Ludwig, 17
Rouser, Kathleen, 185
Royal Blend, 114
Royal Coffee, 105
Royal #6 roaster, 129
Royal Roaster, 111
R. Poursini and Company, 33
RT Coffee, 172
Rue de la Course, 96, 99, 114
Ruffner, McDowell, and Burch, 46
Ruliff, 33
Rumford, Count Benjamin, 186
Rwanda, 174, 175
Ryu, Airi, 25

Saint-Domingue, 22, 28, 53–55, 56
Saint-Domingue Creoles, 57
Saint-Domingue refugees, 61

"Saint-Domingue Revolution" (Bradshaw), 53
Salvation Lass (steamship), 46
Sam Stone and Co., 73
Sanderford, Brice, 137–38
Sanders, M. J., 44–45
San Franciscan Coffee Roaster, 112, 118
Santiago, Cuba, 57
Saurage, Henry Norman III, 175
Saurage, Matt, 173–74, 176
Saurage, Norman "Cap," 172–73
Saxon, Lyle, 61, 86
Sazerac Coffee House, 60–61
Sazerac Company, 60, 143
Sazerac House, 143
Scherck, Lewis A., 64
Schilling, Timothy, 175
Schlumbohm, Peter, 188
Schwarz, Leonora, 80–81
Seaman, Craig, 102
second-wave coffee movement, 95–96, 114, 196
Seeds for Progress, 136
Shared Source, 131
Shaw's Louisiana Coffee and Spice Mills, 33
Siemers, Bill and Kathy, 111–12
Silocaf of New Orleans Inc., 162
Simmonds, P. L., 89
Simpson, Todd, 164
single-origin coffees, 16, 92, 103, 108, 124, 127, 129, 138
single-serve coffee brewing, 192–93
single-use pods, 192–93
Skillman, Orville T., 72
slavery, 77–79
Smith, K. Annabelle, 90
Smith, Kiara, 120
Smith and McKenna, 33
Smucker Coffee Silo Operations, 52
Society of New Orleans Baristas (SNOB), 99
soft drinks, 25, 67
Sonnier, Cheramie, 177
South America, 35
South American coffee, 51
Southeast Asia, 8
Southern Coffee Mills, Incorporated, 33
Southern Coffee Mills, Ltd., 80
Southern Coffee Polishing Mills, 33
Southern Pacific rail system, 37
Southwest Airlines, 174
Spain, 28, 51, 56
Spary, Emma, 58
specialty coffee, 3, 15, 94–148; Alinea Coffee Roasters, 132–35; Applied Arts Coffee, 126–27; Cherry Coffee Roasters, 104–7; Coffee Science, 113–17; Congregation Coffee, 117–18; Cora's Girls Coffee, 120; CR Coffee Shop, 127–29; defined, 94–95; Del Alto Valle Coffee, 124–26; Delicious Sips, 120–21; and Ethiopian coffee ceremony, 141–42; French Truck Coffee, 121–24; future of in New Orleans, 144–48; HEY Coffee Co., 107–8; Junk Drawer Coffee, 138–39; Mammoth Coffee Company, 129–31; Mojo Coffee, 108–10; NOLA Coffee Festival, 142–44; Orleans Coffee, 111–13; Pretty Coffee, 118–20; Riverboat Coffee Company, 137–38; and second-wave coffee movement, 95–96; and third-wave coffee movement, 98–100; Try-Me Coffee Roasters, 102–4; and Turkish coffee, 139–41; Undergrowth Coffee, 135–37
Specialty Coffee Association of America (SCAA), 13, 94, 100, 112, 115, 130, 144, 167
Specialty Coffee Expo, 100, 109
Specialty Turkish Coffee, 140–41
spot buying, 50
Sri Lanka, 21
Stall, Buddy, 86
Stamp Act of 1765, 24
Standard Coffee Company, 170
Starbucks, 1, 15, 99, 175, 176
steamboats, 29–30
"Steamboats" (Gershon), 29

Stein's Deli, 104
Stevens, Ryen, 41
Stewart, Melissa, 126–27
Stir the Pot (Bienvenu), 181
Stone, Suzanne, 30–31, 90
Stonebreaker, Michael, 178
The Story of the Old French Market, New Orleans (Cole), 71, 77, 80
Stoughton, WI, 87
Stoughton Coffee Break Festival, 87
Strachan, Sue, 66–67
The Strange History of the American Quadroon (Clark), 54
St. Roch Market, 127–29
Stumptown Coffee Roasters, 193–94
Sucafina Specialty, 107
Sucré, 99
sugar, 54
sugar contracts, 36
Sugar Equalization Board, 40
Suleiman the Magnificent (Sultan), 19–20
swill milk scandal, 91–92
Swiss Water Process, 17
Symington, William, 29

Tales of the Cocktail conference, 143
taxes, 24, 89
Taylor, Sewell, 60–61
Tea Act of 1773, 24
Tet Festival, 159
T. G. Mandt's Wagon Factory, 87
Thiot, Jean Baptiste Hyacinthe, 61
third-wave coffee movement, 98–100, 109, 117
Thompson, Benjamin. *See* Rumford, Count Benjamin
Thompson, Charles L., 70
Thompson, Steve, 153
three waves of coffee, 14–16
Times-Picayune (newspaper), 39–40, 42, 43, 44–45, 46, 162, 164, 171
Timken Center, 84
Timmerman, Savannah, 102
Toddy Coffee Maker, 164
Toepfer, Brenda, 162
Tooker, Poppy, 166
Townshend Acts, 24
trade: during the Civil War, 34–35; and coffee shed, 46; and coffee terminal, 44–45; J. Aron and Company, 32–33; Napoleon's Continental System, 88–89; and New Orleans in the nineteenth century, 27–29; New York Coffee Exchange, 35–36; and railroads, 37, 44; and restrictions during World War I, 39–40; and steamboats, 29–30; trade shows, 16, 144; and Vietnamese, 152; Westfeldt Brothers, Inc., 31–32
Treaty of Fontainebleau, 28
Treaty of Huế, 152
Treaty of Ryswick, 54
Treaty of Saigon, 152
Treaty of San Ildefonso, 56
Tremoulet's New Exchange Coffee House, 59
Troy, OH, 182
True Brew coffee cart, 97
True Brew Coffee House, 3, 96–97
True Brew Theater, 97
Try-Me Coffee Mills, 102
Try-Me Coffee Roasters, 102–4
Tự Đức (Emperor), 152
Turkish coffee, 19–21, 139–41
Turkish mill, 182

Ukers, William, 10, 33, 37, 39, 66–67, 182, 185–86, 194
Uncommon Grounds (Pendergrast), 19
Undergrowth Coffee, 135–37
Underhill, Zoe, 117–18
"Understanding the Weird History of Decaffeinated Coffee and How It's Made," 17
Union Coffee, 172
United Nations Educational, Scientific and Cultural Organization (UNESCO), 124
United Natural Foods, Inc. (UNFI), 179

United States, coffee's introduction into, 24–26
United States Shipping Board, 46
"The Untold Story Behind How Café du Monde Stands Ended Up in Japan" (Larino), 81
U.S. Coffee Championship, 132, 133
U.S. Roaster Nationals, 132

vacuum brewing, 186–87
vacuum-sealed "firm packs" of coffee, 172
Vargas, Paul, 72, 80
Vautrot, Leah, 115
Venice, Italy, 22
Vienna, Austria, 22
Việt Minh, 153
Vietnam/Vietnamese coffee, 7; and Café du Monde, 4, 151, 155–57; coffee imports from, 51; and immigration after Vietnam War, 149–50; New Orleans's connection to, 155–59; and refugees in New Orleans, 149–52; steps in preparing Vietnamese coffee, 157–58; Vietnamese cuisine, 153–54
Vietnam War, 149–50
Village de L'Est, 151, 159
Visual Capitalist, 25
Voss, Ashlee, 169

Walle, Bruce, 128
War Trade Board, 40
washed-process coffee, 108
Well, Jay, 46
Westfeldt, Gustavus Adolphus George, 31–32
Westfeldt, Shelby, 32
Westfeldt, Thomas, 32
Westfeldt Brothers, Inc., 31–33, 121, 168
Westfeldt Mills, Shelby, 147
West Indies, 53–54
Whatever Coffee, 119
"What's the Difference Between Cajun and Creole—or Is There One?" (Cleaver), 56–57
white elite, 54
white planters, 55
Whole Foods, 118, 179
Widmann, Gottlob, 191
Wigomat, 191–92
Williams, Caroline "Phant," 96
Williams, Elizabeth, 65–66, 92–93
Wingerter, Pat, 97
women, 23, 69, 76–78, 109–10, 119, 120, 168
"The Women's Petition Against Coffee," 23
World Brewers Cup competition, 140
World Coffee Championship, 133
World Coffee Events competition, 140
World Port Source, 33
World War I, 39–40
World War II, 87, 153

yellow fever epidemic, 32, 34–35, 73
Yildizli, Turgay and Amy, 139–41
"You Can't Beat a Cup of Cajun Coffee" (Bradshaw), 179
Young, Henry, 46

zero-emission coffee roasting, 114–15
Zosel, Kurt, 17–18
Z'otz Café, 99